VICTIMS OF INEPTITUDE

An Insider's Account of Injustice within the World Health Organization

FIRDU ZAWIDE WITH HILARY BASSETT

VICTIMS OF INEPTITUDE

An Insider's Account of Injustice within the World Health Organization

FIRDU ZAWIDE WITH HILARY BASSETT

ARPress
ILLUMINATING IDEAS
EMPOWERING VOICES

ARPress
45 Dan Road Suite 15
Canton MA 02021

  Hotline: 1(888) 821-0229
  Fax: 1(508) 545-7580

Ordering Information:
Quantity sales. Special discounts are available on quantity purchases by corporations, associations, and others. For details, contact the publisher at the address above.

Printed in the United States of America.

  ISBN-13:   Softcover   979-8-89676-437-3
              eBook   979-8-89676-438-0

Library of Congress Control Number: 2025914665

DEDICATION

For my beloved family and in memory of Gregor Watters, Andrew Peter Damon and those international civil servants who lost their lives in the service of the United Nations.

ACKNOWLEDGEMENTS

So many retired and active staff members of the World Health Organization and other United Nation's specialized agencies, far too many to name here, have given me encouragement and moral support in their belief and strong conviction that my story should be told. Some friends and colleagues volunteered to be interviewed, check facts, review drafts, and share their memories. I greatly appreciate their help and thank them for supporting me.

I am especially grateful to the family of my friend the late Dr. Gregor Watters, for their warm hospitality during my frequent travels to Geneva and for standing by my side throughout the legal battle.

Thanks also go to my legal representative, Mr. Edward Flaherty of Geneva, for providing practical counsel after reading the manuscripts. His help in sharing his experience and providing information about other relevant appeal cases is highly appreciated.

My attorney, Mr. J.A. Aggenbach of Koep & Company in Windhoek followed the legal process in Namibia from beginning to end and provided photocopies of the legal documentation which has been referred to this book. I am grateful for his dedication and invaluable assistance.

Hilary Bassett held together the writing process of this book from start to finish, reviewing and synthesizing every document I gave her and scrutinizing every scrap information I provided. Her attention to detail is the rare gift of a skillful writer, and I have relied on her strength and integrity in expressing my views of events and people described in this book. It was a joy to work with her.

Journalist and editor Mr. Nick Worrall encouraged me by writing the prologue and editing the book between his frequent travel overseas as a consult. I thank him for his cooperation.

I could not have survived the stress of travelling, researching and writing of this book for almost three years had it not been for the love and comfort of my wife, my children and a host of relatives and friends. I thank them for their understanding.

Victims of Ineptitude
Second Edition
AUTHOR'S NOTE

In 2007, when the first edition of this book was published, I received comments from readers, most of whom were active and retired international civil servants in the United Nations system and other organizations, friends and family members of Dr. Gregor Watters and Mr. Peter Damon who lost their lives in the accident, and from colleagues who have known me at work during my long service for WHO in several duty stations in Africa and Geneva.

The family members who lost their husbands and fathers described the book as a relief since the WHO administration was unresponsive for their request to get an official account on the cause of the accident. My meeting for the first time after the accident with Dr. Gregor's family in February 1998 at their lively home, just over the border at Divonne in France, was an emotional moment for all of us, especially for Zoila, Gregor's widow, and Aniola, his adopted daughter. As I gave them a firsthand account of the accident that happened on 11 February 1997, I felt it was a necessary part of the healing process since the two women never received an official report from WHO administration about the death of their beloved husband and father. When they saw the body in the funeral home at first, they thought he was assassinated. As we talked, anger again began to surface at the lack of enquiry by the WHO. Zoila was shocked interpreting that the WHO's apparent lack of concern as an insult. The only report she received was that an inquest was held in Windhoek and concluded that her husband died of multiple injuries. There was no further action taken to investigate the case. The Inquest was superficial. The Gregor's family were bruised by unnecessary provocation and frustration in their efforts to get the facts relating to the cause of death of their father and husband. Thus, in August 1998, they asked the Public Prosecutor of the Government of Namibia for an official investigation to be held and state the reasons for not pursuing the case. On the advise of the British High Commission in Namibia, they hired a Windhoek lawyer and set a private legal wheel in motion by prosecuting the WHO driver.

The long legal struggle between the Namibian Government and WHO to get the case against the WHO driver into court that started in October 1999 came to a close on 16 February 2004. It was a relief for Gregor's family although diplomatic immunity was the brick wall that saved the driver from going to jail for the rest of his life. The hammer to break the wall was in the hands of the WHO Director General according to the Ministry of Justice of the Namibian Government. But the Director General of WHO was not approached to lift the immunity of the driver. It is known that far more outrageous things have happened under Diplomatic Immunity by the United Nations employees and have been kept out of the public gaze. The final remark by the Attorney General of Namibian Government, "The attempt to immune a Namibian Citizen from the operation of the general laws in the country on account of him being a driver of the UN Organization may be viewed as an abuse of the privileges accorded to such an organization by the host country…" In this context, the Attorney General's view was giving immunity to the driver was against the Namibian Constitution which needs review by the United Nations General Assembly.

Regarding the death of the Namibian official, Mr. Peter Damon, justice was most certainly not served at all, and I still ask why the Namibian Ministry of Health or the Ministry of Foreign Affairs did not raise this issue. At least WHO should have paid the young widow, Sanya Damon, a part of the insurance claims of the vehicle that killed her husband who was on an official mission. Even if the vehicle did not have insurance, WHO would have done something for her as compensation to help her raise their three children. Peter's sister who lives in the USA sent me a thank you letter for dedicating the book in memory of her brother. His brother from Namibia, who was also a staff member of the Ministry of Health in Windhoek visited the accident site and examined the condition of the vehicle that took the life of his brother Peter Damon, and sent me the photo shown in this book. All the tires were in place without signs of damage except some parts of the car's body. They were very delighted to receive a few copies of the book to share with family members.

The other comments made about the book, apart from being a relief to the bereaved families, were eye-opener, whistle-blower, and controversial. It is an eye-opener because it encourages every international civil servant who has been the victim of injustice to speak out, as they are tied by golden thread, not to write about what happened to them after leaving the organization for fear of losing their benefits and consultancy services. However, it is encouraging to see that after I have spoken out, some colleagues have started writing despite the risks, about their experiences including staff harassment and abuse of authority in WHO. The problem will continue unless drastic measures are taken to punish the wrongdoers. A few months after the Namibian car crash, when the WHO representative in Burundi was murdered at his residence and his body thrown in Lake Tanganyika, the police wanted to interrogate the WHO staff and sought permission from the Organization. It was granted immediately. On the contrary, WHO fought to the highest level to deny us justice under the cover of immunity. The whole High Court against WHO was farce, a charade to deter Zoila Waters from pursuing her civil case. A mockery of local judiciaries. In my case, I have spoken, and the act of WHO as the Tribunal finding put it was "inconceivable".

A friend of Dr. Gregor Watters, who retired from WHO service described the book as terrific and wholistic. He informed me that he has also started writing a book about his experience of working for WHO in hardship areas as European and the challenges he met and the level of support he got from the Regional Office and Headquarters in Geneva. He added a mockery statement which said that he is focusing on work that had a positive health outcome as his boss is still in active service of the organization and he did not want to disappoint him.

The most compelling book published after "Victims of Ineptitude" was "WHOLIGANS"; a witness account of fraud and bullying at the heart of the World Health Organization by Kari Just Laperriere, a former staff member of the WHO Administration with 15 years of professional service as a Human Resources Expert. Her book exposes WHO as the worst UN agency under the authority of the International Labor Organization Administration Tribunal ILOAT in cases of harassment, reassignment, and recruitment. In her own case, she initiated a legal appeal against WHO, a process that continued for 10 years. During this long antagonizing period, WHO escalated the harassment, defamed her, and committed forgery in an attempt to silence her. WHO simply dehumanized her and knowing that its despicable actions against her had led to severe illness, and that she was on strong medication. It nevertheless relentlessly did all in its might to destabilize her. She confessed that there were moments when she had been close to jumping. She concludes her book by a snapshot legacy of Dr. Margaret Chan, the Director General of WHO, who left office in 2016 after two terms service. It was during her reign that Kari Just Laperriere fought a legal battle against WHO and eventually won. She also sent a message at the end of her book about what the new Director General should do to regain the image of the organization and restore the confidence of the hard-working WHO staff across the world. The question is, do the Director General and the Regional Directors want to learn from their mistakes?

Those who commented that the book is a whistleblower may be right in the sense that a whistleblower by definition is anyone who reports wrongdoings within a workplace or organization; abuse of authority, disclosing specific danger to public health, laws, rules, and regulations. In this context, the considerations of the WHO Board of Appeal after hearing my case no. 476 on March 20, 2000, and that of the International Labour Organization Administration Tribunal on November 5, 2002, under case 2190 can be given as evidence for justification of the whistleblower view. In summary, the WHO Board of Appeal noted that although WHO was not in a position to carry out criminal investigation as such investigation was the responsibility of the local authorities. However, in the light of the contradictory statements made by various parties involved concerning weather conditions, and the state of the road, and the gravity of the accident in which two people died and a third was seriously injured. The Board considered that such an enquiry was essential. The Board also noted that the objective of diplomatic immunity was to facilitate the work of WHO's international staff, not to allow individuals to break the law with impunity. They considered that WHO should do everything in its power to facilitate an investigation into the accident by the Namibian authorities, and to ensure that justice was done. Although the Board requested the WHO Administration to release all the documents it had in possession, the Members of the Board concluded that no other documentation existed and noted that there was nothing which indicated that any sort of internal enquiry into the accident had been carried out. Similarly, the judges of the ILOAT, having examined the appeal under my case number 2190, passed their judgement as follows.

"It is incomprehensible that no internal administrative investigation was conducted following an accident which involved a WHO vehicle driven by an employee of the Organization in the context of an official and which caused the death of two passengers, one of whom was a WHO staff member, as well as the serious injuries suffered by the complainant. The fact that the Namibian authorities opened their own enquiry could not in any way exempt the Organization from ascertaining whether the condition of the vehicle. The preparation of the mission, and more generally the circumstances of the accident revealed any administrative failure, the consequences of which it would have a duty to bear. As noted in by the Board of Appeal, there is no evidence to suggest that any internal enquiry whatsoever was conducted in connection with this accident. This failure caused the complainant an injury which the Tribunal considers to be equitably compensated". In Namibia the Prosecutor General failed to proceed with the initial proposal made by the Ministry of Justice to request WHO's Director General to waive the driver's immunity and allow justice to be served. It was his moral duty not to abuse the privileges of diplomatic immunity given to its international civil servants. The high court ruling after the driver was charged in the Magistrate's court with Culpable Homicide because he enjoyed diplomatic immunity from prosecution was against the Namibian Constitution. It is for this reason that the General Assembly of the United Nations should review the limit of the immunity given to its international civil servants and the employment condition of the ILOAT judges which is currently under the International Labor Organization."

Those who described the book as controversial, meant that it may give rise to public disagreement to criticize WHO as it is working hard to save lives. They may also argue that it operates with efficiency and that its workforce abides by established rules, regulations, and code of conduct, and that any credible allegations of misconduct are reported and investigated to ensure that a duty of care is provided to the workforce. On the other hand, a controversial book sparks public debate, challenges prevailing social or cultural norms, tackles sensitive subjects like sexual and professional harassment, and leads to heated discussions, differing opinions, and significant emotional responses similar to Gregor's widow and Kari Just Laperriere cases. The last chapter of the book, "Long Live WHO" clearly demonstrates that the book is not against the Institution's existence and its immense contribution for global health. Instead, the Organization whose budget was frozen for 13 years chose to spend hundreds of thousands of dollars from an unknown budget source by going to the Tribunal and the Namibian High Court to protect an employee who at best was incompetent at his job. At worst, he was a menace and a liability who might yet cause the death of more eminent, skilled people the world can ill-afford to lose.

Who cares? Few people, because the money did not come out of the pockets of individuals but from the bottomless purse of faceless bureaucracies, sheltering so-called leaders and directors who have long ago lost any consideration or concern for their hardworking staff and the Organization's reputation and effectiveness, or above all, compassion for the millions of Africans dying of disease. It seems to me that a controversial book gets better public attention. The controversy is about the leadership and bureaucracy and not about the work of the Organization to which it is committed.

CONTENTS

PROLOGUE

You could easily argue that one of mankind's greatest achievements – far outreaching the killing power of the atom, the phenomenal speed of the flying machine, the growth of communications to disseminate information and entertainment – is the progress that has been made in the past century to improve the health and longevity of men, women and children. This, on a worldwide scale, though Natural always seems to find a way of fighting back, to challenge the scientist further and in greater complexity.

There are many organizations committed to the fight against ill-health, the best known being the World Health Organization, founded in 1948 and funded from the pockets of ordinary people and their governments. Consider the extraordinary battle the WHO waged against smallpox in the 1970's – and won; the crippling and disfiguring scourge of Yaws, which afflicted 50 million people in the 1950s, is virtually forgotten; and other killer ailments that arrived in epidemic, even pandemic form, only to be neutralized through tenacious assault by the international health professionals.

The latest and probably the toughest challenge so far, is that of AIDS, currently disabling and killing millions of people worldwide and leaving behind hordes of tiny orphans. The WHO has been one of the leaders in this war which is being waged by its determined international civil servants. Their primary interest – one must believe – is not – only the welfare of the world's vulnerable populations, but also of their own staff and agents whose exploits among the deadly bacteria and viruses pose intense personal risk and present truly a heroic undertaking.

Those facts and ideas are reflected in this book by a former professional staff member who travelled for more than two decades in hostile places with scant regard for his own good health and security, in the fight for better health and living conditions among some of the world's poorest and more vulnerable people. It comes as a shock, therefore, to discover that in the writer's experience, the WHO can be a cold and heartless organization which shows precious little respect for its own hardworking staff and is considerably wasteful, misspending its precious public funding to pay for errors and mismanagement. This is a story of human tragedy and massive disillusionment. It will, page after page, severely anger readers of reason and goodwill who will surely find it hard to believe the administration of such a large outfit with such great responsibilities can behave in such disgraceful and uncaring manner.

The casual, wasteful and, at times, vindictive operation of the WHO is scrutinised in expert and deeply moving detail by the experienced official. He believed that WHO was "a body which many of us loved and respected; by and large it was held in high esteem by the rest of the world; it stood for high ideals, which inspired its staff, many of whom had died for them."

Ethiopian born, Firdu Zawide, and his two valued professional colleagues, Dr. Gregor Watters of British national and Mr. Peter Damon of South African, origin venture to remote part of Namibia on humanitarian journey for the WHO official mission. The story relates what becomes of them, the callous treatment they and their families receive, the extent to which the WHO Administration – right to the very top of Organization – has been prepared to go to evade their responsibilities to their long-serving employees.

In such an uncertain era as today's it should not be surprisingly to find that one huge international agency, charged with improving the health of the world's peoples and living off great sums of public money, should care so little about the people who staff it, many of them utterly devoted to bettering the lives of those less fortunate. But that is the disgraceful and saddening picture painted in this book by a long-serving and highly placed official who writes movingly from his own experience. It is a fight for justice which at the time of writing has yet to come to an end.

Nick Worrall – journalist and editor

WORLD HEALTH, ONE STEP AT A TIME

For years, ivory-tower academics and political leaders have cried *'Reform!'* to the World Health Organization and the United Nations in general. But change doesn't happen overnight, so it is left to the staff of International Civil Servants to grapple with the real difficulties the academics and the politicians discuss. Our work in distant lands among foreign cultures is hazardous and lonely, exacerbated by the lack of support from above. Should we fail as a result of the weaknesses the academics theorise about, no blast of grand talk at a conference, no high-flying plan on plush paper, will save millions of dollars in aid money from sinking into sand like water. The individual human story I am about to reveal illustrates why, at the micro-level, Africa remains the most disease-ridden continent in the planet.

'For the want of a nail, a shoe was lost...' I hope to show that simply by treating its own staff according to the mores of good management, the World Health Organization, the other specialized agencies and the United Nations could probably be much more effective. This is unashamedly personal story, which I hope will touch people's hearts in a way that dry academic reports, mouldering on musty shelves, do not.

It seemed a routine enough mission. As the 737 touched down on Windhoek's scorching tarmac at the end of my long journey from Brazzaville, in the heart of Africa, I felt tentatively optimistic about our prospects. On this Saturday in February 1997, my job as Environmental Health Adviser for the World Health Organization in Africa seemed fruitful and fulfilling. I was here by invitation, after all: the result of the Namibian Government's positive response to our acceleration towards the goal of 'Health for All by the Year 2000'. We'd been beating this drum on numerous international platforms for years, following the historic Alma-Ata Declaration of 1978 which spelled out the minimum activities governments should aim for in implementing the World Health Assembly's agreed priority of primary health care.

This Declaration had been a victory for common sense in improving the world's health. It stated that the delivery of sound primary health care such as good nutrition and safe water should be a top priority in every country, since these things were ultimately far more effective in preventing sickness than trying to deliver miraculous drug-based 'bullets' for individual diseases. Health was increasingly seen as a vital prerequisite for social development and justice; yet it could not be bought, or bestowed on any country which was not prepared to do the groundwork. Good health depended on the provision of good primary health care, and this in turn depended on the ability and political will of individual nations. If leaders valued guns, fancy palaces or even education more highly, their people would remain as weak and sickly as their health budgets.

With the millennium almost upon us, the pressure was on for myself and my colleagues to find, in this case, a sensible health route for all Namibians. They needed one, for their lives at that time were, for the most part, distinctly insalubrious. No doubt Namibia *did* want better health for its citizens, or we wouldn't be there. Yet the young, developing country was feeling overwhelmed by the massive scale of its communicable disease burden. It couldn't do without modern hi-tech healthcare, for all its fabulous cost, yet at the same time it recognized the urgent need to upgrade the appallingly inadequate and patchy basic health services bequeathed by the country's colonial masters. There was a need for thorough planning, reaching into every corner of this vast mostly empty land. The new Master Plan must integrate all the components of healthcare including adequate safe drinking water, sanitation, hygiene education and so on, not to mention basic first aid. This required taking a lot of concepts into account such as equity, effectiveness, affordability, community participation, inter-sectoral collaboration and the use of appropriate technology.

'The number of water taps is a better indicator of how much leaders care about their people's health than the number of hospital beds.'

Welding all these things into a clear plan of action was a complex undertaking – which is where the World Health Organization came in. The Ministry of Health had requested the help of experts from WHO's African Regional Office (AFRO) in the form of myself and a colleague, Dr. Gregor Watters, from WHO headquarters in Geneva, to help formulate an effective national policy on sanitation, plus strategies for putting it into practice.

Pledging countries to do this unglamorous but fundamental work had been my job for nearly 20 years. However, since my transfer in 1991 to the Regional Office in Brazzaville, I'd been largely desk-bound, gathering reports and analysing figures. So I very much enjoyed times like these when I could stretch my legs over the local terrain and see for myself what the real difficulties were and what could be done about them.

My remit covered 46 African countries, so there was plenty of variety. My duties were to promote environmental health programmes within the primary health care framework, so as to slash the communicable element of many misery-causing diseases. Factors such as unsafe drinking water and lack of hygienic sanitation; exposure to indoor and outdoor air pollution; poor quality housing, drainage and waste disposal; exposure to toxic chemicals and unsafe food, and occupational hazards, all fell under my portfolio.

Astonishingly to people in the West, one out of every two people in the developing world suffers from the diseases carried in their water and food, and an estimated 30,000 people die *every day* from water-related diseases. Environmental health, or lack of it, thus accounts for about a third of the burden of unnecessary morbidity and mortality in Africa.

I am a sanitary engineer by profession, with a background in public and environmental health – a common enough species in WHO in 1981 when I joined, but rarely sighted today, particularly in Africa. Out of the thirty-plus WHO sanitary engineers employed at that time, in the African Region, only a handful now remains at local level, and until my retirement in 2004, I was the only survivor at international level. I find this distressing, because no matter how technologically advanced treatment becomes, it still makes more sense to prevent illness in the first place. Given the appalling conditions extant in much of Africa, these elementary first steps are all that's needed to cut out a vast amount of misery.

In the 1970s, before it lost its way, the World Health Organization focused on public health policies such as immunization, nutrition, safe water and sanitation, maternal and child health and healthy lifestyle. Today, despite the Alma-Ata Declaration and other fine-sounding words, WHO has largely succumbed to political pressure to prioritise recurring illnesses by spending millions on first-world drugs. The original philosophy was excellently promoted in Africa by Dr. Comlan Quenum, first African Regional Director of the WHO African Office (1965-1984) and a charismatic advocate of community health. He told Member States that 'If there is to be Health for All by the Year 2000 we must [address] all basic problems which no technocratic structure has been able to solve.'

Sadly, Quenum died in office of a heart attack in 1984 in his fourth term as Regional Director, after returning from intensive field visits to several countries. But he laid down an excellent blueprint in his book *Twenty Years of Political Struggle for Health.*

Dr. Quenum's African community health paradigm was wholeheartedly endorsed at global level by his contemporary, the great Dr. Halfden Mahler, Director General of WHO 1973 to 1988. Dr. Mahler believed that the number of water taps is a better indicator of how much a country cares about its people's health than the number of hospital beds it provides. If the world forgot this, he predicted, the number of hospital beds would ultimately far exceed the number of water taps – which indeed has been the case. Today countless water supply sources have dried up due to drought and neglect, with the result that infectious diseases such as cholera, malaria and bilharzia, have flourished through contaminated water and other environmental factors. This totally unnecessary disaster is on top of tragic new diseases such as HIV/AIDS, which are over-crowding hospital beds beyond belief, and way beyond capacity.

Mahler and Quenum were two great international health leaders, and they worked together as colleagues and friends in an exemplary way. They demonstrated mutual respect and genuine support for each other without rivalry, a standard which alas, subsequent leaders were unable to sustain. Their aim in the 1970s and 1980s was to assist Member States in achieving the objective of 'health for all by 2000'. Their policies contributed to the eradication of smallpox and laid the foundation for control of malaria, guinea worm, onchocerciasis (river blindness) and other tropical diseases. Never again were leaders of the World Health Organization to be so clearly focused and so immune to politics and the maneuvering of multi-national pharmaceutical companies.

Under subsequent leaders, international politics played a great part. Power struggles, rivalry and the interests of the global drug trade gradually overpowered those who had at heart the interests of millions in far-flung countries such as Namibia, dying like flies from the easily-preventable diseases. The approach to health gradually became top-down, the priority given to curing diseases through medication, high-tech treatment and expensive drugs, which were accessible to the rich minority instead of the rather more numerous humble peasant. The major emphasis on old-fashioned, common-sense ways of preventing illness, dried up along with the taps. It simply wasn't sexy enough for the space age.

That's not to say that the Organization hasn't achieved an immense amount of good, of course. The World Health Organization's objective in 1948 when it was founded remains the same today; 'The attainment by all people of the highest possible level of health'. And health is defined in its widest sense – as meaning complete physical, mental and social well-being, not merely the absence of disease and infirmity. Its strategy for achieving this high ideal is to act through Member States, advising their governments on technical matters so as to strengthen their health services.

The Organization also finances the training of local health professionals and tries to encourage policy decisions based on research and epidemiological evidence. Many a fanfare about ways of improving public health has been sounded internationally, with Decades of this and Years of that. And these events have achieved a great deal, as we shall see. It is easy – and popular – to mock them, and indeed United Nations and Bretton Woods Organizations such as the World Bank have often invited criticism by launching such grandiose-sounding, hot-air programmes at glittering banquets, attended by chauffeur-driven Ministers flown into New York from round the globe at a cost which probably exceeds many a country's entire health budget.

At grassroots level, we, the civil servants, have a different perspective. We need such goals to work towards, and often assist in their formulation. But, while acknowledging their importance we also know what their achievement costs in human terms. It isn't just a question of providing the money, though that helps. It is also necessary to provide the right staff and to give that staff the best possible management and support. Because to us falls the lonely, difficult work of translating grandiose plans into concrete reality. Persuading poverty-stricken, starving and illiterate people to alter their way of life fundamentally by adopting new standards of hygiene, for instance, doesn't happen overnight. It takes months of hard unremitting slog, based on sound psychology. It takes in-depth knowledge and understanding of change, and the way people react to it, work with it and internalise it before it actually happens. You can put on paper any number of targets, theories, diagrams and dreams but if you ignore real people, progress will be as slow as a stream in a drought, and just as likely to dry up.

In the more than fifty years of the Organization's existence, WHO officials have learnt some hard lessons about this. There have been spectacular successes, such as the eradication of smallpox – quoted ad nauseam. And there have been some lesser known but equally dramatic failures. Wonderful, fruitful work has been done in defining and publishing standards, epidemiological intelligence, and protocols for healthy practices that slash the rates of disease dramatically. Many useful books have been published, including comparative health statistics for every country in the world, which enable nations to see how well or how badly they are doing. This engenders awareness, rivalry between countries, and efforts to improve which are enormously gratifying, and have often led to the recovery of some very sick health budgets!

Nevertheless, there remains a long and shocking list of things that have *not* been achieved. Not only have plagues such as AIDS been allowed to flourish but hundreds of millions of people have not been given even the most basic prerequisites for civilised living; safe water, adequate sanitation, and information about the importance of both. These people still defecate in the open, so that what little water they have is contaminated further. Small wonder that half Africa suffers from water-borne and excreta-related diseases.

If you ignore real people, progress will be as slow as a stream in a drought, and just as likely to dry up.

The Africans and others who drink polluted water and live in contaminated environments pay the costs in the currency of illness, death and stunted lives. Neglecting their needs costs far more in the long term than the meeting them. Massive immunisation drives, and even fancy clinics, achieve little when people are dying in their millions from conditions such as diarrhea.

Many people in the West feel that the problems of Africa are overwhelming; that the continent is a lost cause, its people fundamentally helpless – the victims of never-ending crises, bad governance, disasters and catastrophes. African people are despised, because it seems they cannot solve these problems themselves but must forever be begging rich and powerful nations to intervene. But those of us who have not only worked in Africa but belong to its soil, like myself, know the simple truth: that if you patiently educate people, instead of dictating to them, they, like people everywhere, will choose what is in their own best interests and change their personal habits willingly.

The World Health Organization has been held in high esteem for its struggles to protect mankind from scourges and the misery of diseases both communicable and non-communicable. Although we believe that the high esteem is deserved, we shall show how its struggles are compounded by a sickness at its very core, preventing the Organization from achieving anything like its potential. We understand that this is why it has lost its status as the unquestioned leader in global public health, as evidenced by the fact that many bodies today outstrip it in health-spending power. They include the World Bank, UNICEF, UNDP – and most recently even UNAIDS. All have dropped WHO as the executive agency for their public health and water and sanitation projects, preferring to do the work themselves.

In revealing my own experience and that of colleagues in the international civil service, it is my hope that the people and nations who entrust this Organization to look after global health, will examine more critically how that job is being done. I hope that they will demand it be done better. Because not only money is invested in the WHO but also the hopes of people everywhere for a better world, in which human suffering is reduced and poor people are genuinely helped to live a socially and economically productive life. When such bodies fail because they mismanage their own staff, the very people who must ground their vision if it is to work, it is as if the billions of dollars they are entrusted with, are so much water poured into the sand.

This is the story of a mission that went horribly wrong. But, in a wider context, it is about what can happen when an antiquated approach to management is applied to human beings. For years, critics have said the United Nations and its specialized agencies were in need of reform. But while academics theorised about it in their ivory towers, we, the international civil servants, struggled on the ground, our jobs made harder by knowing that should we fall prey to any of the ills the academics pointed out, we would have no recourse to justice. And so it was to prove.

The story illustrates, as no dry study can, what can happen when leadership is inadequate; when it is above the law and accountable to no-one. It's about the fight of one individual against a vast implacable bureaucracy which had no interest in people skills; about a leadership which, instead of trying to motivate and inspire, was concerned only with protecting itself from accusations.

Far from being noble and above petty squabbles, the WHO is deeply embroiled in them. It is time governments insisted that it modernize and manage its human resources in line with the best, not the worst, practices. Only then it can achieve its goal as a dynamic 'World Health Organization'.

CHAPTER ONE

AN UNFORGETTABLE ADVENTURE

B*efore narrating the disaster that befell me in Namibia, we backtrack to how I came to be visiting the country. What sort of people are hired by the WHO? Are they, mostly westerners, 'deeply convinced of the superiority of their own values and of the supremacy of their technical knowledge; as Graham Hancock says in his book 'The Lords of Poverty'?*

I am an Ethiopian, raised under the stable, if autocratic, regime of Emperor Haile Selassie. In the four-plus decades of his rule, from the 1920s to 1974, Haile Selassie transformed and modernised Ethiopia. The Emperor had a strong conviction that the key to modernization was the development of a sound education system. As evidence of his firm commitment, the education portfolio in his cabinet was held by himself. Given the immensity of the reconstruction problem following the Italian occupation of Ethiopia in 1941, the achievement of Selassie's government in terms of education is worth noting. The Emperor took special pride in providing education free for Ethiopia's youth, from primary to tertiary level. Occasionally he took time off from his busy schedule to visit schools in person; once a year he would offer Christmas gifts to thousands of school children who assembled at his old palace in Addis Ababa. The finances of local education institutions were supplemented by overseas grants and some friendly countries offered technical cooperation. I was among the young Ethiopians who benefited.

Ethiopia's international obligations became more complex during Haile Selassie's rule. Thus as a boy in Addis Ababa, I'd watch, fascinated, as buildings such as the Headquarters of the United Nations Economic Commission for Africa rose up near my parents' house. I would dawdle by the construction site for a few minutes every day on my way to school, watching as form works were made, reinforcement bars cut and concrete mixed and poured onto columns, slabs and beams. This made engineering a natural career choice for me, and on leaving school with good marks in maths, I had no trouble securing a place at the College of Building Technology, later part of the Haile Selassie University, now renamed Addis Ababa University.

In my final year, my fellow-students elected me head of the home improvement community service project. Every Saturday we'd go out and work on people's houses, helping with the unglamorous but satisfying jobs of constructing pit latrines, painting walls, replacing worn-out corrugated iron roofs and digging drainage around the houses to prevent mosquitoes breeding. I became so fascinated by the relationship between health and a clean environment that I soaked up WHO texts on water, sanitation, and hygiene. Not surprisingly this paid off when it came to exams, and I was one of the top students. But I had ambitions for more than good marks; I wanted to contribute to people's welfare. So, while other final-year students wrote their dissertations on designing fancy buildings and so on, I took myself off to a remote farm for several months, and got the utmost satisfaction from designing and constructing a rural water supply system.

My subsequent career will give you an idea of what the WHO was seeking from the people they employed in those days. After graduating in 1966, I spent two years gaining hands-on experience as a construction engineer for a national building contractor in Addis Ababa. Then I won a scholarship from the British Council to do post-graduate study in public health engineering at the University of Newcastle-upon-Tyne in England. Greatly delighted I travelled there in 1968, and studied for a further three years, adding public health, epidemiology, water and waste water engineering and environmental health to my engineering portfolio.

At the time, Ethiopia had less than half a dozen sanitary engineers, so I expected that my impressive qualifications would mean I was welcomed home with open arms. But alas, that is not the way of human nature. Although I had no trouble getting a government job with the Ministry of Public Works, my specialisation made me a threat to the jack-of-all-trades civil engineers who were then the people to design and supervise systems for water supply and waste treatment. So after two years I quit and got a job with a parastatal, the Awash Valley Authority. The project I was to work on was executed by WHO and financed jointly by the United Nations Development Programme (UNDP), the Food and Agricultural Organization (FAO) and the Ethiopian Government.

With their cotton robes and wild warrior-like hair... they were the object of curiosity and fear.

I joined a team comprising a WHO Epidemiologist (Italian), a WHO sanitary engineer (Malaysian), a national sanitary engineer (myself) and a public health officer (Ethiopian). The Awash is one of the longest rivers in Ethiopia. Its upper reaches cross a huge savannah with scrub, shrub bush, scattered trees and tributaries that run into the Awash when there is rain in the highlands hundreds of miles away. The middle and lower valley stretching from Amibara to Tendaho is fertile, with dark, thick soil suitable for agriculture. We travelled extensively throughout its basin, carrying our tents and food, and conducting environmental and epidemiological surveys. Crossing the semi-desert, sleeping in tents, interacting with indigenous people and sharing their food: all this added up to an exciting and unforgettable adventure for a young man of 30.

A key objective was to settle the Afar nomads who wandered the length of the valley, living a primitive life. These nomads travelled half-naked with herds of camels, sheep and goats. Each night they assembled their huts, dome-shaped structures made of sticks and grass mats. With their cotton robes and wild warrior-like hair, sharp dangerous-looking pointed knives dangling from leather belts, they were the object of curiosity and fear whenever they appeared in villages and small towns. They wandered freely under the warm open sky in search of pasture for their camels, which were their major asset. They fed on camel milk, corn porridge, beef and goats' meat; they drank polluted water from rivers, ponds and small streams. They defecated in the open and, unless the weather was bad, they cooked outside their huts. They had few material possessions, the lifestyle limiting them to what they could carry.

This gypsy life may sound romantic to those of us who are deskbound in a smog-riddled city, but the reality was not so great. The freedom from materialism cost the travellers dear in terms of health; they suffered from malnutrition and constant infectious diseases – malaria, diarrhea and schistosomiasis, for instance, were rife. Much of this illness was due to ignorance and could have been prevented through attention to sanitation and hygiene, drinking unpolluted water, and eating a more balanced diet.

Our team put a lot of effort into settling these people, trying to engage them with the work on state-owned commercial farms. But agriculture was looked down on by the nomads as a dirty job, better left to the lower castes, the farmers. An Afar nomad with a small herd of cattle was superior in his own mind than any rich, successful farmer. This concept is an important element of the Afar psyche, as is attachment to clan and herds of cattle. The goal in life was to raise more and more wealth from cattle, even though they were destroying the fragile ecosystem on which they grazed their herds.

It wasn't easy to persuade them to change their traditional way of life, even when we told them that wearing better clothes such as shoes would save them from parasitic diseases such as bilharzia and worm infestation. We tried to train them in the use of latrines and tap water, and encouraged them to eat vegetables and other food items available in the market.

When people are allowed to choose what they get, they get what they want.

The government hoped to improve their quality of life by teaching them to grow crops; by settling them near state-owned commercial farms, where extension workers would show them farming techniques, and by training them to use farm tools. Ultimately it was hoped they would become normal, tax-paying citizens. However, there was another stumbling block in the way of this aim, in the form of the chiefs, who received indirect tax from the nomads. These chiefs were highly influential and vowed to disrupt the government's plans to settle the nomads unless they could have a say in them first. The net result was that we succeeded in settling only 140 families during the initial phase of the project.

In *Lords of Poverty*, Hancock pours scorn on our efforts on behalf of the Afar. 'Their traditional dry-season pasture lands have been sown with cash crops and surrounded with barbed wire, so they are today reduced to absolute penury, their independence gone, their way of life shattered, their dignity destroyed as they queue in rags for food handouts', he writes. Yet it seemed to us at the time, a worthy effort, because there wasn't much dignity in dying from malnutrition and disease either. Part of the subsequent trouble arose because when the nomads were paid in cash, they used the money to buy firearms. They thought this was the best investment they could make, protecting themselves from tribal enemies – just as the wealthiest nations in the world do today, so who can blame them?

Nevertheless, this illustrates how complex the business of settlement is, and how much we had to discover. By the time I went to Namibia, as we shall see, we had learnt many lessons. Far more emphasis was given to participatory approaches in which communities are asked to identify their own problems, analyse them and find solutions. Then the government can support them in providing the necessary facilities. When people are allowed to choose what they get, they get what they want.

Apart from our doubtful struggles with the Afars, however, our team was able to do some good. We designed and constructed water supply systems for commercial, private and government farms along the Awash River. We built demonstration houses and latrines. We established a Public Health and Environmental Control Laboratory; we carried out a water pollution assessment of the Awash River and its tributaries, the first ever river pollution study in the country. We also surveyed the industries which were discharging waste into the Awash River and its tributaries. We produced impressive reports on the baseline health and environmental conditions, which subsequently helped planners to decide on development priorities for the area.

To further this work, the WHO awarded me a fellowship to go and study river basin development in the United States. So, in June 1974, I set off for an extended tour of 15 American States, mostly in hot, semiarid areas such as Texas, Arizona, and New Mexico. I visited the Tennessee Valley Authority, the Delaware River Authority, the Ohio River Sanitation Compact (ORSANCO) and several training institutions.

This was my first visit to America, and I was delighted by the warm welcome extended to me everywhere I went. I made many friends, some of whom I corresponded with for years afterwards. I also visited a Puerto Rican self-aided housing project and studied their environmental health management programme. En route for home I stopped off at the WHO's Eastern Mediterranean Regional Office in Alexandria for a one-week field trip. I wanted to see first-hand their measures for controlling bilharzia in irrigation canals on the River Nile.

After this enriching experience, I naturally looked for opportunities to work for WHO in my chosen field of sanitary engineering. However, despite their generous sponsorship of my American trip, I was told that although my qualifications were right, I must gain at least five years' practical experience before being considered. This was the time when professionalism was the major criterion for appointees to international posts in WHO, not, as was later the case, political attachment, personal contact, gender or geographical representation.

This Junta was soon up to its elbows in blood.

My job with the Awash Project came to an abrupt end in 1976, the indirect result of the toppling of Emperor Haile Selassie by a military coup two years earlier. The people of Ethiopia had a great faith in the Emperor, hoping he would make their country into a democracy one day, one which would still accommodate the monarchy. Unfortunately, his love of power and his unwillingness to share it with his subjects made this unlikely, and led to his downfall at the hands of his own soldiers.

A proclamation by the Military Coordinating Committee, known as the Dergue, on 17 March 1975, abolished the monarchy, bringing to an end to the Solomon Dynasty which had ruled Ethiopia for over 250 years. Emperor Haile Selassie was assassinated in the same year while under custody of the Junta. This Junta was soon up to its elbows in blood; sixty former civilian and military officials were charged with maladministration, corruption and gross abuse of power while plotting to overthrow the military government, and were executed. A struggle for power within the Junta went on for two years, with Colonel Mengistu Haile Mariam finally gaining the upper hand, becoming Ethiopia's new army dictator.

All too soon the Dergue descended into violence and horror, as Mengistu's regime instituted a campaign of urban counter insurgency which he called, in fond recollection of the French and Russian Revolutions, the Red Terror. Anyone who opposed the regime was labelled reactionary and anarchist, and soon ordinary citizens were being purged through house-to-house searches and indiscriminate night raids in residential areas. The raids ended in summary executions on the merest suspicion of opposition, and had soon escalated into mass killing of citizens without process of law. No-one was spared, old, young, even children. As the wanton killing continued unabated, the terror of living in Addis Ababa became unendurable.

In 1976, I had married Mereb Shiferaw, and the first of our three children, a daughter, Tikikil, was born in 1977. One afternoon when my wife was still pregnant, we found, on returning from work, that our flat was surrounded by heavily-armed soldiers. These soldiers had already forced their way into the flat on a search for firearms and documents relating to anarchist organizations. Fortunately, they found nothing and we were left unharmed. But the incident sent shivers down our spines.

By the summer of 1977 the first round of Red Terror had broken the backbone of the any counter revolutionary elements. But then second round began, uprooting citizens from all cities and major towns. By the end of 1978 several thousand mainly young lives had been lost, including some of our close friends and relatives. The cruelty and lack of discrimination of this monstrous process remains a crime against humanity, and is by far the darkest chapter of Ethiopian history.

I steered clear of politics as far as I was able. Later two of my younger brothers emigrated to Germany and the United States. My father had also been a career civil servant in the Haile Selassie government, gaining the rank of 'Grazmatch' the traditional title granted by the Emperors to patriotic citizens who had fought against the foreign invasion of Ethiopia. He retired, but the new government confiscated the land and rental property he'd secured for his retirement. However, life had to go on and I was fortunate to obtain a non-government post with the Urban Water and Sewerage Authority, as water supply project engineer.

This project, financed by the German government to the tune of some US$ 15 million, entailed the construction of piped water supply systems for twelve medium towns. It provided me with valuable experience in supervising a complex, multi-million dollar scheme. I got on well with the German Water Engineers who were consultants for the project, and learnt much from them, while they fully cooperated with me in providing a design that used local materials and appropriate technology.

Nonetheless, when the two years of my contract were up I decided against renewing, as by now I had my license as a consulting engineer. I felt the time had come to start my own business. So, in January 1979, I sank every cent of our savings, and launched 'Sancon Engineering'.

This Consultancy had offices in the capital, Addis Ababa, and it turned out to be a good move. Contracts came flowing in from private consultants, government agencies and the university. Within two years my small company could (and did!) boast of designing water supply and waste treatment plants for two major new breweries and several industrial complexes. I had carried out environmental impact assessments for six tanneries, and designed the utilities for several complex buildings. I also lectured part-time at the College of Technology and the School of Architecture. In fact, I did so well that by 1981 I had expanded the business considerably and was able to build my own house.

I mention this success not merely to boast, but to challenge Graham Hancock's somewhat contemptuous description of international civil servants as 'a tribe of highly-paid men and women who are irredeemably out of touch with the day-to-day realities of the global state of poverty and underdevelopment which they are supposed to be working to alleviate'. He continues: 'These over-compensated aid bureaucrats demand – and get – a standard of living often far better than that which they could aspire to if they were working, for example, in industry or commerce in their home countries.'*

At all levels there are fine professionals in the employ of the World Health Organization and the United Nations.

I would like to correct this impression. I think at all levels there are many fine professionals in the employ of the United Nations and the World Health Organization – doctors, public health experts, nurses, health economists, sanitary engineers, chemists, epidemiologists, translators, accountants as well as public health administrators and business managers – who could have earned as much if not more if they'd stayed at home. Certainly, some friends of mine who qualified at the same time are now better off than I, through having become consultants and contractors.

However, if there are those idealism has been dampened and diverted into self-seeking, one reason is undoubtedly the poor staff management that has crept over the World Health Organization like a thick fog in the years that I have worked for them. The sense of being treated like an impersonal cog in a huge uncaring machine, driven ultimately by the political demands of donor nations and Member States, as well as by the personal ambition of Director Generals and Regional Directors, is not conducive to inspired vision or selfless dedication.

It was at this time, in 1981, that I received a letter from the WHO reminding me of my previous application, and asking if I would like to apply for a post that had recently become available in Sierra Leone.

The offer was tempting. Despite my booming business the blood-thirsty regime my poor country was labouring under made the decision a fairly easy one. We had had our share of horrific experiences under the Red Terror, and the idea of working in another country seemed highly attractive. I counted myself lucky not to have been persecuted, but I was still scared. And of what use was money when the Socialist Military

Government dictated how you spent it? We were only allowed to own one house; we were not permitted to educate our children abroad or to travel overseas on vacation, and the business tax was horrendously high. It seemed likely that things would get worse before they got better.

Besides, with my idealism and strict Coptic Orthodox Christian upbringing, I felt I should be doing something more constructive. Having been born and bred in Africa I knew its strengths as well as its weaknesses, and I wanted to help the continent heal by making my contribution. I had seen enough of suffering, and I believed I could serve humanity a whole lot better in another country, under the auspices of an Organization which I wholeheartedly admired. So, I accepted the WHO offer and, out of three candidates put forward by WHO to the government of Sierra Leone, I was the one selected. My career as an international civil servant had begun, initially on a fixed-term contract of two years. I thus joined the rapidly-growing, dynamic, public health engineering team of the African Region. Dr. Comlan Quenum was our leader, and our mission was to accelerate the provision of safe drinking water and basic sanitation to all of Africa.

Lords of Poverty Graham Hancock, Camerapix Publishers International, 2001, p32

CHAPTER TWO

NOTHING HAS MORE MEANING

L ife as international civil servant, working in foreign countries, surrounded by unfamiliar languages, cultures and beliefs, takes patience, courage, understanding and perseverance.

Good, caring leadership and wise support is vitally necessary.

But as events were to prove, at heart the WHO administration is shockingly cold.

'Serving WHO is a privilege,' Director General Dr. Gro Harlem Brundtland said in her inaugural address to the WHO staff in 1998. 'We can make a difference. We can help build healthy communities and populations. We can combat ill-health. We can do our part to combat poverty and suffering. Nothing in life – as I see it – has more meaning.'

These were fine, inspiring words. And back in 1981 when I went to Sierra Leone, it was the kind of motivation that empowered us. We were confident that the leadership was behind us. But we shall see that by the time Dr. Brundtland left WHO, many staff had become disillusioned, feeling misused and betrayed by leaders who seemed to put a higher priority on politics.

Graham Hancock wrote: 'At every level of the multilateral agencies, maladjusted, inadequate, incompetent individuals are to be found clinging tenaciously to highly-paid jobs, timidly and indifferently performing their functions and in the process betraying the world's poor in whose name they have been appointed.'

He goes on: 'It simply seems to be taken for granted by the UN ...that the experts and advisers it sends to Third World communities at the expense of Western tax payers are not only competent and able but are also well motivated and appropriately experienced. The key questions never get asked. Are these guiders and managers really equipped to render direct and useful service to the poor? Do they have sufficient humility and insight – which presumably, are at least as important as technical know-how? Perhaps most important of all, do the poor actually require the kind of guidance and management that wealthy foreigners can provide?'*

My experience in Sierra Leone shows that WHO and suchlike international bodies can provide useful guidance, but success depends on having properly-selected staff who are trained, rewarded and encouraged in their efforts. It is not an easy road and, as Hancock intimates, far more than mere technical knowledge is required.

Sierra Leone is on the West Coast of Africa, between Guinea and Liberia. Its population today is about 4.5 million. It had thrived in the nineteenth century as a Crown colony, the main base for enforcing the 1807 law that ended the slave trade. Many Africans rescued from slave ships settled there; by 1961 it had become an independent state within the Commonwealth, and in 1971 a republican constitution was adopted. In 1978 however, following a referendum, it became a one-party state.

Though the British claim to have left the stamp of their English civilization upon their colonies, less than 10 percent of the Sierra Leoneans were literate when the country gained independence. Nearly two hundred years later, the Creole descendants of those freed slaves were a distinct but tiny minority of some 60,000 people representing the well-educated elite of the country. In the first decade of self-rule, mismanagement and corruption were rife throughout the state-operated sectors. Roads, schools and hospitals deteriorated and new constructions were concentrated in the country's three main cities, Freetown (the capital), Kenema and Bo. Subsistence existence in the villages became even more difficult.

The substantial foreign funding I was able to mobilise was one reason for my popularity.

By the time I arrived, the average baby born in Sierra Leone had about a one in ten chance of surviving a host of infectious diseases and chronic malnutrition to reach adulthood. Having done so, men could expect to live up to the age of forty-one and women six years longer. Infant mortality was high: 154 of every 1000 babies died before their first birthday. Maternal mortality was 700 per 100,000. And for those older children and adults who fell ill, scant curative facilities were available. Fewer than 150 doctors – many of them foreigners – treated the whole population in a patchwork of hospitals and clinics nationwide that provided only 4000 beds. Under these circumstances most of the population, especially in rural areas, sought medical help from traditional herbalists.

My assignment in Sierra Leone was as Technical Adviser to the Ministry of Health and the Water Supply Department. Later, as I gained seniority among the WHO team, I acted as the WHO Representative when that personage was out of the country. My initial contract was for two years but it kept being renewed, and in the end we stayed for eight – the eight most productive years of my life. The Government was reluctant to part with me; we left for personal reasons to do with our children's education.

The substantial foreign funding I was able to mobilise was one reason for my popularity. I started with a project of US$2 million – a soft loan from the German government to improve the waste management of the capital, Freetown, and the surrounding area. Greatly encouraged, I forged ahead with the extensive provision of public toilets, the development of refuse disposal sites, and the provision of facilities for septic tank emptying. I also embarked on biogas recovery from sanitary landfill, for the production of electricity. The project was extended for six more years with an additional loan of US $ 6 million from the Germans.

We re-organised the Environmental Health Unit of the Ministry of Health and trained health inspectors in waste management, food safety, water supply and sanitation. The Public Health Inspectorate was upgraded to department level and a national sanitary engineer was appointed at its head. The Ministry of Health changed its name to the Ministry of Health and Sanitation. And despite the civil upheavel the country has gone through since, this infrastructure remains firmly in place today.

With the financial support of WHO, we established a public health laboratory for environmental health surveillance and monitoring. When a new Department of Community Health was established at the University of Sierra Leone, I was invited to teach environmental health. For five years I lectured to international students, mostly medical practitioners and senior health superintendents. But the conditions were appalling – the School of Hygiene, where I taught for two hours a week, was housed in a dilapidated building at the government wharf. I felt this neglect was inappropriate, and convinced my German colleagues to propose a project to the European Union, so that a new school of hygiene would be included in the paramedical school they were putting up in Bo. It gave me great satisfaction to see this new building in place, and the School of Hygiene relocated there, before I left.

When I first went to start to Sierra Leone we prepared a national action plan for the United Nations International Drinking Water Supply and Sanitation Decade (1981-1990). Graham Hancock derides such ponderous titles, saying 'none of these observances, past or current, has made the slightest difference to the state of the world we live in. Nevertheless, their proliferation within the United Nations system tends to be confused with action.' Well, I don't know about the examples he cites, but I do know that this particular decade generated similar actions and plans to those of Sierra Leone all over the continent.

By the time it ended it was my job to correlate the results from the whole of Africa, and I found that enormous strides had been made. In 1975 less than five percent of the rural population of many African countries had access to safe drinking water and adequate sanitation. By the end of the decade (1990) the urban water coverage had reached almost 80 percent and the rural coverage 35 percent. During the same period urban sanitation coverage increased to over 75 percent and rural sanitation about 45 percent. Taking the population increase during the same period, this was a significant achievement; thanks to the external support agencies and national governments. It was an indirect result of this activity that took me to Namibia...but I am jumping ahead.

When such gestures are neglected, the wheels fall off.

As part of our plan, we established a national coordination committee composed of representatives from every Government ministry involved in water supply and sanitation, plus UNICEF, UNDP, NGOs and the donor agencies represented in Sierra Leone. We prepared projects for the expansion of urban and rural water supply. We hold monthly meetings to review our work plan and monitor progress. We introduced the concepts of community participation and hygiene education, without which such projects usually fall flat.

At one stage the World Bank arrived, with a proposal that an autonomous parastatal urban water supply company be established for the country. It was a good idea and after some discussion the Government agreed. However, the World Bank then reneged on its promise to make a loan available for the project. The national authorities were disappointed and turned to the WHO for help. I convinced my supervisor in Brazzaville to grant financial aid for the preparation of legislation and the necessary institutional structure by hiring a WHO consultant. The national authorities pursued this initiative and eventually, to my great satisfaction, launched the Sierra Leone Water Company – a major breakthrough in institutional reform of the urban water supply sub-sector, through which we forged ahead with an exemplary programme.

In the rural water supply and sanitation sub-sector, the communities took responsibility for providing local materials and unskilled labour, and committed themselves to ongoing operation and maintenance. We used a mix of technology, such as spring development, small piped supply, rainwater harvesting, hand-dug shallow and deep wells with rope and bucket, hand-pumps and mechanically drilled boreholes with submersible pumps. It may sound unexciting, but it was a first because it integrated education, technology and local participation – the three factors that are vital, for without any one of them the other two fail. I was delighted.

I got excellent feedback from my boss in Brazzaville, and felt that my efforts at furthering the work of WHO by building this good relationship with the Sierra Leone Government were appreciated. 'I shall recommend you get a double-step increase in your annual salary, Firdu!' he told me. And he was as good as his word, for in the appraisal report – the decisive document for the extension of contracts and the termination of employment by the WHO's staff administration – he included this recommendation honouring his promise. However, personnel didn't act on it and I was already on the upper salary scale of WHO professionals working in the field, so I didn't demur. But I valued my boss's encouragement almost as much as I would have the increase. In any Organization staff morale is boosted by such gestures, which help to oil the wheels. Conversely, when they are neglected, the wheels fall off.

In those days we would get a letter at Christmas from the Regional Director, Dr. Quenum, and the then WHO Director General Dr. Mahler, thanking us for our work and wishing us and our families a healthy and successful new year. It was a simple enough gesture, yet it made a difference. In later years it fell away, as their successors distanced themselves from their field staff. This illustrates an important point: considering how spread-out the global staff of WHO are, and how many nationalities they represent, it is remarkable how little is done to foster cooperation or to build a sense of belonging. Our dedication is taken for granted.

Although well trained in technical matters, we would have benefited immensely from training which took into account the difficulties of dealing with different cultures in different languages. When people outside WHO hear that this training is not given as standard procedure, they are usually incredulous.

Some UN Country Representatives took it upon themselves to create a sense of family among the international civil servants' community by inviting the various UN bodies to social events at Christmas and so on. The Representative of the United Nations Development Programme in Sierra Leone, at that time Mrs. Henry Hesse, from Ghana, was particularly interested in bringing us all closer. The WHO Programme Coordinator, Dr. Marcella Davies, also brought together the WHO family in social functions aimed at creating good relations among staff. But generally, we were pretty isolated. And when disputes and misunderstandings arose – inevitable in a foreign environment when you are trying to get people to work together and to uphold standards that came from afar and cost a lot to implement – it could get lonely.

I recall a few misunderstandings I had with national authorities. One day I returned to my office after visiting a fishing village outside Freetown together with field staff from the German Technical Agency (GTZ). We were considering a new project with GTZ to improve the sanitation, water supply and health of the fishermen, and I had been asked to draw up a sanitation proposal. On my return, I found a message on my desk from the Chief Medical Officer, whose adviser I was on environmental health matters. 'Mr. Zawide, please be so good as to come and see me!'

I went to her office the next day, and was received with an icy politeness quite unlike her usual friendly manner. We'd had a good working relationship until now, and I admired her – she was a medical doctor and a public health specialist, so we understood each other. 'What exactly,' she now demanded, in angry tones, 'did I think the role of the Ministry of Health *was* in rural sanitation?'

'The Ministry is playing an active role in promoting sanitation with the Water Supply Department,' I replied evenly. 'Several of your health inspectors are involved in the construction of pit latrines and hygiene education in rural areas. It's a highly effective programme, and the Ministry of Health is playing a useful role, even if it is the Water Department that is actually coordinating the programme.'

This, as it turned out, was the problem. The ministerial feathers had been ruffled because, after the GTZ group had paid her a courtesy call to discuss the fishing village proposal, which they were keen to support, she had naturally assumed that the Ministry of Health was to get the job (and the kudos) of implementing the project. Now it transpired that the Water Department was to be in charge after all. 'You should have warned me, Mr. Zawide,' she fumed. 'I would have seen to it that the correct agency was given the job.' I calmed her down and promised to give her monthly progress reports on the project.

The next day she called again, asking to come and see her immediately. This time I kept her waiting; I was no doormat. However, when I finally got to her office she welcomed me most warmly and was all apologies. 'I want you to know how much we appreciate the work you are doing in the Ministry, Mr. Zawide! Please forget our little misunderstanding.' She had a good heart and supported me throughout my stay in Sierra Leone. But it was a reminder of the delicate footwork we had to perform to keep everyone happy.

On another occasion the senior health inspectors got angry with me because I had recommended a re-organization plan which led to the establishment of a new Department of Environmental Health. The plan was approved by the Chief Medical Officer and the Permanent Secretary, which meant that senior health staff had to be transferred from the provinces to Freetown. They sent a deputation. 'Do you realise,' their leader demanded, 'that this plan will mean we lose out on considerable perks?' Whilst in the sleepy provinces they had plenty of free time to do private business. Now, in Freetown, they found they had more responsibility and closer supervision. 'We are angry and disappointed, and we blame you!' was the gist of their message, although more diplomatically expressed. I hastened to reassure them that because the move constituted a promotion, I would see to it they got more money from the Ministry. I also promised to ask WHO to award fellowships to enable Unit heads to go abroad for further training in their areas of specialisation. As time went on, they came to understand me better and we got on well. But such gaps in coordination between different departments and levels of government were a potential landmine in this field. Hancock was indeed right to ask 'Are these guiders and managers really equipped to render direct and useful service to the poor? Do they have sufficient humility and insight – which presumably, are at least as important as technical know-how?' We were given no help at all in developing much-needed skills such as conflict resolution and negotiation.

Life as an international civil servant, always working in a strange country, often surrounded by foreign languages and cultures, takes patience, courage and perseverance. Good caring leadership and wise support is vitally necessary. But, as events in my own case were to prove, at heart the WHO administration is shockingly cold.

Time to move on

While in Sierra Leone my two daughters finished primary school and our son, born there grew ready to start school. When it came to high school, we wanted a higher standard than was available there for our daughters, so I requested reassignment. At that time Zimbabwe had a good education system and the then Regional Director, Professor Monekosso, heard my case and reassigned me there as a reward for eight years' satisfactory service in Sierra Leone.

My new job was based in the sub-regional office in Zimbabwe, and meant constant travelling since I was now serving 14 countries in the South and East of Africa. I was mostly engaged in reorganizing environmental health services within the framework of the Three Phase Health Development programme at district, provincial and national levels. This concept was evolved by Professor Monekosso, building on Dr. Comlan Quenum's foundation in terms of the approach to health development. I helped these countries reorient their environmental health activities at different levels, and prepared projects for external funding. I had to be available to fly at a moment's notice to wherever an epidemic had broken out – to help, for instance, with outbreaks of cholera in Mozambique, Tanzania, Zambia and Zimbabwe.

But in 1992 our lives were again disrupted when the Zimbabwe office was closed due to reorganization. Some colleagues lost their jobs, but I was lucky and was offered promotion to the Regional Office in Brazzaville, capital of the Republic of Congo. Professor Monekosso valued my work and said so in my annual performance report – this was by way of reward.

However, it was not all plain sailing. The Congo was a French-speaking country, and there were no schools that taught in English. Although I had managed to learn French while in Sierra Leone, which was a great help to me, it didn't help the children. With a heavy heart, I realised that the time had come to part with them, as they must now join the legion of international civil servants' children who must be schooled in foreign lands. Whatever the benefits and perks of our lives, this is without doubt the heaviest cost.

Some of us have to pay with our lives.

Being without your family is stressful but necessary, since it is impossible to give children a good education when you often have to work in countries with low educational standards or a different language. Critics such as Hancock are scathing about the amounts we get paid, but without being complacent, one must take into account the personal sacrifices we make to do this work. Many WHO staff are hard-working idealists, with the interests of the poor at heart. If you doubt this, remember that some of us pay with our lives when we are sent into the epicentre of new outbreaks of disease. And when there's an Ebola crisis or some totally unheard of new virus such as SARS, WHO experts are first in line – and often, the first to die.

After much deliberation we sent the two girls to a boarding high school in the United States. Our son was still very young, so we decided to keep him with us for two or three more years. Eventually, when he was 11, we sent him to a boarding school in England. Later we transferred him to America, and started travelling regularly to the States. My wife remained with me in Brazzaville most of the time, and the children would come and stay. But family life thereafter was intermittent, and the family got used to being dispersed. I worried that the young ones might be lonely in a strange country. Life was never straightforward again.

Lords of Poverty Graham Hancock, Camerapix Publishers International, 2001, p98

CHAPTER THREE

INCENTIVISING AFRICA

*R*egional Directors hire and fire at whim, which enables them to run their empire with no restraint from Geneva. This causes fear and insecurity among staff. There is, incredibly, no effort at team building or overcoming the distrust and misunderstandings that arise....

Dr. Comlan Alfred Quenum, the first African to be appointed Regional Director, served from 1965 to 1984 and as we have seen, was an inspired leader. He wrote:

'In the field of Environmental Health, which is so much in the news today, I am sad to say that we have been overtaken by the twin evils of urbanization and industrialization even before we have managed to solve the basic problems of water supply, drainage and sewerage, waste disposal and adequate housing for the majority of the population. It has been said that people who feel they have no further contribution to make, seize upon imitation as some kind of cultural reprieve. We are therefore skeptical of that particular concept of development, especially in the health field. We think it is less a question of catching up with the most technically-developed countries, which should not be used as models anyway, than of reaching a minimum standard where basic needs will be met. When we have reached that minimum level, we can then strive for greater and higher things.'

As regional adviser I was responsible for promoting the WHO's environmental health programme throughout the African region, particularly its water supply and sanitation component. Our major role was in advocacy, training, monitoring and development of policy and strategy. We also provided technical support for projects from start to finish.

One of my first jobs in 1991 was to prepare an evaluation report on the International Drinking Water Supply and Sanitation Decade (1981-1990) in Africa. I had to establish how far the 46 countries in Africa had come in their efforts. It wasn't easy for them, for many countries were desperately poor, and struggled to implement WHO standards. And of course some had less worthy priorities. Sanitation and hygiene are not such sexy items on a country's budget as, say, arms or education, no matter how unhealthy its people.

Water problems are not unique to Africa – global demand has increased more than six-fold since 1900, while the world's population has tripled and economic growth has mushroomed. The United Nations has sternly warned that unless there's better management, two-thirds of the world's people will suffer severe or moderate water shortages by 2025. Countries that find it difficult or impossible to meet their water needs face severe stress.

It is easy if you live in a developed country to forget how recent its development has been. Although latrines dating back 10,000 years have been excavated in the Orkney Islands, and the Romans at Pompei had sophisticated flushing toilets similar to those invented by Sir James Harrington in 1596, modern concepts of water and sanitation are less than a century old in most of the world. Piped water wasn't introduced into industrialised countries until the late nineteenth century; water-borne sewage even later. Even then most countries weren't able to provide those services to rural populations until the mid-twentieth century. So Africa has not lagged so far behind, especially since many countries only gained independence during the past 40 years. Now all that's needed is for Africa to manifest the political will to mobilise its own human and material resources. The WHO provides a great incentive to do this by comparing the progress made by different countries – comparisons which have only been possible in the past 30 years.

A fundamentally new approach was needed, one that involved far more respect for local communities.

In our report we were able to compare such factors as the levels of service coverage in each country; how many houses had taps; how many public water points; what percentage of each population was served by sewers; how much of the drinking water was disinfected: how many schools incorporated health education into their syllabus: and how advanced was each country's plan for improving these things. Also, what was their total investment in the health sector.

Results ranged from big blanks from countries such as Burundi and Guinea Bissau, to total coverage for countries such as Mauritius and Algeria. It was interesting to note how many different agencies, UN bodies and ministries were involved in this work. It was clear that coordinating their efforts was vital. In spite of the constraints involved, both water and sanitation coverage increased markedly during the International Drinking Water and Sanitation Decade. They rose from 32% water coverage in 1980 to 49% in 1990, and from 28% sanitation coverage in 1980 to 56% in 1990. The WHO sanitary engineers assigned to the countries were greatly instrumental in bringing about this gratifying result.

All this culminated in the next phase of my work, which was the launch of 'The AFRICA 2000 Water and Sanitation for All Initiative' in September 1994, intended to keep the momentum of the Drinking Water and Sanitation Decade going beyond 1990. Attended by the Ministers of Health of 46 African nations, it was hailed as a major step forward in realising the potential of African countries to take charge of their own development. It recognised the need for local solutions and for establishing new partnership with development agencies.

A later regional consultation brought together some 140 participants, including senior government officials in the water sector, from almost every country in Africa. It also included representatives of UN Organizations, development agencies and non-governmental Organization. The purpose was to review progress and create a common vision for the future. Among them were Peter Damon of Namibia and Dr. Gregor Watters from WHO Headquarters in Geneva, two men whose ill-starred destiny came to be so closely linked with my own.

This consultation resulted in the 'Brazzaville Declaration', endorsed by 108 policy-makers from 46 African governments. This constituted a new vision for providing safe and adequate water and sanitation for all Africans. The Declaration was distributed to the 46 heads of state and within a year, over 25 countries had organized national consultative meetings and formed national action plans. These included demonstration projects in rural areas hard-hit by drought and cholera epidemics. An 'AFRICA 2000 village' was one in which self-help and community-managed water and sanitation projects were working. They became increasingly popular throughout Zimbabwe, Zambia, Mali, Ghana, Uganda, Botswana, Swaziland, Kenya, Benin and Tanzania.

We had learnt a lot from the activities of Decade, but there was one key lesson that impressed us greatly. This was, that a fundamentally new approach was needed, one that involved far more interaction with, and respect for, local communities. Thus in 1993 a far more satisfactory way of doing things was ushered in. It had yet another tedious and mind-numbing acronym: PHAST, which stood for 'Participatory Hygiene and Sanitation Transformation'. But its message was far more inspiring than its name, for it taught that there could be no lasting change in people's behaviour until they were properly educated about what creates health itself. If you know nothing of germs and how they are spread, a toilet can seem to have many useful purposes other than the one for which it was created. And why waste precious water washing hands? To change such ingrained and personal daily habits, these people had to *want* to change. Only when they understood these things would they want to learn how to maintain the equipment. No more supplying them, from a position of superiority, with stuff they neither understood nor wanted, because it was 'good for them'. It's so obvious a truth that one suspects only colonial attitudes obscured it in the past: when people *understand* why improved sanitation is to their advantage, they act.

It became so popular and effective in Africa that other regions of the world began to take notice.

PHAST had grown out of another initiative: SARAR, standing for Self-esteem, Associative strength, Resourcefulness, Action planning and Responsibility. This popular methodology developed in the 70s and 80s from integrated rural development projects, which enabled people to identify their problems, plan for change and then implement and monitor that change. Its two main principles are that people solve their problems best in a participatory group process, and that the group collectively has enough information and experience to begin to address its own problems. So PHAST also acknowledged that individuals within a community in fact already possessed a great deal of health-related experience and knowledge, and they were quite capable of determining their own priorities for disease prevention. It was a very different approach to that of experts going in and forcing change on people, as we had in the Awash Valley in Ethiopia.

One problem was that to get agreement took skilled facilitators and a shift in understanding. However, we were motivated and excited because we knew that in the end, this approach *worked*. Africa's health problems, amongst the worst in the world, could gradually be solved if it were to be universally adopted. So all the agencies – UNICEF, UNDP, the World Bank Water and Sanitation Group – joined forces with WHO to promote PHAST in the African region, convinced that at last, we could make real progress.

A 1994 report on the seven countries which piloted PHAST confirmed this optimism. Among the comments were: 'Trust and communication between communities and extension workers have increased. This has led to addressing real but unrecognised problems.' (Botswana). And from Uganda: 'The urban pilot project was a great success. Within a few months latrines had been built, drainage improved and garbage collection instituted. Groups also embarked on income-generating activities. Major achievements in rural areas were that:

- communities became willing to pay for the operation and maintenance of their water points;
- they were increasingly committed to the concept of community management;
- they requested extension workers to come more often and when they came, attendance at meetings increased;
- there was increased appreciation and understanding, which led to more installations of latrines with hand-washing facilities;
- communities wanted to monitor and evaluate their own progress and designed billboards to publicise their campaign.'

Following the success of this pilot phase, an African network was established to scale it up and several more countries, including the French-speaking West Africans, adopted the approach. A few even reached an advanced stage by institutionalizing PHAST as a tool for changing behaviour and empowering communities to take responsibility for their overall development. It became so popular and effective in Africa that other regions of the world began to sit up and take notice; we were approached by WHO Regional Offices in the Western Pacific and South East Asia for advice on training field workers.

Another activity which gained momentum in the wake of the Drinking Water Decade in Africa, was the tackling of key constraints in water supply and sanitation systems. Many countries had reported that their urban water supply was intermittent and few rural systems worked at all. Similarly, the majority of countries reported that no treatment was given to sewage discharged from public sewers. Overall, water and sanitation systems in Africa were experiencing severe operational problems. So collaboration was enhanced by the setting up in 1991 of an Operation and Maintenance Working Group of the Water Supply and Sanitation Collaborative Council. A network of key institutions and professionals oriented towards the promotion of good practice in Africa began to operate, helping each other and spreading information. WHO workshops and training courses were organized at all levels, with the technical and financial support of international and bilateral agencies. Two vital foci were identified, of universal importance: human resource development in all its forms and at all levels; and community participation, especially of women.

Practicing what we preached?

Now we return to the start of this book – the time when, in pursuit of these aims, I was invited to Namibia in order to help the Namibian Ministry of Health to implement the strategies that, it was hoped, would set their nation on its feet as far as health was concerned. I was joined in my mission, if you recall, by Dr. Gregor Watters, an expert who had flown in all the way from Geneva from the headquarters of the World Health Organization.

Greg Watters and I were old friends, and we shared a passion for this work. We were optimistic that this new approach was, at last, the right one, and that implementing it in Namibia would save many lives. We had no illusions – we knew that implementation entailed a long, uphill path. But the major stumbling blocks are common wherever you are, and we were sanguine that the advice we had to offer could save Namibia much time, effort and money.

First, we had to convince health officials that people must come first. Success lay in everyone understanding and accepting this, from the top down. It was a matter of education, psychology and tact – a simple but profound shift from the bad old days of colonial interference when international civil servants automatically assumed their job was to impose their superior knowledge and demand obedience. We aimed at helping Namibia motivate her people, so that long after we, the 'experts', had departed, the systems they had chosen for themselves in far-flung dunes and villages would go on operating. People must first be treated with respect, so that they developed new inner strength as well as better health. These things would, as they had elsewhere, give Namibian communities the necessary willpower to browbeat politicians until clean water became a priority. At present health ranked way too low here, although it had a better record than many an African state, where guns rated infinitely higher.

Yet as I thought over this approach, and surveyed our prospects in Namibia, I was uncomfortably aware that the Organization I represented didn't follow its own advice. For these fine ideals about how to treat people were totally ignored when it came to the WHO's own human resource management. The culture that ruled at Brazzaville was one of arbitrary favouritism, where an individual staff member's inner strength and self-esteem seemed to matter as little as a grain of Namib sand. The discretionary authority of the Regional Directors to hire and fire staff encouraged them to run their own small empires without restraint, causing immense fear and job insecurity. There was no effort at team building or overcoming the distrust and other complications that arise when people of different nationalities, languages and cultures are thrown together in the workplace. As a result, many staff felt misused and betrayed. This had led to a plummeting of staff morale and, consequently a decline in the Organization's credibility. This in turn, as many commentators have noted, directly affected its competency in fulfilling its responsibility as a global health authority.

This serious blindness of the WHO to its own inadequacies was now to have a profound effect on our mission. What happened to us illustrates the way that grand-scale plans can fail when the details are ignored. Amongst the UN staff too, people must be treated with respect, and those who are trusted to implement the plans must be honoured, as in any decent society. But because the Administration disregarded these fundamentals, thousands of man-hours and millions of dollars of aid money, was poured away. The promises made to the humble people of Namibia were pushed off the agenda for years. And the Organization was not held accountable for a single cent of the money or a single subsequent death that could have been prevented.

CHAPTER FOUR

ONE BIG SANDPIT

Prejudiced Western cynics ask, 'What else can you expect in Africa? Aren't all its people stunted, and backward, unable to initiate or maintain progress, especially once their colonial masters have departed?' The truth is that often their colonial masters created most of their problems, as the history of Namibia demonstrates.

Before recounting the dramatic events that overtook our mission, I would like to set our work within the context of the bigger picture: the way the World Health Organization seeks to achieve its ambitious goal of 'The attainment by all people of the highest possible level of health'.

In order to do its work, the WHO depends on its Secretariat, its highly-qualified technical staff, its Executive Board and its great Assembly. Its financial resources are paltry – astonishingly, the annual budget amounts to less than what it costs to run one large district hospital in a developed country. It is less than New York City's annual cleaning bill. During the biennium 2004-2005 an amount of US$960,111,000 – nearly one billion US dollars – was approved by the World Health Assembly under the regular budget. An additional US $1,824,500,000, approximately, was allocated to individual programmes such as the tropical diseases research programme, which are financed from other sources. So the total effective budget under all sources, was US$2,784,611,000. It is this pitiful amount which trickles into six regional offices to address the vast health problems of the world.

On the other hand, the Organization boasts assets which can't be measured in dollars, such as the virtual universality of its membership; the high regard in which it is held in medical and public health circles, and its position as final forum for international health consensus. It is this high regard that prompted the Namibian Government to request our help in drafting its health development policy. The Organization relies on such invitations, for without them it may not operate in a country. Even when governments do decide to spend their money in this humane way instead of on armies, limousines and palaces, it takes immense commitment from the people, not to mention substantial resources, to make a real difference.

WHO's financial resources are less than New York City's annual cleaning bill.

It's a big task, to expect health officials such as ourselves to come into a country and persuade them to adopt an approach which may be totally foreign to the way they think. So how did we plan to go about it?

To understand that you need to know more about Greg Watters. A silver-haired Scot who'd never lost his attractive Scots burr even after years of working for the WHO world-wide, Watters was a much-liked man. His reputation for kindness was deserved and he had a sense of humour such that few could tell a story like him. Greg was friendly, humorous and somehow, joyful. He had an incredibly sharp memory, with a special gift for recalling what was said in meetings. He would record every word in writing later. He was good company; a convivial dinner companion, but even better, someone who could enliven the dullest technical discussion with the most sober of ministers with a light story or an amusing joke. This charm was a valuable asset in our work, for we often had little time to establish a good rapport with government ministers and officials, vital if we were to succeed. Charm like Watters' could make or break a mission, no matter how many years of behind-the-scenes preparation had gone into it beforehand. Little wonder then, that I loved working with him.

I had often been thankful for Greg Watters' support in my job as Regional Adviser. It was good to know that someone in the remote, pristine offices in Switzerland felt as strongly as I did about the importance of this work. I often felt even more lonely than I had in Sierra Leone, as my job entailed constant travel throughout Africa. And by now I had little family support, as my children were at school in

England and America, and my wife had to divide her time between all three continents. Although the WHO and other UN bodies give their fixed-contract staff education grants for their children, it sometimes seemed scant recompense for the loss of family life.

Dr. Watters specifically had been invited to Namibia in his capacity as head of the joint WHO/UNICEF programme for developing water supply and sanitation monitoring systems throughout the world. We'd been on several previous missions together, to Lesotho, to South Africa, to Benin and to Botswana. In 1995 we had spent weeks in South Africa, at the invitation of Dr. Nkosasana Zuma, who later became Foreign Minister. We travelled extensively there, preparing a proposal for improving the water supply and sanitation facilities to rural clinics and schools. We also made available some WHO seed money to get this project off the ground. Later this project was incorporated into the country's Reconstruction and Development Programme, and the upgrading of facilities continued along the lines we'd drawn up. Dr. Zuma sent a letter of gratitude for our contribution to the WHO Regional Director.

Greg Watters and I had a lot in common, even though we'd been raised on different continents, at different times and in different cultures. One thing that bonded us was our alma mater – we'd both done post-graduate studies in public health engineering at the University of Newcastle-upon-Tyne. We were both progressive, deriving satisfaction from building a better world in the most down to earth way. At 53, I was slightly younger than Watters, whose 57th birthday it would be on Friday, February 14, 1997. He'd already planned a surprise dinner on this day for the WHO team accompanying him in this mission.

'Pretty stones'

I arrived in Windhoek on Saturday February 8. As I flew over the small capital, I looked down on neat white colonial houses, replete with blue swimming pools and lush green gardens, and was struck as always at the amazing contrasts of Africa. All around the town parched red plains stretched emptily away towards mountains. And I knew that scattered among the dunes were a million poor, in desperate need of water. In fact, the country was obsessed with it – the cracked dry plains created a never-ending battle with thirst.

Namibia was the baby of African nations, having gained independence a mere seven years earlier from its rich and powerful neighbour, South Africa. The infant was having problems getting on its feet, but on the whole it was doing well. In its favour was one of the best constitutions in the world, and fabulous natural resources.

Diamonds for instance. In 1884, a German named Adolf Lüderitiz had taken ownership of vast tracts of the Atlantic coast, where diamonds were so abundant they were kicked around by boys playing in the sand. Known to the indigenous people as 'mooi klip' (pretty stones), some of these gems were so fabulous they afterwards became the stuff of legends. And they made a pretty amount of money for the Germans too, as Namibia began to produce so many that the country topped the tables in terms of world production. At its peak, Namibia provided thirty percent of the world's gemstone diamonds. But not much money flowed back to the people who lived there. Between 1908 and 1915, the country exported 5.5 million carats in diamonds, which gave the German tax collector, not the local one, a magi's gift equivalent to Rand 6 million.

What's more, diamonds are not the only stones for which Namibia is famous. The country has a hoard of semi-precious ones, extraordinarily beautiful, with names to match: agate, amethyst, tourmaline, rose quartz, aquamarine, garnet, chrysolla, chalcedony and dioptase. Today these are polished and carved into a myriad of ornaments, jewellery and objets d'art for the tourists who increasingly favour this quiet, safe corner of the world.

On top of all this, Namibia also boasts some of the world's largest deposits of uranium, a much-in-demand mineral in this nuclear age. And there are still rich reserves of other minerals, including copper, lead, zinc, magnesium, cadmium, arsenic, pyrites, silver and gold. So, this must be a wealthy country, well able to afford decent sanitation, right? Wrong.

At that time, nine out of ten households – 90 per cent of them in rural areas – had no toilet or running water. Their occupants had to defecate in the desert, like animals. This often led to contamination of what precious water they had. Little wonder that over 2000 people died each year from diarrhoea alone; or that vicious African diseases such as cholera, typhoid and guinea-worm infection caused enormous suffering.

So why did this country, so rich in things the whole world wanted, have so little money that it failed to meet its citizens' most basic, elementary needs?

Prejudiced Western cynics may shrug and ask, what else do you expect in Africa? Aren't all its peoples stunted and backward, unable to progress or transform? Especially once their colonial masters have left, abandoning them to their own devices?

But the truth is that invariably those very colonialists caused most of their problems in the first place, as is borne out by Namibia's history. For centuries before the Europeans arrived, many tribes co-existed more or less amicably, breeding cattle and bartering between themselves. The names of the various ethnic groups read like poetry – the Himba, San, and Ovambo; the Damara, Nama and Herero, the Mafwe, Masubis, the Tswana and the Basters. These groupings developed in isolation, conserving their energies under the hot sun, searching for food and water and protecting their livestock. 'They were cut off,' says geographer J H Wellington in his book *SWA and its Human Issues* (Oxford, 1967) 'from the great streams of human progress where clash and competition had strengthened the sinew and sharpened the wit.'

But European minds could neither comprehend nor forgive this so-different, so-primitive way of life. The country was basically one big sandpit, which is why Europeans largely ignored it when Africa was being sliced up among them like cake in the nineteenth century. But when, gradually, this 'crumb' turned out to be much richer than the settlers had imagined, they made amends. Bismarck, a latecomer to the Scramble for Africa, and jealous of his European neighbours' colonial empires, proclaimed Namibia (then South West Africa) a German protectorate in 1884.

For the next century, Namibia's was the usual history of colonial exploitation, expropriation of the indigenous peoples' land and neglect. At first the Germans magnanimously allowed the locals to occupy about 25 per cent of the decent terrain that could be used for farming, but they soon decided they'd been too generous. More and more land was claimed by Europeans, until the pitiful patches left for locals could sustain neither them nor their animals. This led to a brave rebellion on the part of the Herero people in 1904. But alas, they were no match for the coldly efficient guns of the usurpers, and 65,000 men, women and children were slaughtered like cattle by the German troops. The tribe never recovered from this genocide; today they still number less than 70,000.

In 1920 South Africa took over South West Africa, and treated the country like another province. Apartheid was harshly applied: nine out of ten of the black people who had occupied the entire area from the dawn of time, were now forced into crowded reserves which occupied 40 per cent of the land – that part, of course, which was least habitable. They had little dignity, being treated like temporary sojourners in a white area. Choice was non-existent – new laws dictated where they could and could not shop, be educated, worship their God, be entertained and receive medical treatment.

People don't have the remotest idea that washing hands before meals or after defecating is one way of avoiding manifold diseases.

When the country finally gained Independence in 1990 things began to change. Its health services made great strides, changing direction, on WHO's advice, from high-tech, curative health programmes for the few to a cost-effective, preventative programme for the many. However, the sanitation situation remained a nightmare and could not be changed overnight. By the time of our mission, most Namibians still lived a miserable life. A mere fifteen per cent – some 240,000 people, mainly Europeans – lived in sophisticated Windhoek, with its gay night-clubs, casinos and impersonal skyscrapers in glass and steel towering above the many attractive, timbered colonial buildings. Beyond this, beyond the game resorts and gleaming guest lodges, it was a different matter. The remaining 85 per cent of the population were poor beyond European imagining. They occupied isolated pockets, dunes and sandy hovels the length and breadth of the country. It was these people we had come to help.

To the Namibian poor, fresh clean water on tap was and still is for many, an impossible dream. Living in isolated pockets hundreds of kilometres apart, a piped-water system will never be feasible. They can only imagine it as they swelter under a burning sun and trudge weary distances every day to a communal tap or borehole often shared by cattle.

Not surprisingly these small buckets of brackish water, obtained with such effort, don't encourage the washing of hands. Especially when people don't have the remotest idea that washing hands before meals or after defecating is one simple way of avoiding the untold misery caused by the manifold diseases that ravage and kill them.

It's ironic that a civilised place like Windhoek, where at a touch, taps can gush fresh water (much of it from recycling plants), exists in the full view of people whose lives are made so miserable by the lack of it. Dubbed 'a dry place between two deserts,' the country is vast, its 824,269 square kilometres adding up to more than Britain and Germany combined. And it's the most arid country on earth: water is a national obsession. Talk of it creeps into every conversation; farmers in remote areas – there is no other kind – sometimes have to lay a hundred kilometres of pipe to transport a meagre trickle to their homesteads. When the inevitable drought comes, these tough men have no choice: they must sell every last animal and hunker down to wait out the siege.

One-fifth of the country is occupied by two deserts: the Namib to the west and the Kalahari to the east. With an average rainfall of 270 millimetres, little land is valuable for cultivation and about an eighth of it is totally uninhabitable. What little rain that falls, falls in an antisocial manner. The North is bordered by a tangle of great rivers – the Kunene, the Okavango, the Zambezi and the Chobe – and therefore has less need of water, yet it gets 600 mm of rainfall annually, while parts of the interior get a meagre 200 mm a year. Much of that evaporates before the farmers, who employ nearly half the people, can conserve it. To add insult to injury, what rain there is comes in a brief, heavy rush, and carries away precious topsoil, adding soil erosion to the long list of problems with which Namibians struggle.

You've got to be tough to stay in Namibia, which is why it's one of the most sparsely-populated countries on earth. There are only 1.83

million people, an astonishingly small population – far less than many a city. And as you would expect, the number of educated and skilled people is not enough to run a country, especially one that's suffered such neglect. Consequently, there is an acute shortage of human, technical and financial resources.

Forging ahead

Even so, to the Namibians' great credit, about 15 per cent of the total government expenditure is allocated to public health. It's one of the largest fiscal allocations per head for health development in the world, let alone in Africa. Nevertheless, the shortage of skilled manpower makes health development difficult to manage. And this presents a complex challenge, because public expectations are rising, and AIDS is beginning to extort a heavy toll. The already overloaded system faces political pressure to provide more resources.

At the time of our visit, the Ministry of Health was doing its best by defining priorities for policy analysis and programme development. They were working out a policy to strengthen primary health care services at operational levels by involving the communities and reinforcing intersectoral collaboration and coordination. This was why, in January that year, they had approached the WHO in Brazzaville for help and technical advice. We proposed that they broaden their scope, and develop a comprehensive policy on environmental health and sustainable health development.

Between us, Watters and I had nearly 70 years of valuable hands-on experience. We were ready to get their programme off the ground. We knew we could help them with the most cost-effective way to reach the minds and hearts of their people. We were excited, for our small contribution could make a big impact. But some treacherous hand, human or divine, had other plans.

CHAPTER FIVE

THE SEEDS OF SUSPICION

Graham Hancock refers to the United Nations system as 'self-perpetuating bureaucracies… empires created within the system by ambitious and greedy men, and then staffed by time servers and sycophants… the goal of helping the world's poor to achieve a better life, often ends up being relegated to second or third place or completely forgotten. At all levels, staff show tendency to become side-tracked, indeed obsessed, by issues of a personal nature notably their pay and privileges'.* Indeed there are some WHO and UN employees who fall under this category.

Arriving in Namibia, I was picked up from the airport by Mr. Niklaas Mootu, the driver who was to play the major role in turning my world upside down. A black Namibian with the usual fairly light skin typical of the area, he was of average height, well-built and physically strong. He spoke slowly and looked gentle, although I subsequently heard that he was a war veteran, having fought with the freedom fighters. I was told he was a member of SWAPO, the South West African People's Organization, which was now the majority party in the multiparty democracy. Whether this is true or not I don't know.

Aged about 45, Mootu had been employed by the local office of the WHO for some years, as he reminded me on the forty kilometre-drive to the city. He remembered me from my previous visit, when I had come on a fact-finding mission shortly before Independence at the request of the United Nations Development Programme. I had joined a team from the World Bank and UNICEF and we prepared the Water Supply and Sanitation sector assessment report on which Namibia's policy framework had subsequently been based.

Mootu was breezy and cheerful, pointing out various improvements along the way such as the widening of the road, which had led to a substantial drop in traffic accidents. Nevertheless, there was something about him I instinctively felt uncomfortable. It was hard to pinpoint – a certain unrestness in his face, perhaps; a brash confidence in his abilities as a driver. He boasted that he had been given a merit award for his safety record by the WHO office in Windhoek. Later these words came back to haunt me.

When he collected me that Saturday afternoon, Mootu handed me a hand-written note of welcome from an old colleague, WHO administrator Miss Aster Gashaw, inviting me to tea later at her home.

Aster Gashaw was a compatriot of mine from Ethiopia who, when I first met her in 1980, had been secretary to WHO's Ethiopian programme coordinator in Addis Ababa. In 1982 she was recruited to the Regional HQ in Brazzaville, also as a secretary. Subsequently she became embroiled in the political intrigue which swirled around those corridors, inevitable in an Organization which employs most of its staff on a two-year fixed-term contract basis. As I've said, this impermanence breeds great insecurity among staff and gives the Regional Director undue power. If he is prone to favouritism – and most, being human, develop that tendency – then those who are not in favour may find their contracts inexplicably terminated. Some Regional Directors and Programme Managers are quite shameless about this, and the lobbying for power that goes on in Brazzaville makes it an uncomfortable place in which to work.

This politicisation is a decidedly unhealthy aspect of the World Health Organization. Graham Hancock refers to 'self-perpetuating bureaucracies...empires created within the system by ambitious and greedy men, and then staffed by time servers and sycophants.' He was referring to the fact that when a new Regional Director or Director General is elected, his own people are appointed to his staff. The existing post-holders, no matter how skilled or experienced, are often overlooked when it comes to promotion or new appointments, which naturally leads to bitterness and backstabbing. All this and more seethed away in the feelings of the faceless bureaucrats at Brazzaville.

Little wonder then that 'staff show a tendency to become sidetracked, indeed obsessed, by issues of a personal nature: notably their pay and privileges,' as Graham Hancock observed. He went on: 'The goal of helping the world's poor to achieve a better life, often ends up being relegated to second or third place – or completely forgotten.' This was true – one doctor in charge of a major programme confided to me that he did not care what assignment the Regional Director gave him even if it was outside his profession; he would do it as long as he got his salary. Serving the poor of Africa, as Hancock claimed, was often the last thing on some people's minds.

Those who are not in favour may find their contracts inexplicably terminated.

Aster, however, knew how to succeed despite this poisonous atmosphere. She proved to be a hard working and ambitious lady, and was soon promoted to Assistant Administrator in the Regional Director's office. By the time I arrived from Zimbabwe, she was firmly entrenched – and already a controversial figure.

On the contrary it so happened that a young, female, Ethiopian doctor was one of the victims whose contract was inexplicably to be terminated. After five years of dedicated service in the WHO country office in the Congo, working among people who needed her desperately, her post was going to be abolished without offering her reassignment – she was in difficult circumstances, being a widow with two young children. Naturally she was deeply upset. This is because when her supervisor recommended six possible positions in the Region for which she might be considered, the Regional Director refused to consider her for any of them. It was a relief when two weeks before the end of her contract this doctor got a WHO posting outside the African region on her own efforts.

Interestingly, when in 1995, a new Regional Director was elected, this doctor was called back to Africa and given a better position. She proved to be efficient and highly dedicated to WHO's mission, which proved that for whatever reason her contract was terminated, incompetence wasn't one of them.

Aster stayed in Brazzaville until her immediate boss, the Regional Director was ousted in 1995, after which she requested reassignment. My wife and I were saddened by her transfer as by that time she was close to us. After she left, Aster kept in touch, often telephoning and expressing her continued friendship with the family. And we reciprocated. It had been Aster who first told me that a mission to Namibia was in the offing, ringing me in Baltimore one Christmas while I was on vacation. She sounded excited about seeing me again. So now we were to meet for tea.

Aster collected me from the hotel after lunch, and we drove to her house to meet another lady, also her friend from Ethiopia. We chatted about people at the Regional Office, and I brought them up to date on the changes that had occurred since Aster's time. We called up from her home, to let my wife know I had arrived safely in Windhoek. I spoke to my younger daughter too and was thrilled to hear that she had been accepted by the college of her choice in USA. Aster too was pleased – she had been especially fond of my daughters.

I was happy that my daughter was fulfilling her potential, and sanguine about the choices and sacrifices we had made. I felt mellow and comfortable with our old friend, Aster the Administrator. I didn't suspect for a moment that our mission was to be bungled.

Lords of Poverty Graham Hancock, Camerapix Publishers International, 2001, p83

CHAPTER SIX

A MISSION MANGLED

A lmost as soon as we arrived in the WHO office, we sensed that *something was wrong. For one thing, the atmosphere of welcome and cooperation seemed to have evaporated.*

We spent a relaxed weekend, Greg Watters and I, dining together on the Saturday evening. I discovered that he was unhappy about the itinerary that had been planned for us. The programme consisted of little else but field trips, which might have been nice had we really been in it merely for the pay and the ride, as Hancock implies. But we knew all too well how much work was required, and there was no time to waste.

Was Namibia, we asked ourselves, one of those countries that preferred to stick to the comfortable old way of doing things, in which experts gave advice and technical assistance and then departed, without probing beneath the surface at the real change needed? Did the Ministry want to avoid the delicate business of tackling people's traditional customs? If so, our work would be harder, for most of today's illness was too complex for that simplistic approach. When, in the seventies, the WHO had scored its greatest triumph – the eradication of smallpox, to which we shall return – the parameters were clear: all that was needed was a clear-cut treatment programme. Now we were tackling the deeper, underlying causes of ill-health, so factors such as culture, people-skills, behaviour and the use of local materials had to be considered or the programme would only partially succeed, if not fail totally.

We needed several different ministries to cooperate, since finance, education, agriculture, public works, water resources, environment, and health were all interlinked in our approach. There was also a need to bring on board external agencies such as UNICEF and the World Bank. Getting all these complex bodies to work together was Watters' forté. He was admired for it round the world, and he hadn't come all this way to admire the scenery, beautiful as Namibia's sculpted red deserts were. We needed in-depth discussion if we were to educate the educators.

We wanted them to grasp that education was the priority. The perception that prevailed in many rural areas was that toilets and latrines are primarily status symbols – unnecessary luxuries which could be used for any old thing once the 'experts' had driven off in their four by fours. That's how come so many well-meant projects fail – as soon as the dust settles, and the novelty wears off, the water closets become storage cupboards or chicken coops! Civil servants and health officials despair, and write reports to their political masters; but whoever heard of hygiene education in an election manifesto? Even if you re-label it as something altogether sexier such as 'Wellness programmes,' it's hardly the stuff of dynamic vote-catching. So part of our job was to insist that awareness programmes were part and parcel of the overall plan.

Every tiny community had to be asked basic questions such as, 'Does each household recognise the need for improved sanitation so as to value it? Do they know the changes they need to make in their way of life to gain the maximum health benefits? Do they understand the recurrent and capital costs and environmental considerations of the different types of sanitation system, so that they can decide which is most appropriate? And what contributions can each household make in terms of physical involvement, to reduce costs?'

The cost issue was a delicate one. Considering the extreme poverty of these people, it sometimes seemed unreasonable to expect them to pay, even for maintenance. However, it has become more and more apparent that communities only value that for which what they pay. The Namibian Government, following our advice, had already decided to charge; also to come down heavily on excessive water use. The aim we considered reasonable was to provide 20 litres of water per person per day within 1000 metres of every homestead. This was the absolute minimum – 30 to 40 litres a day, within 250 metres of every home, is the normal standard for adequate personal and domestic hygiene. But this was one big desert, and they had to start somewhere.

Before he arrived, Greg Watters had already tried to get our field-trip schedule changed. He was annoyed at the waste of time involved in travelling the length and breadth of the country, when we badly needed to talk with government officials. He felt it boded ill for our mission.

A meeting sabotaged?

After our relaxed weekend, on the Monday morning we were raring to go, and we set off for the WHO office in good spirits. However, almost as soon as we arrived, we sensed that something was wrong. For one thing, the atmosphere of welcome and cooperation seemed to have evaporated. Aster Gashaw, in particular, was a changed person. She appeared fussy and officious, full of her role as administrator and demanding to see our travel authorisation. This was so unusual (and unnecessary) that Dr. Watters had not even brought his with him to Namibia. However instead of getting annoyed he humoured her by putting through a call to Geneva, and asking his secretary to fax the document.

Aster informed us that our crucial first meeting with the Minister of Health and other top officials had been confirmed for three o'clock, and suggested we be at her office at least half an hour earlier so the driver could get us there in good time. We then had a preliminary discussion with Dr. Paul Rojas, the Namibian WHO representative, and a man from the United Nations Children's Emergency Fund (UNICEF). This Organization, with which we worked closely, had been running a pilot sanitation project in the area we were to visit the following day.

Also present was Andrew Damon, the cheerful young South African from the Namibian Ministry of Health, who would be accompanying us. We had met before in Brazzaville when he'd represented Namibia at the Africa 2000 Conference. He was now acting Head of Environmental Health Services, a responsible post for a man of only 38.

Our remonstrance regarding the field trips was heard and it was agreed to reduce them by half. After a good morning's discussion, we went off for lunch, returning to the office in good time. We were looking forward to meeting with the Minister.

However, no driver appeared. We began to get anxious, especially since neither the Administrator nor the WHO representative were around either. As the minutes ticked by, and we sat in an anteroom in solitary impatience, we became more and more agitated. No-one could enlighten us as to what was happening – all the secretary could say was that Dr. Rojas was out of the office. This seemed extraordinary – was he not going to join us for this important meeting, central to the work he'd been appointed to do in Namibia? He had given no indication of it that morning. Could some accident have detained him? How come he hadn't let us know? And where, oh where, were the Administrator and the driver?

Our eyes glued to the clock, we became more frustrated by the minute. Two forty-five approached, and passed. There was now no way we were going to make the meeting on time. But despite our urgent importuning, the secretary could do nothing. As three o'clock passed, our frustration and anger seethed. But it was not until three-fifteen that a secretary ushered us into a room where the driver, and the administrator were seated. I raged at her, telling her that she was undermining our entire mission. It was a disgrace for WHO officials to be so late for such an important appointment with top members of the host country's government. And where was Dr. Rojas, I demanded? 'He was supposed to join you,' she said. 'I have no idea where he is.'

In retrospect her whole demeanour, not to mention her lack of an adequate explanation, seemed completely at odds with the professionalism incumbent upon her. However, we were extremely anxious to be off, and made no further enquiry; we would follow it up later. We left immediately for the Ministry of Health.

Once there, Dr. Watters' famous charm came into full play, and I had never before been so thankful for it. Feeling deeply ruffled myself, I was enormously impressed by his ability to remain calm under these extraordinary circumstances. After a fulsome apology, he charmed the Minister with an amusing story about a welcome he had once received from a paramount chief in a remote village, where he and a team of WHO workers had gone to preach sanitation. The Minister laughed, and responded with an anecdote of her own, about sanitation problems in the camps where she had spent her exile as a freedom fighter with

SWAPO. My tension soon dissolved in the atmosphere of friendliness and warmth, and it turned into a thoroughly productive meeting – a good omen, we felt, for our mission.

Sadly, we couldn't have been more wrong.

That evening we reviewed progress and turned in early, for we were due to leave on our first field trip, due to last five days, the following afternoon. We would travel to the North-East of Namibia to assess the needs of the people living on communal land. Our actual destination was Katima Mulilo, a small but important town, the capital of Caprivi and on the border close to Angola, Zambia and Botswana. Although boasting several fine guest lodges and a nine-hole golf course, its streets were dirty and pot-holed and its council was owed millions of Namibian dollars in water bills. We were interested in seeing UNICEF's latrine-building pilot project there. We wanted to see how much local material could be used, and to hear the problems people were experiencing.

In the morning, we met Andrew Damon, who would be accompanying us on this mission. He seemed competent and very interested in the work. After discussing the mission with him and his boss, we returned to the hotel for an early lunch. Greg Watters went to change some money, then we settled our hotel bill, and sat down to wait in the lobby.

The car, driven by Niklaas Mootu, arrived promptly at 1:30. The first stage of the journey, to a guest lodge en route was expected to take four hours. Allowing for a 30-minute break in Otjiwarongo, a favourite tourist stopping place on the long haul to the famous Etosha National Park, we expected to arrive at six that evening. But we never made it.

CHAPTER SEVEN

A MAN POSSESSED

N*o vehicle older than five years should be used for long field trips, because of the wear and tear they suffer on many African roads. Yet this one had been made in 1990.*

'The WHO country representatives are the weak link in an already weak chain of influence from the Organization's headquarters in Geneva through its six regional offices into national ministries of health. Seen as political appointees they are given no structured training and few resources and they are often poorly motivated.'

'WHO in Crisis' by Fiona Godlee. British Medical Journal, 26 Nov 1994, p1425)

Every detail of that journey on February 11 is imprinted on my mind as clearly as a photograph. I have gone over it again and again, trying to see whether I was wrong in any particular about the facts as I am about to relate them. This, to the best of my recollection, is exactly what happened.

As the driver loaded our luggage into the white Toyota Land Cruiser, Dr. Greg Watters and I settled into our seats, both sitting in the back so that Andrew Damon, whom we were going to pick up next, could sit in front. The first thing we noticed was that there were no seat belts in the vehicle, other than that of the driver. The wearing of seat belts is compulsory in Namibia, as in most countries. Even if this hadn't been the case, their absence was a direct contravention of WHO regulations which clearly state that unless staff members are wearing seatbelts, they will not be covered by insurance. When this regulation had been circulated at headquarters in Geneva a year or so earlier, Greg

Watters had retorted with a memo of his own, pointing out that if this was so, seat belts must be more strictly maintained, since they were often stolen or cut out from vehicles. Strangely – and somewhat suspiciously – this memo appeared to have disappeared into thin air when, later, his secretary tried to locate it in the files.

Another anomaly was the age of this car. According to the rules, no vehicle older than five years should be used for long field trips, because of the wear and tear they suffer on many African roads. Yet this one had been made in 1990. The Windhoek office would, I estimated, have had three vehicles at its disposal. To whom could the other two have been assigned? What work could have a higher priority than this, which we had flown across the world to carry out? It didn't make sense. However, we weren't about to demand a different car – we wanted to get under way. We just added these annoyances to the long list of things that had made the mission seem jinxed from the start, and decided to raise our questions with the Administrator on our return.

We went to pick up Peter Damon, who was waved off from his home by his wife and three small children. Then the driver threaded his way through the spacious suburban streets of Windhoek. Soon we were exiting the small city on the B1, the major road that bisects Namibia from top to bottom. Of the 5,450 kilometres of tarred road that have been laid down in the country in the past 30 years, the B1 is the showpiece, the main artery from which a network of fine-veined gravelled roads spread out to the east and west, carrying four-wheel drives laden with tourists to the spectacular red dunes for which the country is famous. Vehicles often speed unthinkingly along these minor roads, and because they are loose-gravelled, accidents and blowouts are common. But the B1 is as safe as any major highway anywhere; it is a smooth masterpiece of modern engineering. Mootu seemed to enjoy its let-rip surface, for the four-by-four picked up speed and was soon barrelling along so fast that Damon asked him to slow down. But Mootu seemed in a hurry, and the needle on the speedometer crept steadily and consistently over the official speed limit of 120 km/h. It seemed to us that we were hurtling along quite unnecessarily, and Damon gently remonstrated with Mootu several more times. But he didn't take the warning seriously. 'Don't worry, you're in good hands', he said gaily,

'I am an excellent driver. I have even been given merit awards for my driving!'

This hardly seemed an appropriate response, but we didn't argue with him, even though his words lingered in my mind. I, for one, was uneasy, thinking he was tempting fate. After the initial pleasantries none of us spoke much. It began to rain slightly, and Mootu was excited. Rain in Namibia is like gold dust, and he exclaimed that we must be lucky people to have brought the rain with us. However, it was little more than dampener and the road was soon as parched as ever.

Once again this lack of training in people skills had shown up as a glaring lack in WHO affairs.

There was little of interest in the scenery – nothing but endless sandy scrub-like plains stretching away on either side, dotted here and there with twisted, black, camel thorn trees. But we were used to the vastness and isolation of Africa, and enjoyed the landscape sliding by. Its emptiness and sheer scale reminds me forcibly of man's insignificance in the greater scheme of things; but today we had more immediate problems on our minds. I was brooding over the inexplicable delays of the day before, and Dr. Rojas' absence. We had not been back to the office in the intervening time, and no-one had phoned to apologise. What reason could there have been to cause us such embarrassment, and show such discourtesy to the very people we were there to woo?

Perhaps this WHO country representative (WR) was the kind of person that critic Fiona Godlee had in mind when she wrote in the *British Medical Journal*, 'The WHO's country representatives are the weak link in an already weak chain of influence from the Organization's headquarters in Geneva through its six regional offices into national ministries of health. Seen as political appointees, they are given no structured training and few resources, and they are often poorly motivated.' *('WHO in Crisis' by Fiona Godlee. British Medical Journal, 26 Nov 1994, p1425).* Once again, this lack of training in people skills, cultivated so assiduously in multi-national conglomerates, had shown up as a glaring lack in WHO affairs.

Namibian tour guides like to boast that this is one of the oldest countries on earth, proving it with proudly-displayed fossilised dinosaur footprints sealed in the volcanic rock. Probably not much has changed since the giant creatures roamed these plains. In later centuries the route we now travelled had carried caravans of traders, linking the North with the copper and tin mines mined by the Ovambo people centuries before the Europeans appeared.

About 70 kilometres from Windhoek, the monotony of the empty road was broken by the small fortress town of Okahandja, a Herero name meaning 'place where the rivers meet.' This is an important cultural centre for the colourful Herero people, who gather here each year for a festival. It is also a Mecca for woodcarvers. As we passed through, we observed the huge Mbangura Market underway, with piles of hand-carved animals such as hippos, giraffes and elephants lying on display by the side of the road.

By and by the thrumming of the wheels made us sleepy and Greg Watters, sitting beside me, dozed in the heat, his head resting on his jacket, wedged up against the window. In front, Damon was reading a book. None of us had the slightest intimation of danger.

The speed of the vehicle still bothered me.

About an hour and a half after setting off, having travelled over 200 kilometres, we felt the need for a break, and told Mootu to stop at the fast-approaching town of Otjiwarongo. The town is 245 kilometres from Windhoek and popular with tourists en route for the famous Etosha National Park, one of Africa's biggest game reserves. But we had personal reason for stopping there too: Andrew Damon had an appointment with the local health inspector – and had arranged to have a cup of tea with him. So we were looking forward to our stop. We eyed the landscape, now dotted with scrawny cattle for we'd reached ranch country.

The speed of the vehicle still bothered me, though I couldn't see the speedometer from where I was sitting, which was directly behind the driver. I kept my eye on Mootu, because something about him troubled me. He kept shaking his head from side to side in a restless, excitable way. Was he perhaps trying to keep himself awake? Was he in pain? Or was he – as I have asked myself repeatedly since – debating with himself between two courses of action?

I had no reason to distrust Mootu, but I was the more concerned at his behaviour because we were travelling so fast. The road ahead was clear and straight, with nothing but a shimmering heat haze in view. I glanced behind – there were no other vehicles in sight and the road stretched emptily away in an unbroken line. It seemed I had no reason to be afraid. On either side were the fenced-in lands of a cattle ranch. There was no sign of man or beast or any other danger. And yet Mootu's whole body conveyed tension. The engine purred smoothly – this high – speed cruising was what it was designed for. But it was decidedly not designed for what happened next.

'We were going to roll...'

Niklaas Mootu looked over his shoulder, as if making sure the road was clear. I can see his profile now. Then suddenly, and with no warning, he wrenched the steering wheel hard down to the right. As the tyres screamed across the road, the centrifugal force that was propelling the heavy load forwards took over. In one spectacular second of indecision every bolt and panel of streamlined steel protested in agony. Then the vehicle's tyres left the road and I realised we were going to roll.

That split second of warning was enough to save me. Instantly, the instinct to survive took over, blotting out every other thought. As the Land Cruiser reared sideways up into the air and, incredibly, turned its first somersault, the image of what I had to do came instantly to mind. The emergency evacuation lessons I'd heard from countless air hostesses in bored, sing-song voices in aeroplanes all over Africa saved me now: put both hands on your head, lean forward and keep your face down. My reaction was utterly automatic, as it needed to be. I put my head down and brought my legs up, curling into as much of a ball as I was able, so I could roll with the impact.

The car reared up into the air in true Hollywood car-chase style, then it crashed down onto its roof with such sickening force and speed that its doors burst open. As we bounced back up into the air, I hung on to my knees, oblivious to my fellow-passengers. Again, we bounced and rolled, and again. I wound myself up tighter so that only my shoulders and forehead took the knocks and my body rolled, spreading the impact. Finally, after no fewer than six sickening somersaults, rolling down a bank for a distance of 30 meters, we came to a shuddering, jarring, upside-down halt. As we did so, my head hit something hard, sending a shattering impact throughout my body. I crashed down, landing on the now stationary roof. The impact was so harsh that it sent a searing pain through my pelvis, and I knew instinctively that bones had broken. But I was alive, and basically in one piece, although almost unconscious with shock.

I suspect I passed out. When I could gather my senses, I found myself in a nightmarish space, lying on the ceiling of the car. I was facing Mootu, the only other person visible. There were mechanical clicks and groans as the heavy car, rocking gently, settled into the sand. Despite the pain I wriggled over to the window, and managed somehow to pull myself through the broken glass. I slithered down to the ground in agony. Then, anxious in case the fuel caught fire, I clutched at bunches of grass, pulling myself up the slight incline towards a tree a few metres away. There I collapsed, gasping in breaths of air and taking in the terrible scene before me.

Scarcely before I'd had time to wonder what had befallen Greg Watters and Andrew Damon, I heard a terrifying sound. Not far away lay Andrew, stretched out, leaning on his shoulder. He was screaming in agony, a primal sound that made my heart turn cold.

Of Greg Watters there was no sight or sound. The first time the car hit the ground, I learned later, he had been tossed out, my wonderful friend and colleague, like a rag doll.

I lay there, feeling helpless, appalled, useless, while Mootu ran up and down like a man possessed.

Part of one's mind, I discovered, detaches and goes on operating when horror is too much to bear. I noted that my documents were strewn all over the car. My briefcase must have burst open, for there, directly in my line of vision, was my picture of Saint Mary, placed inside my passport by my wife whenever I travel, to keep me safe. It was a comfort, and a reminder of how lucky I was to have survived. I closed my eyes and thanked God for saving my life.

St Mary, it seemed, was keeping a careful eye on things, for a few minutes later I heard a shout and saw a white man running down from the road, some 30 metres away. He spotted me under the tree and called over his shoulder that there was a survivor, and to call an ambulance. The word 'survivor' chilled me. I worried desperately about Greg. Then the stranger was beside me, holding my hand, reassuring me that help was on its way. He whipped out his cell phone and, in just the calm capable manner one longs for at such a time, reported the situation to the police. He told me to lie flat, so that I could easily be transferred to a stretcher. He asked if I had medical insurance and where I was working. It later transpired that his name was Graham Snyman, and he was the manager of a private medi-clinic in Otjiwarongo.

How had the accident happened? he asked. I told him it was because the driver was going too fast. In the irrational way one's brain works in shock, I became obsessed about the need to gather up my documents, now dispersing in the wind. It suddenly seemed to me vital to rescue these shreds of my life, and get them, at least, under control. Within ten minutes uniformed traffic officers appeared, running down to survey the still-hissing vehicle. As they approached I beseeched my rescuer to gather up the papers. He looked a little shocked, but he reassured me that he would save them, and that I would get them back the next day. He was as good as his word, for my plane ticket, my passport, my Laissez Passer (the UN passport), my wallet, credit cards, ID document and money were all safely handed over to me in the clinic, thus saving me a great deal of trouble later.

Now, as pain shot through my hips, I surrendered to the identity of 'accident victim', and allowed myself to be lifted gently onto a stretcher. It felt so good to be in caring, capable hands. A mere twenty minutes later I was lifted onto a table in an emergency room, bright lights glaring down at me, nurses and a doctor busying themselves with tubes. While they bustled round with their drips and needles, I asked them the question which was hammering away at my mind: how and where were my fellow passengers, Dr. Gregor Watters and the young Namibian, Andrew Damon? I dreaded the answer, which somehow I already knew.

The medics looked at me sadly. Both men had died at the scene, they said. Greg Watters had been almost decapitated and had died instantly. Andrew Damon suffered internal injury and bled to death.

It was the most devastating moment of my life. I turned my head away and wailed.

View of damaged vehicle after the accident (first from right)

CHAPTER EIGHT

THE PAINFUL AFTERMATH

'*United Nations Staff members give everything they've got to save people living in the worst circumstances on earth; they should not have to give their lives.*' — *Catherine Bertini, Former Executive Director, World Food Programme.*

Had Greg Watters or Andrew Damon known in their souls they were going to die, as some say? I kept going over those last two hours of their lives, trying to grasp the fact that they were dead. 'It's a bad omen,' I recalled Damon saying earlier in the day when, entering his boss's office for our meeting, we found the man hadn't arrived. Now the memory sent shivers down my spine. At 38, Damon was young to be shouldering so much responsibility, and undoubtedly, he had a distinguished career ahead of him. In the few years I'd known him I'd been impressed by his quiet intelligence, his willingness to tackle the big issues that faced his country. With its desperate shortage of educated manpower, neither Namibia nor his native country, South Africa, could afford to lose such a man.

Later his brother sent me a moving tribute, describing Andrew's childhood. The sixth of ten children, he grew up in Upington, South Africa, where his father was a teacher. As a coloured boy in the apartheid era, he was politicised early and often challenged his teachers. But it was a happy time, with memories of rough and tumble with his brothers in the open veld. Later Andrew entertained the youth of the town with a disco in the family garage. He enrolled to do a B.Sc at the University of the Western Cape in 1978, but this time apartheid did intervene, for the campus was seething with politics and he found study impossible. So the following year he enrolled for a three-year course in Public Health at the Peninsula Technikon, emerging as a health inspector in 1981.

Andrew married social worker Sanya Keyser, and in 1982 they moved to Windhoek, Namibia, where his brother John was living. Andrew took up an appointment as a meat inspector at an abattoir, while both brothers fought the municipality over remnants of apartheid in the form of separate abattoir facilities based on colour. This did not make him popular but it must have made him noticed, for in 1990, just before Namibia gained its independence, Andrew was appointed by the Ministry of Health and Social Services as a health inspector. Here he began to flourish and soon gained a reputation as a tireless worker. In 1991, he and a colleague started Windhoek's first training facility for environmental health assistants.

Andy was soon promoted to the food hygiene unit at the Ministry of Health head office, where he monitored imported foodstuffs. This was the work he was doing at the time of his death. He and Sanya had three children, Angelo, Stefan and Andrea. Still less could the world afford to lose Greg Watters. 'Never travel with me, Firdu' he'd once joked, when, on a flight from Maseru to Johannesburg, we'd been hit by severe turbulence which tossed the small plane about in the sky. 'There's always trouble when I travel.' The prophetic words took on a more sinister meaning now. His loss and the unnecessary cause of it, would cause me agony long after my body had healed.

International civil servants are no strangers to risk – a certain amount of it comes with the job. It is in part a justification for the salaries which, while no means as lordly as critics would have us believe, are comparatively good. World Health Organization staff are especially vulnerable, since whenever there's a highly-infectious new virus such as Ebola or SARS, nurses and doctors are among the first to die. Even I, a sanitary engineer, had faced risk, being sent to Rwanda at the height of the genocide, and often visiting areas ridden with malaria and cholera. Greg Watters too had been exposed to his fair share of danger, and had once had a particularly narrow escape in Yugoslavia just as bullets started flying. But to lose his life this way, at the hands of a WHO employee, when there was no hint of any other danger, seemed bitterly ironic.

My mind churned over the events incessantly. The more I grieved the cutting short of my friend's life, the angrier I became. I had loved Greg, as had colleagues all over the world. He'd dedicated his life to our work, and done it with distinction. He had so much still to give and his expertise was sorely needed, especially in Africa. He would be deeply missed. He was so far the opposite of Hancock's epithet 'overpaid freebooters living off the fat of the land' that it made me angry to read that phrase.

Already I yearned to understand this tragedy better. I longed to know what had caused Mootu's madness, and to see him held accountable. Justice needed to be done, if for no other reason than to honour these two distinguished men.

Over the next few terrible days all this simmered in my mind. At first, when I heard that the men were dead, I was being stabilised and it was almost more than I could bear. Weak with pain and shock, I could scarcely take it in. The grief ran through me like a river and I could not stop the tears. I started to scream and thrash around, to the extent that the nurses had to hold me or I'd have fallen from the bed. I cried as though my throat would burst. Finally, the doctor warned me that if I did not calm down I might suffer cardiac arrest and die as well, for my heart was under severe strain from my injuries. So a nurse gave me a tranquilizer, and I shivered and slid into a troubled sleep.

Later, drifting in and out of consciousness, I was aware that John Damon, Andrew's brother, was beside my bed, looking terribly sad. Later still Dr. Rojas appeared, enquiring anxiously how I was. No-one knew at this stage how serious my injuries were, but I suspected I'd broken my pelvis and had been warned of possible further internal damage. My head had taken a hard knock, I had bad cuts and I was suffering blurred vision. Who knows how I would have fared had I not followed the emergency landing procedure? Without the restraint of a seat belt, I was extremely lucky not to have broken my neck and be facing the rest of my life in a wheelchair. Meanwhile Niklaas Mootu was walking around barely scratched. Why? Why?

I assumed that our employers would be as keen to know the answer as I was. But I was wrong.

Next morning I was surprised to hear a nurse's voice asking brightly, 'Are we ready to go for a shower now?' Not thinking – or perhaps having too much faith in her superior medical knowledge – I started to sit up. Immediately pain shot through my right side and I began to shake. Getting out of bed, let alone walking, was simply impossible. However, the nurse called a helper and between them they carried me to the bathroom where I showered with their assistance. In retrospect I quake – who knows what damage they might have done, had my spine been seriously injured? It was a huge relief to be back in bed, and even to suffer the indignity of bedpans and towel washes. No-one else attempted to get me to a bathroom for another eight weeks. But the incident was to have repercussions later when the Organization wanted to send me to a station where the medical care was below par.

After 52 years of being mobile and independent, never suffering so much as a serious illness, the identity of 'patient' took getting used to. Arrangements were made to transfer me by ambulance to the more sophisticated medi-clinic in Windhoek, and I left Otjiwarongo the following day, feeling as if part of me would remain there forever. We set off at about 10 am, a nurse beside me taking pulse and blood pressure measurements every half hour. Soon we passed the scene of the accident and I shuddered to see the broken fence and the Land Cruiser still lying upside down in the sand. How impossible to think that only 24 hours since, it had been a proud, ordinary vehicle and our lives had been full of purpose, vigour and promise. The journey back to Windhoek was slow, tedious and immensely sad.

By afternoon I was safely installed in another hospital, and soon afterwards Aster Gashaw arrived. Her strange behaviour of two days earlier was fresh in my mind, and I was angry and distant with her. She had seemed so bossy and officious, and later, so strangely reluctant to tell us where Dr. Rojas had got to. I blamed her for our embarrassing delay, and now I was in the mood to heap much more blame on her head. Wasn't she, as Administrator, responsible for assigning us the inadequate old Land Cruiser, the so-negligent driver? What was she thinking, to send us on such a long journey without seat belts? I told her all about the driver's actions, hoping that, as Administrator she would pass this on at the internal investigation. But I was in no position to send her away, so I bit my tongue. I would ask questions at the right time, in the right place.

Meanwhile, Aster seemed solicitous and full of concern, and expressed anger with Dr. Rojas because he hadn't asked her to accompany him to Otjiwarongo to see me at the clinic the day before. I stared at her, unable to say what was on my mind. She looked confused, and didn't know what to say. Then she recalled herself, and asked if there was anything I needed. On Aster's advice I repeated the whole story to Dr. Rojas later, detailing Mootu's actions. He promised to follow up.

Dr. Rojas brought some of the WHO staff with him. At his suggestion, I finally called my wife, Mereb, in Baltimore where she was staying with my two daughters. I had asked that she not be told of the accident until I was ready to speak with her. When I got through I made light of what had happened, not mentioning that people had died; I didn't want to give her too much of a shock. So I told her I was okay and expected to be out of hospital in two or three days. Perhaps I hadn't fully grasped the seriousness of my injury myself; I didn't realise that months of recovery lay ahead.

After such a shock to the system, the pain, fear, and reality of being helplessly dependent on others all take a while to absorb. Despite my gratitude at being saved, I found it hard to accept not being able to get up and walk. Lying there brooding, staring at the ceiling hour after hour, in between X-rays and examinations, I began to get irrational fears that I might never walk again. Although comforted by telephone calls from distant relatives and friends, I'm afraid I gave the nurses a hard time, especially at night when nightmares caused me to shout out loud.

The Regional Director did not bother to put out an official communiqué about the crash.

'When I saw Mr. Zawide on February 14th, he had a very high fever and was slightly confused but did not complain of severe pain,' wrote Dr. O J Oosthuizen to Dr. J Nel, that Friday – the day that would have been Greg Watters' 57th birthday. I thought about the evening of fun and celebration he'd planned. Instead, incredible as it still seemed, this was the day his body would be loaded onto a plane to begin its long journey back home.

'The patient's blood pressure was dropping,' reported Dr. Oosthuizen. 'His Hb had dropped from 12.5 to 11. His white count had climbed to 16,200 and his platelets dropped to a low of 29,000. I diagnosed septicaemia... and possibly a rupture of his ascending aorta as the chest X-ray revealed a rather wide mediastinum (the space between the two lungs).

'He was ill, confused, with a temperature. He was very short of breath, and sweating. Cardiovascularly he was in definite right and left cardiac failure with soft heart sounds, a raised JVP and a BP of 90/60. He had fine crepitations in his left lower lobe of the lung.' When a further chest X-ray revealed I had pneumonia, I began to feel very low and hopeless and thought my life was over. And when, four days later, my blurred eyesight deteriorated into a squint (strabismus in medical terms) so that my two eyes went in independent directions, it only confirmed that I had every right to feel depressed.

The sixth day after the crash the doctors did a neurological examination, concluding that the squint was due to a 'sixth nerve palsy'. In lay terms this meant the cranial nerve which supplies the external muscle of the eyeball was paralysed. Luckily the hospital served the more sophisticated and wealthy inhabitants of Namibia, for it boasted a sophisticated MRI scanner – not something you can take for granted in Africa. So I was subjected to a nuclear scan, which revealed a possible bleed in the base of the brain near the nerve's nucleus.

I had an entire menu of medication with which to occupy myself, which helped pass the time between X-rays and cat scans and orthopaedic surgeons shaking their heads and prescribing a corset for my broken pelvis. My mind dwelt continually on Greg Watters. A memorial service was being held for him in Windh3oek, organised by the Ministry of Foreign Affairs and the British High Commission. I was also told about the funeral service for poor Andrew Damon. I was shown the press releases, and the obituaries placed prominently in the local newspaper. The Ministries of Health and Foreign Affairs made a joint statement, to the effect that Dr. Watters had come to Namibia to give the people water, and that he would be remembered for his noble sacrifice. Fine words, but what did they mean? Did the authorities really care about this so oh so unnecessary tragedy? Subsequent events made me bitterly doubt it.

Every visitor who appeared at my bedside, from the Representative of the United Nations in Namibia to the Permanent Secretary of the Ministry of Health, was regaled with my account of the disaster. All looked suitably shocked, and said that the circumstances should be thoroughly investigated. The Permanent Secretary expressed surprise that Mootu was the driver as he knew of his good reputation. This only made me brood more deeply.

I was much cheered by telephone calls from my family at least twice a day, and relatives and friends kept the operator so busy her patience was tested. I could not complain of neglect. Among the stream of visitors I was touched to meet two Ethiopian families, unknown to me but living in Windhoek, who came simply to offer support to a fellow-countryman.

By contrast I heard not a word from my many friends and colleagues in Brazzaville, which I found very strange. Only later did I discover the reason: most unusually under these circumstances, the Regional Director had not bothered to put out an official communiqué about the crash. Consequently, very few staff knew about the death of one of their most senior and highly-respected colleagues, and the serious injury of another. Why, I wondered, had it been kept so hush-hush? I found it disturbing and suspicious.

Aster Gashaw was a regular visitor, her manner friendly, sympathetic and concerned. But although she fussed over me and offered to bring me extra food, I noticed that her talk was all about herself. One day a group of WHO staff came to visit, and there among them, skulking in the background, was Niklaas Mootu. I could scarcely believe that he, whom I considered guilty of manslaughter at the very least, would have the gall to show his face. I glared at him, but no words were exchanged. After he left a reaction set in and I began to feel frightened. I remained scared for my life for the rest of my hospital stay.

Dr. Oosthuizen informed me that pelvic surgery was necessary to fix the broken bone; I told him I would have it done in America where I would be close to my family. Dr. Rojas confirmed that WHO would foot the bill for my evacuation, and within a few more days I had improved to the point where the long flight was viable. I had arranged to be admitted to one of the world's great hospitals – Johns Hopkins in Baltimore. For this I had my daughter Tikikil to thank, for she was studying Public Health there, which helped me to gain admission at short notice. All that remained was to find someone to accompany me. My wife had wanted to come over, but getting a visa would take too long. Who else could put their life on hold at such short notice?

We breathed a sigh of relief when a solution appeared in the person of my wife's niece, Zini, who happened to be holidaying in Addis at the time. Zini left Ethiopia in 1977 to study in England, and subsequently became a British citizen. Her British passport meant she didn't need a visa for Namibia or the USA. Enormously kind, she offered to break her vacation and accompany me to America.

Knowing that one of the family was going to be by my side was tremendously reassuring, and I relaxed a little. Aster offered to put Zini up, but we declined. Although I found it hard to believe that anyone, least of all a friend, had planned to have us killed, my confidence was so shaken I didn't know what to think. I only knew that my trust had been shattered. Something evil, unexpected and totally out of the ordinary had occurred on that road to Otjiwarongo, and until I knew what was behind it, I looked on everyone, even the kindly and inoffensive Dr. Rojas, with suspicion.

Zini stayed in a guest room annexed to the hospital. She arrived three days before our departure, and I immediately felt safer. Nevertheless, I advised her not to walk alone on the street. Could I be sure that my life, and even hers, was not in danger? It felt unreal, but I reserved the right to be neurotic.

And indeed I was beginning to suspect that this crash was going to be swept under the carpet – that it would not get the investigation into every aspect that would be standard procedure in many countries. No police had yet appeared at the hospital to take my statement, and I kept reminding Aster and Dr. Rojas to chase them up as the day of departure drew near. Finally, they arrived, on February 27 just as I was getting dressed to leave. With barely two hours to go before my flight, and a long journey in the ambulance to cope with, I was preoccupied, anxious and in pain. Flustered, I could not give them my full attention. I wanted to get the statement over with as quickly as possible. Was this what they'd planned perhaps?

The police showed me photographs of the vehicle, taken on the day of the crash. I gave them my account of events, stressing that there had been no rain, no other car in sight either in front or behind, and that no tyre had burst – as the photographs confirmed. There had been, in short, no reason for the car's going out of control other than the driver's negligence. I did not emphasise the speed, or accuse Mootu more definitely, because I had very little time. I signed the statement quickly without even reading it through. Their strategy, if that's what it was, was effective, and I had plenty of time in the months and years ahead to regret my hasty action.

In no time the ambulance had arrived and I was carried on, with Zini and a nurse by my side. Aster and Dr. Rojas came to the airport to say goodbye. As I was unable to sit in a wheel chair, they opened up a hatch at the back of the plane and I was stretchered on board.

Ahead of me lay a long, painful journey to Baltimore, and my family, whom I longed to see. The surgery and extensive treatment was not a pleasant prospect, but then, I was extremely fortunate to be going anywhere. The families of Greg Watters and Andrew Damon were now facing the kind of loss that means life will never be the same again. While I slowly recuperated, they had to come to terms with their grief, and start to build new lives around the gaping hole left by their respective men – breadwinners, lovers, fathers and mates.

Peter Damon and wife Sanya in their home before the accident

CHAPTER NINE

THE LAST GOOD-BYE

*I*nternational civil servants don't have statues, streets or grand buildings named after them. Yet quietly, anonymously, they make the world a better place.

They deserve acknowledgement and respect.

Even before Greg Watters' departure for Namibia, this particular mission presented unusual elements which, in retrospect, seem ominous. Normally Greg greatly enjoyed his field trips since he felt that's where WHO's mandate should be.

One thing about the Namibian mission that upset Greg Watters particularly was the itinerary, because it included many long journeys to remote villages. This did not comply with the terms of reference, which were to work out a national policy of water supply and sanitation with the Ministry of Health. But he didn't want to rock the boat – he never had, except when fighting for staff rights and improved pensions. So, feeling tact was required, he decided to wait and take it up with officials once he was in the country.

Just before leaving office for Namibia he had informed Dennis Warner, his supervisor, that he would be taking early retirement the following year, which would mark his 25 years' service with WHO.

WHO provided no official communication and information to the family of Greg Watters concerning his death. The wife of Greg Watters was informed of his death by four family friends and colleagues late at night in hers and Greg's home on the 11th of February. She was told there had been an accident, but they had received no other information. In the following days, Greg's widow pursued WHO's Department of Personnel for more information regarding the circumstances in which the accident had occurred, the manner of Greg's death, whether he had suffered, where the body was, when he would be returned to her, and a host of other questions, natural at such time. The WHO was unable to provide her with any answers but instead sent her their bill for the newspaper announcement of her husband's service-incurred death. Finally, a member of the Department of Personnel had to remind her that because of her and her need for more information, he was in the office till late at 1800 hrs.

It was on a Saturday February 15 that Greg Watters' body was flown to Geneva where he was taken to a funeral home and from which point on wards his family did not leave his side. The memorial service was held on the Sunday.

This was packed with WHO staff. It was addressed by Dennis Aitken, the WHO's Assistant Director - General for Administration And Finance, who said that Greg had represented the best of WHO. "Through all these years he upheld the highest standards of honesty, courage and dedication to his work and to his co-workers," he said. On Tuesday Greg's body was flown to Scotland for his funeral in Crieff. The church was so full, the mourners spilled out on to the pavement. Greg's daughter spoke for the family in her moving tribute to her father. "His keen intellect, together with his principled and upright approach to life – nothing and no-one excepted – made him invaluable in any situation. All his actions were governed by what he believed to be just and honest. He was a remarkable man...a wonderful human being on every level."

For months afterwards, the family continued to receive tributes to Gregor from all over the world.

In order to pay tribute to Greg Watters and his work and to show what calibre of man he was, I should like to dwell briefly on the condolences his family received. They show not only that he was loved ("This awful news paralysed the whole office this morning") but that his influence was wide. International civil servants tend to be self-effacing and modest; they remain anonymous – no-one names bridges or grand buildings after them – but quietly, behind the scenes, they do the real work of making the world a better place. Greg Watters was a dedicated international civil servant and deserves great acknowledgment and respect.

Tributes

An editorial in a newsletter for international civil servants outlined Greg's career thus: 'Greg joined WHO/EURO in 1971, first as a consultant, and then as a staff member. He held a PhD in Sanitary Engineering and soon became a key professional. In 1984 he joined HQ where, among his many contributions to the Division of Environmental Health, he was responsible for WHO's global monitoring of water supply and sanitation services and helped establish the WHO/UNICEF Joint Monitoring Programme for drinking water supply and sanitation. He was a conscientious and devoted professional who applied the highest standards to his work.

'Greg was greatly appreciated by his colleagues for his constant, cheerful disposition and friendly attitude. He seemed to know everybody in the Organization and always showed concern for staff matters. Greg belonged to the staff committee from 1977 to 1992 as first and second vice president. He was very active in FICSA and a strong advocate of staff interests and defender of staff pensions. He was respected for his loyalty to those he represented, never sparing his efforts or time defending their rights. His innate sensitivity to the problems of others and his availability to listen and discuss were appreciated immensely. In addition, he entertained his colleagues with lively stories in his characteristic Scottish accent, adding a light touch to any situation.'

A friend summed him up well: 'Greg was a kind, honest man; he had a twinkle in his eye and a fine sense of humour. He embraced life with gusto, and knew what was right.' Another pinpointed what his colleagues loved about him: 'Greg always had the time to listen carefully to other people's problems, which he would take seriously; he would invariably come up with good suggestions and solutions.'

Another described him as 'a very rare personality ... never losing sight of what ultimately counts and fighting for it.'

The range of Organizations which wrote to the family included every regional office to the WHO. A colleague from Copenhagen wrote: "In the chaotic and pressurised world of WHO, one works with people for several years and then loses touch because paths diverge. Greg was an outstanding colleague and I know more than most, of his successes during his time in Europe, perhaps outstandingly in Kosovo."

'A friend from the Federation of International Civil Servants (FICSA) described Greg as "a good colleague and friend for whom I had a lot of respect. A true gentleman – so thoughtful and considerate… calm and dependable. He did much work behind the scenes for staff."

Staff at the Division of Water Sciences, Unesco, said, "He will be greatly missed…. It is difficult to believe he will not walk in the door again one of these days, sit himself at whichever computer is available and just get on with it as usual – always with a kind word and consideration for those around him." A man from UNICEF in Guatemala wrote of Greg's "tireless commitment to the work we did together during the last six years in Latin America." And from UNICEF, New York, came a message signed by ten people, reading: 'It is a loss for the sector as Greg was an institution and cannot be replaced." They ended, touchingly, "Having known him and worked with him made a difference in the lives of each one of us."

A man at the Hydrology and Water Resources Department of the World Meteorological Organization wrote "We knew him in two roles – as a conscientious and effective professional officer responsible for water supply and sanitation activities, and as a representative of WHO staff in inter-agency collaboration. In both roles he demonstrated not only an ability for hard work but also a real commitment to causes in which he believed deeply … tempered always with that great sense of humour."

From the International Atomic Energy Agency in Vienna a colleague wrote: "I have known Greg for many years, mainly through our work on the ACC subcommittee on Water Resources. In the many talks I had with him, I developed an immense admiration and liking for him, not only as a scientist and expert in the field of water supply and sanitation, but above all as a colleague and friend who gave immeasurable support and advice to the newcomer I was at the time." The International Water and Sanitation Centre pinpointed his warm personality and the stimulating enthusiasm he displayed while participating in various workshops and meetings.

In addition and as further evidence of the wide-ranging influence a good international civil servant has, they received letters from the Centre for Health Development in Kobe, Japan; the International Hydrological Programme; the Charted Institute of Water and Environmental Management; The United Nations University Office in North America; INSTRAAW; the United Nations International Research and Training Institute for the Advancement of Women; Poland's Ministry of Environment and Protection of Natural Resources; the World Meteorological Organization; UNHCR; UNDP, and the Water Supply and Sanitation Collaborative Council.

Many of their comments are typified by this one: "Our contact with Greg was not that frequent and the sense of loss felt by the staff of this department is indicative of the deep impression that he made on all who met and worked with him. May he rest in peace."

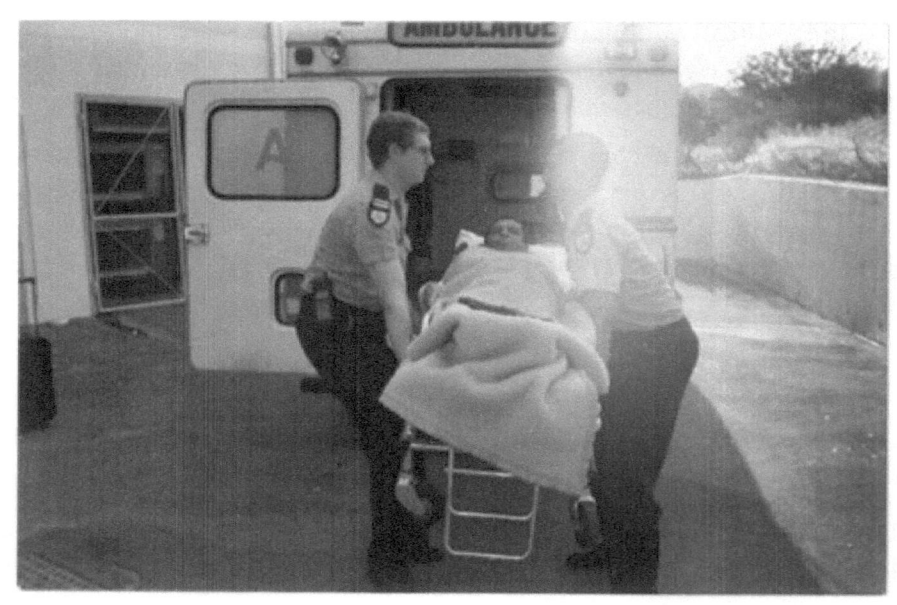

My medical evacuation from Namibia to USA

CHAPTER TEN

JOHNS HOPKINS: HIGH ON HEALTH

W*hen the Johns Hopkins Hospital won its top U.S. ranking in 1997, its Executive Board personally demonstrated their appreciation by being there in person to hand out a small gift, with thanks, to all incoming employees, beginning at 6 a.m and ending at 11:30 p.m. This understanding of the true meaning of teamwork goes a long way towards making Johns Hopkins the renowned institution it is. The World Health Organization operates from the opposite end of the spectrum, lacking a culture of care, support and appreciation for its staff.*

I had no doubt that my broken hip would be knitted up skillfully, but my peace of mind was another matter. I felt shattered by the unnecessary deaths of Greg and Andrew, and on the long journey to the States, brooded over how to word my written report to WHO. My rage with Niklaas Mootu simmered and seethed, never far from the surface. I wanted everything to do with the crash questioned and brought to light. I wanted an explanation, and justice. I knew there would be no peace until the culprit(s) were brought to book.

It was an interesting experience, flying on scheduled flights as a patient. My stretcher was placed across three normal seats on the ten-hour flight from Windhoek to London, likewise on the eight-hour flight to Washington. At Heathrow, between flights, I discovered there was a special ward, cosseted away from the noise and the bustle, for patients in transit. I was escorted there and back by charming air hostesses. Zini and I were soon airborne again, flying business class on a Virgin Airways

747. It was attractive and spacious, with beautiful carpets – perhaps they always are beautiful, and my new vantage point made me aware of them for the first time! At any rate, I was made comfortable and fussed over; even the weather co-operated with a smooth flight across the Atlantic. When we landed, the cabin crew alerted the immigration officers that there was a non-ambulatory passenger and they came on board. They relaxed their usual customs-officer tough-guy act, realizing that we had things other than smuggling on our minds.

I felt quite emotional to see a splendid hi-tech ambulance waiting for me on the tarmac from Johns Hopkins Hospital in Baltimore. It contained two paramedics who helped me off the plane with gentle professionalism – typical, I was to discover, of this wonderful hospital. Not for nothing had it been voted America's best for the past 13 years. As we made our way to Baltimore – the normal 45-minute journey taking twice as long so as not to disturb me – I knew I was in good hands, and relaxed.

Finally, we drew up in front of an old, red-brick, stone-edged building – one of the original 17 buildings, on a site that has now vastly expanded. The unusual name, Johns Hopkins, derives from its founder, a wealthy Quaker who died in 1873, leaving the land and millions of dollars for the purpose of building this hospital. He had been the founder of a chain of a grocery stores and this health project was dear to his heart, although sadly he died never having seen so much as a blue print. Hopefully he's able to peep at it from heaven, for his dream of creating a modern facility that would combine the best practice in training, hospital design and medical expertise, was thoroughly fulfilled.

Hopkins had been raised in a family that rejected slavery, and tried to make amends for its depredations. He set out to relieve the pain and suffering of 'coloured children' by creating an institution that would attract 'surgeons and physicians of the highest character and greatest skill.' In a letter to the First Board of Trustees in 1873, he wrote: *'You will... provide for the reception of... patients who are able to make compensation for the room and attention they may require. The money received from such persons will enable you to appropriate a large sum for the relief of the suffering of that class which I direct you to admit free of charge; and you will thus be enabled to afford to strangers, and to those of your own peoples who have no friends or relations to care for them in sickness, and who are the object of charity, the advantages of careful and skilful treatment.'*

When the buildings went up over a century ago, they were a model of hospital planning, the first to boast of electric wiring, telephones and heating. They've maintained their leading edge ever since. The designer, John Shaw Billings, was fanatical about sanitation, which endears him to me. His ideas were progressive – he was the first to insist that the internal corners of every ward be rounded to avoid the build-up of dust, dirt and insects, which is standard practice all over the world today. He went to enormous lengths to control the spread of airborne diseases, banning elevators in case germs should travel up the shafts. It is fortunate that they've found more efficient ways of controlling germs, for now many of its buildings soar up many storeys.

People who dub Africa's health conditions 'primitive', should remember that little more than a century ago things weren't much better in the West.

From the start, Johns Hopkins aimed high. It wasn't just for the people of Baltimore, but 'for the benefit of the sick and afflicted of all countries of all future time'. That sounds ambitious, but it was not such a challenge at the time for improving healthcare treatment wasn't difficult when standards in general were so low. Medical training was chaotic, with inappropriate people being trained at 'trade schools', from which they were often released to practice as doctors before they had ever laid hands on a patient. When people sneeringly dub Africa's health conditions 'primitive', they should remember that little more than a century ago things weren't much better in the West.

Hopkins earned its reputation through transformational medical research. It pioneered rigid entrance requirements for medical students, and laid down a vastly upgraded medical school curriculum with emphasis on the scientific method. Courses blended bedside teaching with laboratory research, and the School of Medicine was integrated with the Hospital. Amongst its triumphs over the years has been a long list of firsts – the first to admit women; to use rubber gloves for surgery; to develop renal dialysis and CPR. Then there was the first 'blue baby' operation, which led the way to modern heart surgery. Over the years

Johns Hopkins has been the birthplace of many a medical speciality, including neurosurgery, urology, endocrinology and paediatrics. More recently, it has been acclaimed for discovering the brain's natural opiates, such as serotonin, which has had a huge impact on treating depression.

I couldn't help contrasting its sophistication with the people of Namibia, dying in their hovels of dysentery.

I was greeted by name by an elegant and charming lady, Suzi Morris, the hospital's International Relations Manager for Africa – a designation which indicates the size and scope of this vast establishment. Suzi, an African-American, was part of a specialist division coordinating international patients' care; her work included seeing to our personal, cultural and travel-related needs. It was her job to arrange consultations, second opinions and treatment, and to coordinate appointments. The cold depersonalisation that characterises many hospitals was deliberately avoided in this way, I soon realised, for throughout my stay, Suzi was consistently kind, open-hearted, friendly and compassionate. We had already benefited from her efficiency, for it was Suzi who had helped my wife and daughter to ensure my speedy evacuation from Namibia. Not only had she investigated the best surgeon for my case, she had also organised a teleconference between Doctor Oosthuizen in Windhoek and the specialist at Johns Hopkins. She'd also sorted out the insurance details with WHO, and having someone to manage the red tape like this lifted an enormous burden from my family's shoulders. From then on Suzi made it her business to look after me, keeping me informed and becoming a family friend in the process. As I got to know her I learned that her interest in African health was very real, as she had begun her career in missionary service in Ghana. Subsequently she had participated in outreach programmes throughout Africa, and maintained close ties to Africa's faith-based community. After over a decade of dedicated service at Johns Hopkins, she left to carry forward the spirit of the hospital at the African Health Council, of which she was the first Director. This Council strives to mirror the spirit of the original Johns Hopkins, whose reverence for God inspired him to act on behalf of his fellow man.

The first thing I was given on being installed in my room was a copy of the *Charter of Patient Rights and Responsibilities*. Sample: 'As a patient at Johns Hopkins Hospital you can expect... considerate, respectful, and compassionate care regardless of your age, race, gender, religion, national origin, sexual orientation, or physical or mental disability.' And: 'As a patient.... You and /or your representative are expected to provide complete and accurate information about your health, including present condition, past illnesses, hospitalisations, medications, natural products and vitamins, and any other matters that pertain...'

A succession of specialists attended on me – a heart surgeon, a neurologist, and an orthopaedics surgeon. Immediately they ordered tests: my blood, urine, pulse, blood pressure and general well-being were all recorded for posterity. Between tests Mereb and my two daughters arrived. We had an emotional reunion, with much hugging and relief, since they had been under great strain and worry since hearing about the accident and were reassured to see that I did not look too bad – the only visible wounds were a scratch on my forehead and a gash on my shoulder. Later the true extent of my injuries was revealed by a CAT scan, which showed that there was 'a disruption of the symphysis pubis, with evidence of left anterior sacro iliac joint widening'. Translated, this means that the junction line between the bones that form the front and back of the pelvis was disrupted, and the joint that links the rear wall with the wing of the pelvis was getting wider.

Exhausted from the flight, I slept well that night. I was relieved beyond words to be close to my family, far away from whatever mysterious event had caused this accident – if that's what it was – to happen.

I quickly adjusted to life as a patient, though I found it quite surprising. Next morning when the doctor did his rounds I found myself being scrutinised by seven pairs of eyes, as a group of white-coated medical students trailed after their teacher. It was a little unnerving, but probably less so than in most teaching hospitals, for at Johns Hopkins they had their own way of doing things. Instead of the traditional visitation by the God-like medical man, who discusses the patient's condition in terms of an impersonal 'case', as if the real person lying in the bed were a stuffed dummy, the Hopkins approach was people-centred. This followed the conclusion of one of their eminent surgeons – which perhaps seems common-sense to the man in the street, but, like so much else in modern medicine has become far-removed from that commodity – that rounds which focused on the provider of services rather than the patient, were 'a great way to teach medicine, but [not] in the best interest of the patient'.

Peter Pronovost, associate professor of anaesthesiology and critical care, had observed that not only do patients get better quicker when they are treated with respect, but that 'The doctors focused on the physiology, pharmacology and so-called 'available evidence' aspect of the patient, not on creating goals for their recovery'. So today, patients are invited to take an active part in their own healing process.

The way it went was this: the team would visit me for about 25 minutes, starting with formal introductions all round, and explanations as to why each one was there. Then a student would go over the findings and assessments of the previous day. At intervals, they would ask me if this was clear to me, so that I had the chance to comment. Then they would create a plan of care for that day, including step-by-step goals for me. They wanted to know whether I was happy with the nurses, the medication – even if the bed was comfortable. This was so far from my image and experience of hospitals that I began to feel I'd strayed into a five-star hotel – although not even they go to so much trouble. It was a far cry from the grim places portrayed in so much fiction – and fact, for that matter – with cruel matrons, cross nurses and unpalatable food. At Johns Hopkins, every nurse is evaluated on their understanding of patients' daily recovery goals and the work needed to get them to the next level. Not surprisingly, this humane approach pays dividends in terms of speeding recovery and reducing the time spent in hospital.

The nurses were wonderful. Each day as they came on duty they would greet me and introduce themselves. They acted as if they really did care, popping in to see if I was okay without waiting for me to summon them. They not only checked on my condition, they also tried to see that I was comfortable and not too bored. At the end of their shift they came to say good bye and to tell me who my next attendant would be.

One detail stands out in particular as evidence of the way Johns Hopkins achieves this gold standard in innovative and compassionate care. According to their magazine, when the Hospital won its top ranking in the US listings yet again while I was there, its CEO, President and Executive Board made it their business to personally demonstrate their appreciation for the staff. On a chosen day, every single individual who worked there was greeted in person by one of these dignitaries as they came on duty, with thanks for their dedication and a small gift. This effort was all the more extraordinary considering that some shifts started at six a.m, while some didn't start till 11. 30 p.m, yet every one was treated the same. It not only showed rare humility on the part of the Board, it also demonstrated understanding of the true meaning of teamwork. 'The deepest principle in human nature is the craving to be appreciated,' wrote psychologist William James. Had the Administration of WHO believed that and acted on it, this book would not have needed to be written. WHO leaders and managers would do well to realise that the people who do its difficult work need a culture of care, support and appreciation if they are to excel.

It seems that the official view was, 'the less said, the better.'

On the third day after I was admitted, orthopaedic surgeon Dr. James Michelson and his team came to give me the results of the CAT scan. There was no chance of the damage healing naturally, he said; the best option would be to fix the broken bone with a reconstruction plate. New bone would eventually grow across the gap between the pelvic bones, now three centimetres wide, and in the meantime the plate would be screwed in to keep everything in place. I would have to spend the first month in a horizontal position, and then I would progress from wheelchair to crutches. Eventually I should be able to walk as before.

I was warned of the risks attending surgery, and I signed the consent forms. Then the pre-surgery process started and took almost two days. Surgery took one and a half hours – not long as operations go, yet the very word 'surgery' had a sinister ring to one who had never before been ill, let alone cut open. But Dr. Michelson was among the best orthopaedics surgeons in America, and I was lucky to have him.

However, all went well, and when I awoke, I was back in my room and seemed to have a number of tubes sprouting from my body. I had many visitors, and the room was full of flowers. The stitches were miniscule, like a silk thread – quite unlike the ugly scars I'd imagined. The dedicated nurses watched my sleeping position every hour to make sure I did no damage, so when the thread was removed less than a week later, only a thin line was visible, and even this quickly disappeared. On March 12 I was transferred to the Good Samaritan Hospital for physical rehabilitation.

On March 18 I sent off my accident report to Dr. Ibrhaim Samba, the Regional Director of WHO Africa. I outlined the reason for our visit to Namibia, and the events leading up to the ill-fated field trip. I emphasised that only the driver had a seat belt even though the venture was a 1990 model, and would certainly have been fitted with them originally. I said that the speed at which we were travelling at the time of the accident, although I couldn't be certain, seemed to me to be between 120 and 160 km per hour. I stated: 'The driver suddenly turned the steering wheel to the right, missing his lane. He then tried to bring the car back to its lane, turning to the left, but he was unable to control the car since it was accelerating at high speed.' I concluded unequivocally: 'The cause of the accident was the sudden turning of the steering wheel. There was no rain at the time of the accident. The tyres were not punctured. The road was clear. No vehicle was in front or at the back.'

I immediately felt more able to relax, feeling that events would now take their proper course, I imagined that Dr. Samba would call Rojas, Aster and Mootu to account by holding an internal investigation.

What was actually discussed will never be known. I do know that Dr. Rojas was called to Brazzaville soon after the crash to report directly to Dr. Samba. I also know that Aster met with Dr. Samba in Libreville, Gabon in April during the Directors' retreat. I have no knowledge of who Niklaas Mootu reported to or was questioned by. It seems that the official view was, 'the less said, the better'.

CHAPTER ELEVEN

HEALING THE BODY, TRAMPLING THE MIND

H*ad it not been for my resolve to set the record straight, the truth behind the 'accident' would have been buried as speedily and finally as its two victims.*

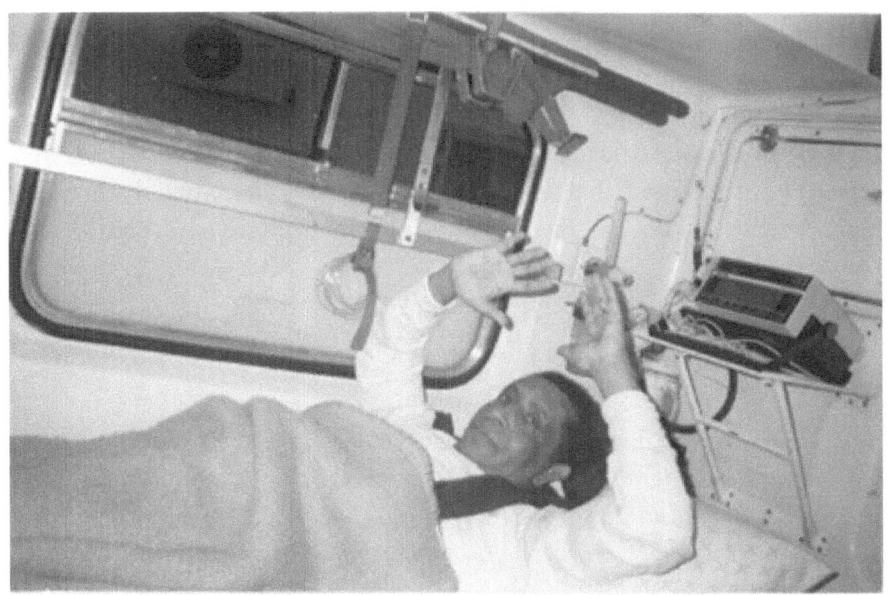

In transit during medical evacuation

While waiting for the wheels of justice to begin churning in Namibia, I was transferred to Baltimore's Hospital of The Good Samaritan for physical rehabilitation. Finally on March 20, I went home to continued physiotherapy. It felt wonderful to be nurtured by my family.

For a month I lay on my back, which created a risk of blood clotting for which I received blood-thinning injections. Washing involved complicated manoeuvres with towels. For six weeks I wasn't allowed to sit up, but at last I graduated to a wheel chair. This was a difficult move involving two people sliding me onto a wooden board because I couldn't put weight on my legs.

By the end of April, the pelvic bone was regenerating, which was a relief. By mid-May I was able to walk with crutches. At last, I began to feel normal. But my muscles had been weakened by inactivity, and my legs wobbled alarmingly. I'd forgotten how to move in a coordinated way, which meant more physiotherapy.

At last, I was able to get dressed and go out with the family. A huge bonus was being able to attend the graduation of my youngest daughter from high school – a family milestone of the kind we international civil servants normally have to forego. By the end of August, I had regained sufficient strength to walk with the aid of a cane. Within two months I was able to exercise, take long walks without the stick, swim and ride a bicycle. By November, the long rest had done its work and friends and relatives commented that I looked younger and healthier than before the accident. I wouldn't recommend it as anti-ageing treatment, I told them.

I was cheered by letters from colleagues in Africa and elsewhere in WHO, wishing me a speedy recovery. One, signed by twenty regional advisers, read:

'All your WHO colleagues who are participating in the Interregional Consultation on Environmental Health take this opportunity to send you best wishes and hopes for your speedy recovery. We are aware that your recovery and rehabilitation from the tragic accident in Namibia in February has been a difficult and painful time for you. Perhaps you can take some comfort in knowing that you are very much missed here. The annual Interregional Consultations are not the same without you. Your absence only highlights how much we need you. Beyond your important role in WHO, however we want you to know how much your friendship means to us. We look forward to the day when you will be able to return to your duties and

resume working with your colleagues. Please give our good wishes to your wife and children. And please remember to call on us if there is any thing we can do to assist during this period of rehabilitation.

This warmly personal, human intervention was in contrast to the indifference to the accident displayed by the WHO hierarchy. The two men behind it were known for their ability in building human relationships with those who worked for them. They were Dr. Wilfred Kreisel, then Executive Director, Environmental Health Promotion, Geneva, and Dr. Dennis Warner, Head of the Rural Environmental Health Unit, also based in Geneva. I had worked closely with Dennis Warner for the previous four years. A former Peace Corps Volunteer, he had worked in Africa for many years and had a passion for the continent. I was touched when, in June, he and his wife came all the way to Baltimore to visit me. Dr. Kreisel later fell victim to the political axe wielded by Dr. Brundtland as Director General, and became WHO Representative to the European Union.

To while away the long hours while recuperating I took the opportunity to continue my studies. In 1994, I had begun work on an external Master's degree in Environmental Management from the Imperial College of Science, Technology and Medicine, University of London. To me this seemed essential because of the fundamental shift in direction being taken by the WHO away from ill health *per se* towards helping countries achieve health within the context of sustainable development and poverty reduction. This was a wider concept than simply controlling or eradicating disease, an attempt which worked only in rare cases such as smallpox where there was a clear medical protocol to follow. There was now recognition that most ill-health results from social, economic and environmental conditions and any improvement must take them into account. In tandem with this was the acknowledgement that resources must be used wisely and preserved for future generations. In sanitation terms this meant it was no use going into countries with super-sophisticated models for onsite disposal of waste. Rather, local materials must be used, and local people taught how to build and maintain the systems they'd chosen.

This approach had been articulated by a WHO Commission on Health and the Environment, a follow-up of the 1987 report

Our Common Future by the United Nations World Commission on Environment and Development (WCED). Although the link between the environment and health was not detailed in this report, concern was implicit. The WHO Commission assessed the health consequences of environmental change in anticipation of the United Nations Conference on Environment and Development (UNCED), known as the Earth Summit, which was held in Rio de Janeiro in June 1992. The WHO Commission had a central role in shaping the health-related aspects of Agenda 21, the action plan negotiated and adopted by 150 Member States of the United Nations during UNCED. Dr. Gro Harlem Brundtland, who led the work of WCED, was keen to see this direction followed. One of her first actions as Director General was to create a special body dealing with sustainable development and healthy environments.

So I felt it was incumbent on me to update myself, as Regional Adviser tasked with helping Member States to integrate health and the environment in their national plans. The shift in mandate at the top had changed the type of work we were expected to do, but I had little expertise in this new area. I was constantly amazed that the WHO gave staff no help or encouragement in updating our training, even refusing to meet any part of my study costs. It was another example of a break in the chain of management, from fine-sounding policies at the top to an utter lack of support for staff who wanted to implement them on the ground.

At least I had no financial worries during this period. For the first time since joining WHO I was able to take advantage of one considerable benefit of working for a United Nations body: I was automatically entitled to sick leave on full pay until I was cleared by my physician to resume duty. In this respect Graham Hancock had a point when he called us `a privileged aristocracy, effectively insulated from the exigencies of everyday life'. Most US employees would have to work 14 years with no sick leave whatever to qualify for over six months' sick leave on full pay. Not only was I on full pay, but in March I filed a claim for compensation for medical expenses in respect of my injuries. In April the Advisory Committee on Compensation Claims decided that since those injuries were service-incurred, every cent would be fully reimbursed. Presumably this money came out of the insurance cover for WHO staff, which takes account of our often dangerous circumstances.

By November I was fit enough to travel to London to sit the University examination and in December I was awarded a postgraduate degree in Environmental Management.

The cause of death was given as 'multiple injuries.'

All this time events were moving along in Namibia. We will never know what was said behind closed doors, but right from the start it appears that Dr. Rojas was in close touch with the police over the matter. He received reports that were never shown to me or the Watters family. Had it not been for my resolve to get the mystery out in to the open, the events surrounding the crash would have been buried as speedily, quietly and finally as its two victims.

On May 7, a quick inquest was held in Otjiwarongo on the death of Dr. Gregor Watters. An unusual aspect was the total lack of communication about this. No-one told me about it, even though my name was included among the list of witnesses and the evidence included the statement I had made to the police on my departure. I had clearly understood that in the event that the driver was prosecuted for culpable homicide, I would be called back to give evidence in person; it was one reason why I had given my official statement less attention than I should have. The British High Commission were not informed of the inquest either, although, since Dr. Watters was a British citizen, this would have been standard procedure.

The net result was that there was a delay of some weeks before all the parties concerned heard the result, which was communicated to me by means of a terse memo from the regional commander of police, which was forwarded by Dr. Rojas. It read:

'The above said case was forwarded to the Public Prosecutor for decision and he has declined to prosecute.

An inquest was held by the local magistrate to establish the cause or probable cause of the death of the deceased.

Attached hereto a copy of the J 56 issued by the magistrate.' He indicates the cause of death.

On this form, the cause of death was given as 'multiple injuries.' *'State whether the death was brought about by any act or omission prima facie involving or amounting to an offence on the part of any person,'* the form demanded. Underneath was typed in capital letters one word: *'NONE'*

I was dumbfounded. On what grounds had the magistrate come to this conclusion? What had become of my statement to the police, in which I laid the blame fair and square on the driver? As I wrote to the widow of Greg Watters in September: 'I have seen photographs taken by Otjiwarongo traffic police at the site of the accident.... There is a comprehensive report with the photographs, prepared by the traffic officers who visited me at the hospital in Windhoek before my departure to the USA. I have noted differences in the information about the inquest sent to the British High Commission, and that sent to the WHO. In WHO's copy, nine witnesses were named, including me and John Damon, Andrew's brother. In the High Commission document, eleven witnesses were named. [These were not eye witnesses but included people such as Graham Snyman, who had come to my rescue, and police officers.] The latter was signed and stamped with the official court stamp, the former was not.'

These discrepancies in the forms indicated that there was more than one official version, and caused me grave disquiet. It suggested to me that something untoward was going on. When, furthermore, I heard that WHO had reinstated Niklaas Mootu, the driver into his post, and he was even now putting WHO staff members at risk, I began not for the first time to wonder whether there was more to all this than met the eye.

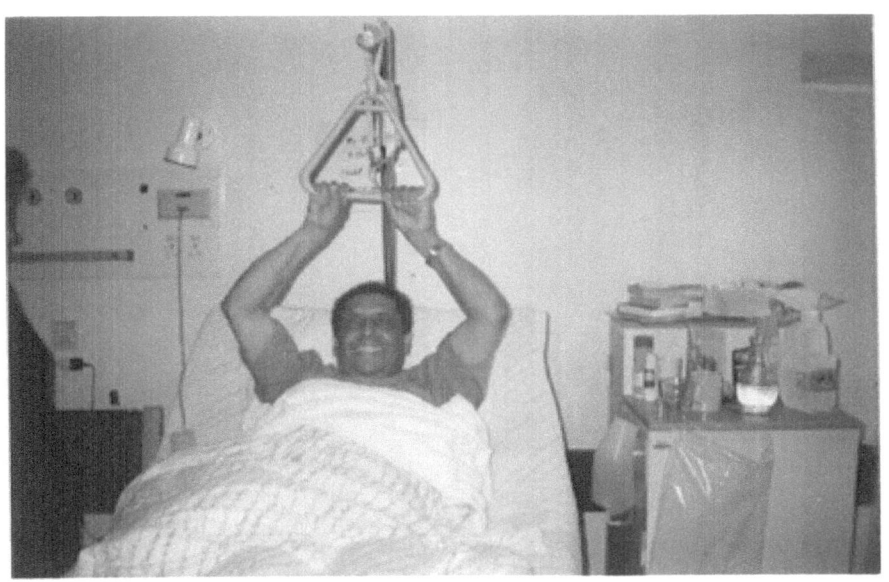

Admission to Johns Hopkins Hospital in Baltimore

CHAPTER TWELVE

BACK TO HARNESS

*C*onsidering one victim was a senior member of the Organization, another a Government official; that the costs ... were extensive; that an expensive vehicle was a write-off; and that the driver might be a menace to others, the lack of investigation seemed extraordinary.

After sitting my exam in London I travelled to Geneva at the end of November. There a WHO doctor examined me and pronounced me fit for work. I would need sophisticated medical care for some time, however, and would be limited to sedentary work, so Dr. Celton, Director of the Joint Medical Service and Dr. Kreisel, Executive Director, Environmental Health reassigned me temporarily to Geneva. However, the bureaucracy of the WHO was so hidebound that it took another three months to sort out the paperwork. This may seem incredible to those in the private sector, accustomed to acting as if time is money. But first the approval of the Regional Director had to be obtained; then the paperwork transferring the budget had to be sorted out. Then there was the travel authorisation, without which staff may not travel. I didn't receive this until 28 January because of delays in correspondence between AFRO and Geneva.

Finally, in February 1998 – a year after the crash – I reported for duty at WHO Headquarters. I was to work in the Division of Operational Support in Environmental Health (EOS) on behalf of the African Region, on such matters as preparing for the African Ministerial Conference on Health and the Environment, to be held the following year.

I met with Greg Watters' family and as I gave them a firsthand account of the events of February 11 the accident came back to me in all its horror. However, I felt it was a necessary part of the healing process, especially since the Watters' family had still received no official account of what exactly had led to the death of their beloved Gregor. As I recounted, anger again began to surface at the lack of enquiry by the WHO. It was bad enough that the Namibian authorities had failed to investigate thoroughly, but it seemed inconceivable that the WHO had not satisfied itself as to what went wrong, and were continuing to employ the driver as if nothing had happened. Considering that one of the victims was a senior member of the Organization and another a Namibian government official; that the cost of my medical care and the loss in man hours had been fairly astronomical; that an expensive vehicle was a write-off; and that the driver had to have been either negligent or malevolent, the lack of investigation seemed highly irregular. One could only ask, why not hold one? Clearly in an organization as bound by rigid rules as the WHO, there must have been a protocol to be followed when a driver was involved in a serious traffic accident.

It seemed strange that rules had been bent and that Mootu was allowed to continue putting others in potential danger. The Administration's failure to account to the family of their employee for the way he had died seemed to imply a lack of common decency. Common sense too, for surely the WHO realised the importance of showing staff that their welfare was taken seriously? And that disciplinary action would follow when someone seriously erred?

I mulled over other disquieting factors, such as the fact that no announcement about the crash had been made by the African Regional Office. This was weird, for such a serious event as the death and injury of senior colleagues would normally have merited a circular at least, and certainly a major announcement in the Staff Bulletin. But our case had been met with total silence. Were the authorities afraid to say anything in case it implied responsibility? Or were they – outrageous as the idea seemed – complicit in any way with the crash?

Aster Gashaw had called me in Baltimore in May, and told me in a chatty, casual way that she had been invited to Gabon to join the Regional Director, Dr. Samba, and his senior staff while on retreat. Why?

He apparently had no problem with the fact that she, as Administrator, bore some responsibility for the disaster: she had, after all, flouted the regulations in providing us with a vehicle which was not properly equipped. It seemed to me that he was singling her out for approval rather than accountability.

In the absence of answers, I began to entertain morbid suspicions about the Administrator, the WHO Representative and the Regional Director. Having witnessed firsthand the Red Terror in Ethiopia and the massacres in Rwanda, I knew too well how cheap life can be in Africa, and how the morés of civilised society can be disregarded for seemingly trivial reasons. I could think of no plausible reason why anyone would have wanted to have any of us killed; and obviously the driver, although the only one to be strapped in, had risked his own life in overturning the Landcruiser. It didn't make sense – but then, neither did this bland official passivity. A deliberate cover-up began to seem the most likely – albeit the most shocking – conclusion.

A deliberate cover-up began to seem the most likely explanation.

No announcement about the death of Dr. Gregor Watters had been made by the African Regional Office. I advised the widow of Greg Watters to hire a lawyer in Namibia, and get the case re-opened. Meanwhile I resolved to try and get a hearing within the Organization. It was a body which many of us, myself included, loved and respected. We were proud of the high esteem in which it was largely held by the world. WHO stood for high ideals which inspired its staff, many of whom were prepared to die for them – as indeed many had. But as Hancock had concluded, the United Nations system is not the moral centre of the development business, with lofty and principled aims, as the spin doctors try to convince us.

The problem is not so much that its leaders make mistakes, but that they make them and get away with them time and again, for they are accountable to no-one. Principles, like freedom, require eternal vigilance. Hancock laid bare the UN 's rickety foundations when he wrote,' I came to realise what spurious cant [these ideals are] for the majority of the UN's 50,000 employees, how cynical many of them have become and the great extent to which most merely go through the motions of asking for a better world. Whatever noble mission the UN may once have had has long since been forgotten.... The atmosphere of idealism that had once so uplifted me is, I now understand, just a veneer – or, worse, a mere stage set, a one-dimensional façade that shouldn't fool anybody. Behind it there is almost nothing at all.'*

When I'd read that I'd felt shocked. But now I wondered – if those at the top of the Organization became aware of this crash and its lack of investigation, surely they would step in? How could they care about the world's poor if they cared so little about their own staff?

I felt it was Dr. Samba who should have ordered the enquiry. Though considered tireless and dedicated as a Regional Director, I felt that he had perhaps been too preoccupied by conflict in the Congo to take much note of internal matters at WHO. But then, why hadn't he authorized his personnel officer or the Director of Finance and Administration to carry out an enquiry, at least for the record? The Regional Office was riven with jealousy, insecurity, racial intolerance and political intrigue; it was a generally uncaring and unsatisfactory atmosphere in which to work, and this could conceivably have led to foul play.

Great changes were being forced on this regional headquarters. There had been civil unrest in the Republic of Congo for two years while two militia groups battled for supremacy. One, supported by the existing regime, democratically elected, and the other led by the former president who had left the country and now wanted his power back. The fighting grew so intense in June 1997 that the WHO offices had to be hurriedly dismantled, the staff dispersed. Brazzaville had never been a good place for the WHO to be located – it was a political choice, made in 1952 to satisfy the Francophone countries. By the time I resumed work in Geneva, the African staff had been split into three groups, further complicating their already poor communications. One group had been dispatched to Libreville, in Gabon, a second to Harare. The main administration and executives were offered a temporary home in Geneva by the then Director General, Dr. Hiroshi Nakajima from Japan, but the offer did not last long.

To digress a little into the politics of WHO, this gesture was probably one of reconciliation, for Dr. Nakajima had seriously erred in

1995 by making a serious racial slur which had so angered the African bloc that he nearly lost his job. A Geneva newspaper had quoted him as saying that he 'did not encourage Africans to work in the Geneva Headquarters for three reasons: the climate, the cultural differences, and their poor writing skills'. This created a furore. The newspaper was full of outraged letters; every African diplomat in Geneva protested, and staff from the African Region signed a letter of solidarity condemning Dr. Nakajima. The Director General was still deeply unpopular in Africa even though he'd denied the allegation, saying he had been misquoted. Insults like these are not easily forgotten, and anger was still simmering when the World Health Executive Board met later that year in Geneva. The African Group condemned Dr. Nakajima for his blunder, and demanded his resignation. I happened to be there during the Board's meeting at the time, and witnessed a succession of African delegates getting to their feet to express their dismay. They demanded to know how Dr. Nakajima, a man who could not speak English well himself, or even express himself well in his own vernacular, could make such a statement. It was the ugliest row the Board had dealt with in the history of WHO. Opinion among the staff was that Dr. Nakajima would have to resign, but he rose to the occasion. With a blush and a stammer he made a full apology, and there was a recess in which the demand for his resignation was reconsidered, his apology accepted.

The fact remained, however, that Dr. Nakajima had not been popular with external support agencies since his election in 1988. Ironically his poor communication skills were part of the problem. 'Even Dr. Nakajima's most dedicated staff acknowledges that his severe difficulties in communicating are a major handicap for a United Nations leader,' wrote Fiona Godlee in the *British Medical Journal*, in a detailed critique of WHO which ran over several issues. 'His spoken English and French are poor, and even Japanese delegates and staff find him difficult to understand. When he speaks privately his passion for the work of WHO is evident, as well as his grasp of the problems it faces; but under stress – at press conferences for example – he becomes defensive and incoherent. His attempts to establish what he has called 'a new paradigm for health' have floundered in a maze of incomprehension.'

Moreover, Dr. Nakajima's management of the Organization was considered weak. The London *Times*** commented, when Dr.

Brundtland took over, that 'ten years of corruption and scandal had all but wrecked the WHO's once sound record in promoting best practice'. Several donors withdrew their extra-budgetary funds. Dr. Nakajima was blamed for not supervising and guiding his Assistant Directors-General well, and they were all removed from their posts by Dr. Brundtland. After his election for a second term in 1993, the Japanese man was accused of bribing third-world delegates by promising them WHO posts if they voted for him, irrespective of the wishes of their governments. This was one of the things that reduced the WHO's credibility as the leader in international health. Dr. Nakajima was also severely criticised for his handling of the AIDS pandemic and the bubonic plague outbreak in India.

When civil war in the Congo necessitated a speedy new solution to housing the Afro staff, the Zimbabwean Government, no doubt keen to curry favour when it could, offered to house the entire Directorate in temporary accommodation at Parirenyatwa Hospital, Harare. The offer was accepted, and the offices were subsequently relocated to two floors of the hospital, plus an annex in the grounds.

The irony was that Zimbabwe's health services, once regarded as a shining example, were by now bleeding to death from years of neglect and inadequate funding. They continued to decline while the WHO Regional Office was temporarily located there, to such an extent that by 2001, Zimbabwe was ranked last out of 191 countries surveyed by the WHO. It performed even worse than the strife-driven Congo (DRC), largely due to President Robert Mugabe's involvement in that war. The cash-strapped Zimbabwe government admitted to spending over $10 billion on the Congolese war; the true amount was estimated by economic analysts and international aid agencies to be much higher than that.

These events affected me in another, more personal way. My apartment in Brazzaville was left empty and neglected after the crash in February 1997, and it was now invaded by looters. By the time they'd been through it, it was as if killer ants had devoured every crumb. Apart from furniture, electrical appliances, TV, video and a car – which, although valuable could be replaced – they also took my precious family photograph albums, souvenirs of my life with WHO, academic diplomas and degrees, birth and marriage certificates, and hundreds of books. Of my former life and identity, they left not so much as a scrap of paper. I later received monetary compensation from WHO, but this loss of the stuff of my life was painful. It reminded me that this was no ordinary job – the risks we face as international civil servants operating in unstable nations shouldn't be taken for granted. The only consolation was that my life had not been equally efficiently dispatched. Which begged the question, had anybody tried? And did anybody in authority care?

Lords of Poverty Graham Hancock, Camerapix International p.83-4

** *The Times* (London) May 15, 2000

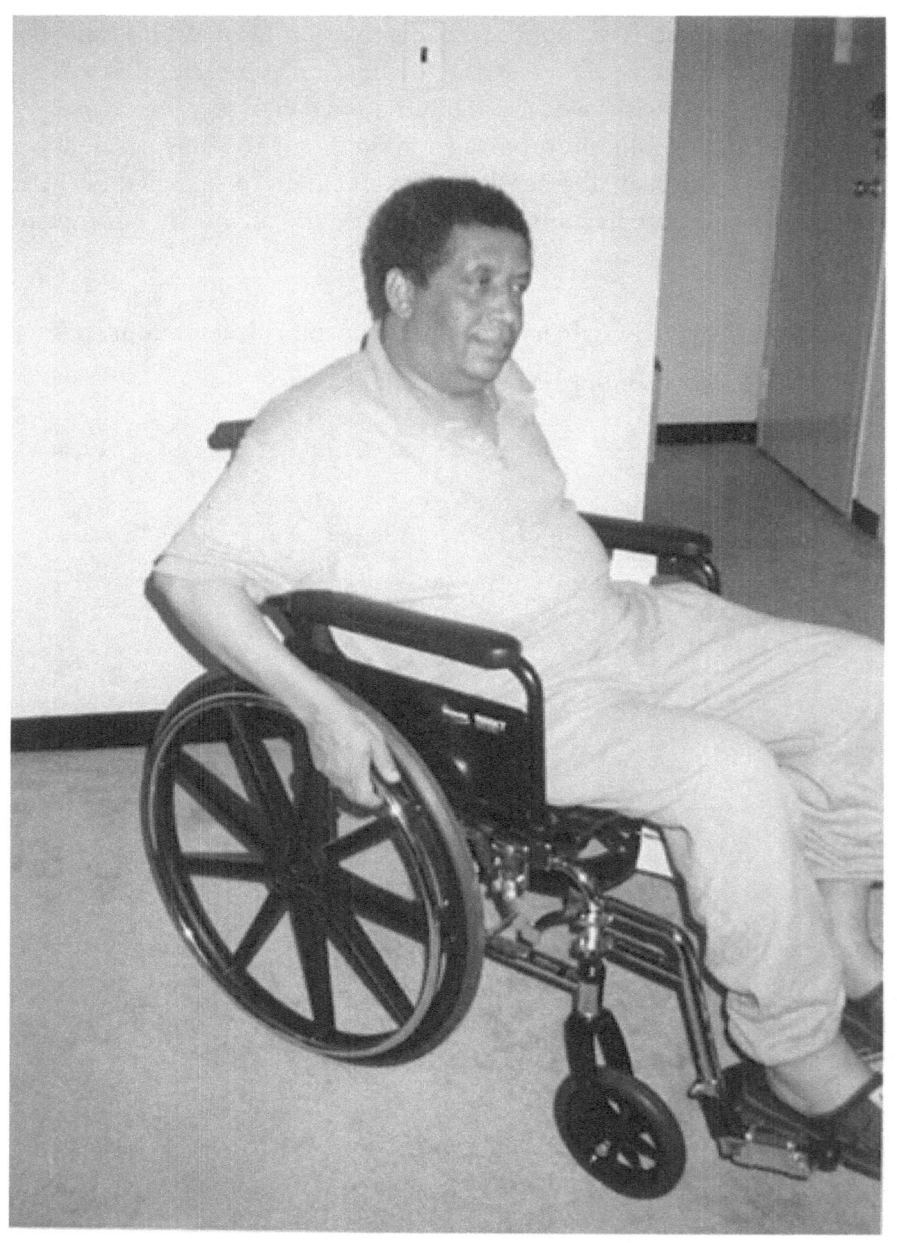

Rehabilitation after leaving hospital at home in Baltimore

CHAPTER THIRTEEN

BIG CRACKS THIN PAPER

*I*t seemed that the WHO's management was as fossilised as the Namibian dinosaurs.

And nobody, given its supra-national character, could force it to be otherwise.

There now began a long-drawn-out battle of wills between the main protagonists in this saga: myself, damaged in spirit as well as in body and seeking justice; and the World Health Organization, too lofty to be bothered about insignificant minions and seeking only to paper over the cracks relating to the crash.

Was WHO too concerned with saving the world (or its image) to bother about its staff, which it treated like unimportant cogs in its great machine-like structure? For the machine was the model the Organization had been based on when it was founded in 1948. Since then, ideas about how such Organizations flourish have evolved, but according to a Swedish study*, the WHO had not evolved with them. Whilst on the ground its staff, as we have seen, preached the importance of building self-esteem, associative strength, resourcefulness, action planning and responsibility, these were the very qualities that were discouraged at the regional offices and headquarters. There, rules came before people every time.

Or was the truth more sinister – did the Organization fear a scandal that might rock its credibility, already at an all-time low? Those who study people management know that treating them like human beings – including listening to their stories – is, not surprisingly, the only effective way to get cooperation, loyalty and commitment. But the

WHO's management seemed fossilised as the Namibian dinosaurs. And nobody, given its supra-national character, could force it to be otherwise. No matter how many critics pinpointed its outdated hierarchical structure as one reason it was ineffective, reform seemed less important than trying to change the world – futile though that endeavour was without the full participation of the staff.

Richard Smith, distinguished editor of the *British Medical Journal*, pronounced the Organization 'over-centralised at headquarters and regions, top heavy, poorly managed, bureaucratic and smelling of corruption'*. Yet no political party falls, no shareholders scream for heads to roll, when bad management leads to plummeting staff motivation and kills zest for work stone dead. There's no doubt that many fine and dedicated individuals work for WHO, yet such a dysfunctional culture is bound, eventually, to undermine their efforts.

One reason WHO gets away with it is that the world is too parochial to care. It is said that the World Health Organization is just another UN body where overpaid bureaucrats carve out their careers. It is too removed from our own world, our own country, for us to notice if lofty schemes which would have uplifted entire regions, fade away through bureaucratic bungling, together with the millions of dollars spent on them. That is, until a Bubonic plague breaks out on our own doorstep! Then we're apt to complain bitterly.

Yet we see televised images of dying, pathetic children, and we *do* care. Via taxes and politicians, it is ordinary citizens who pay for organizations such as this to act on their behalf. They wonder why Africa, in particular, appears to make no progress. When evidence comes to light that the system is failing, they assume that failure will be addressed. It has not been, thus far. We, the authors, hope by shining a light in this particular bit of darkness, to bring a little more pressure to bear. As we shall see, many WHO staffers *were* demoralised, all in their various ways.

By the time I started work in Geneva almost a year had elapsed since the crash. I myself was a changed man. Embittered by the Administration's bland refusal to look into the crash, an omission I found insulting, I had lost some of my idealism. Since the doctors had recommended I do only sedentary work I was given the job of promoting environmental health in Africa from Geneva. I soon settled into the multi-storey, gleaming block with its beautiful gardens. I appreciated the company of old and understanding colleagues, although I was still restricted in movement – I could no longer play squash or go jogging, for instance, so my level of fitness declined. I would require medical monitoring for some time, but I was glad to get back to work. Soon I was busy preparing for an African summit on Health and Environment the following year.

Meanwhile Mrs. Watters continued to request to be kept informed of everything to do with the case, but was left out entirely. Much of their initial information came from the funeral director, from whom they requested photocopies when they realised he had more information than they had. It was he who supplied the death certificate, the certificate of the post-mortem investigation; and a Namibian police report. From this they discovered that a case of culpable homicide was being prepared, which Dr. Rojas confirmed.

Mrs. Watters had still received no official explanation for the accident. She had received only the inquest report, saying that her husband died of 'multiple injuries'.

What future WHO? Bo Stenson and Go Sterky, Health Policy 28 (1994) 235-256

**Quoted in *WHO's Management - struggling to transform a 'fossilised bureaucracy'*. Gavin Yamey, BMJ Vol 325 16 Nov 2002

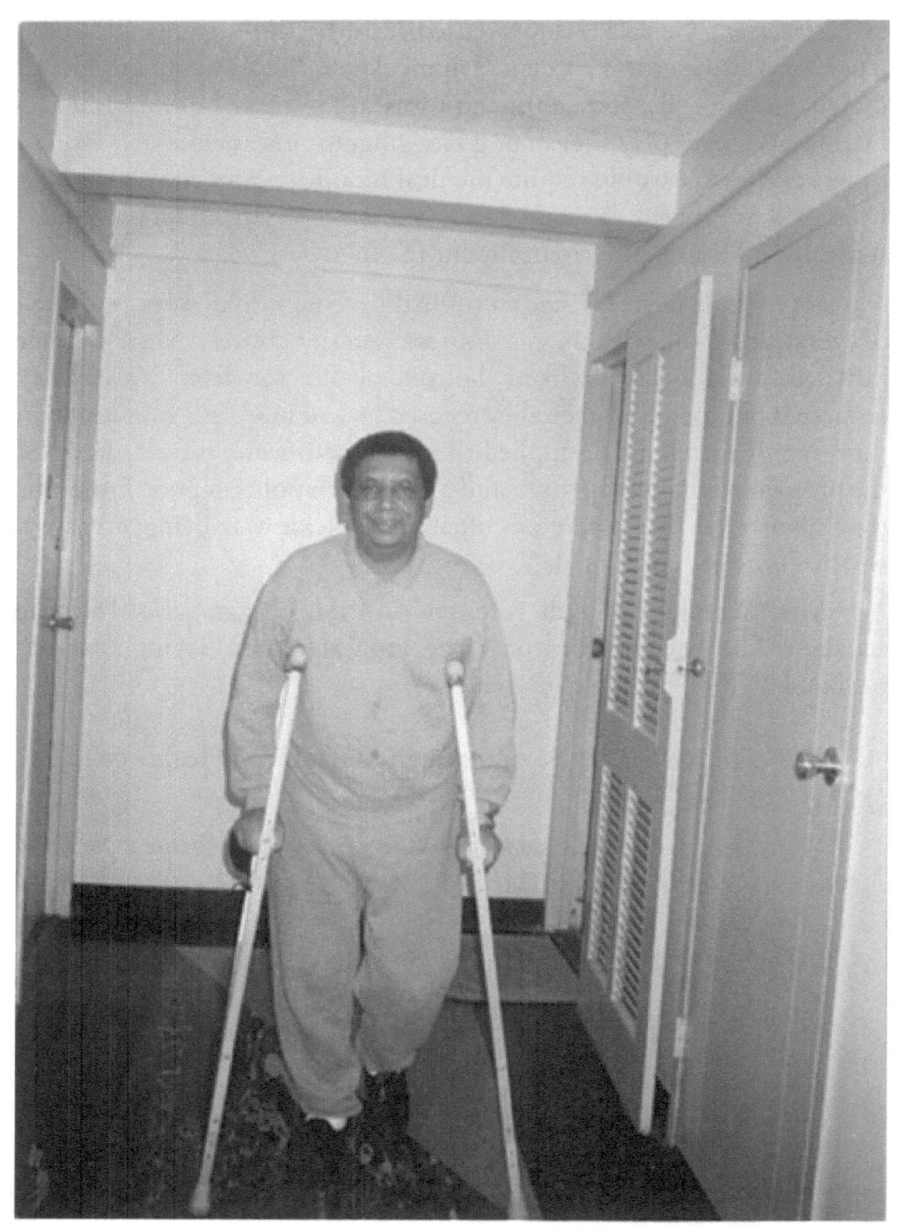

On the way to recovery in Baltimore

CHAPTER FOURTEEN

A LACKADAISICAL INQUEST, AND A LACKLUSTRE NEW LEADER

*P*ossibly the tiny court in the dusty, dry town of Otjiwarongo was presided over by a magistrate as sleepy as the town itself.

That would be the most charitable explanation for the extraordinary conclusion reached by Magistrate A S Venati, on hearing the evidence relating to the crash.

Mootu's statement, hand-printed as if he were unused to writing, read: 'I was driving from Windhoek to Katima Mulilo. I was driving with the speed of 110 km/h. While I was a few kilometres to reach Otjiwarongo Township I realized that the vehicle started swinging and at that time I was trying to control it, but unfortunately it just overturn. I do suspect that one of the backside wheel got burst. I was sober at the time of the accident. I didn't consume liquor at all.'

The police reports make clear however that none of the tyres 'got burst'. No less than eighteen photographs of the upturned vehicle and the site of the crash confirmed this. In particular photos 15, 16, 17 and 18 showed the individual wheels, each in superb condition. In short, not a shred of evidence suggested that anything other than the driver's behaviour caused the accident.

The statements included one from Namibia's Chief Forensic Analyst, a man by the impressive name of Kaapaa Uvatera Kaizemil. It recorded that he had received a blood sample on 14 February (three days after the crash) belonging to Dr. Gregor Watters, and that it had tested negative for alcohol. He did not mention Andrew Damon, or the one man for whom such a test should have been compulsory: Niklaas Mootu. Yet a charge of culpable homicide in such a case was standard procedure – so why were their samples not taken as well? Or were they taken, and then 'lost' in the three days it took for Dr. Watters' sample to be delivered?

The lack of this essential evidence meant that the police were not in a position to confirm or deny Mootu's emphatic denial of having consumed alcohol. By anyone's standards it was an incomplete and bungled investigation. No statement offered the slightest clue as to why Mootu's extraordinary phrases *it started swinging* and *unfortunately it just overturn* should have been allowed to pass unchallenged. Did the magistrate think it was quite natural for a solidly-built, expensive car on a dead straight tar road to start to swing, all on its own, then jump up in the air and overturn?

Graham Snyman, the man who had stopped to assist, was not called to give evidence in person even though, being local, he could have done so with ease. His statement read: *Approximately three kilometres before Otjiwarongo, in a rainstorm, I noticed a vehicle coming to rest on each (sic) roof on the left-hand side of the road, beyond the fence. I stopped my vehicle and phoned the hospital through my cell phone and told them to call the police and an ambulance. I approached the driver and asked him what happened. He responded that he didn't know. Police attended the scene.'*

My own statement, written, as we have seen, under duress while I was preparing to leave for America, differed in one important respect from that of Graham Snyman. It read as follows:

'On the 11th February 1997, we were on our way to Katima Mulilo from Windhoek, on official duties with the official vehicle, a Toyota Land Cruiser. I was the passenger in the vehicle seated right behind the driver. The driver was driving about 120-130 km/h, not very fast, on the road. It was raining on some places and on some places not. About two kilometres before we reached the town of Otjiwarongo, the road was clear, no rain, and no vehicle from behind us or in front. The vehicle suddenly went to the right side. The driver tried to bring the vehicle back to the road. The vehicle accelerated, the driver tried to control the vehicle. The vehicle left the road

and started overturning. Me and the driver remained in the vehicle, the other two passengers were thrown out in the process. Dr. Gregor Watters died instantly and Mr. Damon was taken to the hospital. The driver didn't consume any alcohol and was sober. I was admitted at the Otjiwarongo Medicity and the next day transported to the Windhoek Mediclinic. I sustained serious injuries as follows – a pelvic fracture, and ninth nerve sight damage. I received treatment therefore.'

The police misinterpreted what I said about the speed. And I didn't say that the driver had not consumed alcohol, since I had no way of knowing if this was the case. What I did say was that he didn't consume alcohol after we started our trip, as he was never out of our sight. As Graham Snyman confirmed, one of the first things I told him was that the accident happened because the driver was travelling too fast.

There is a discrepancy between Snyman's statement and my own. Snyman says there was a rainstorm ('It was raining so hard I couldn't see the car clearly,' he said later) while I swear the road was dry at the site of the accident since the rain has stopped. I clearly recall lying on the ground waiting for the ambulance to arrive; my face was not wet, neither were my clothes. However, since neither of us was called to give evidence in person, the magistrate was in no position to judge whose memory was at fault. In any case, while a wet road, if wet it was, might have made the accident more explicable, it certainly would not have exonerated the driver. Landcruisers are not that dainty.

So, when magistrate A S Venatius came to fill in that part of the official form which said *'State whether the death was brought about by any act or omission prima facie involving or amounting to an offence on the part of any person,'* I ask myself, on what could he possibly have based his conclusion, 'None'?

Mrs. Zoila Watters was eventually sent copies of these statements by the WHO, which she shared with me. It raised certain questions in my mind: why, for instance, had Namibia's Ministry of Home Affairs, in the person of Regional Commander A J Louw of the Namibian police, written directly to Dr. Rojas immediately after the inquest to inform him that, based on the magistrate's conclusion, the Public Prosecutor had declined to prosecute Mootu? This was not normally the place of the police, and it suggested that they had been made aware of WHO's special interest in this case, as had the Namibian Government, which was keen to maintain cordial relations with the UN agency. What had been said behind the scenes, I wondered. And why had Rojas promptly reported this news, not to the widow herself but to the Pensions and Insurance department, and the Office of the Legal Counsel? Mrs. Watters concluded that, privately, and for reasons of their own, the administrators of WHO had shown great interest, despite their official lack of curiosity.

The family then turned to the British High Commission for Namibia, since Gregor was a British citizen. They requested that they look into why the inquest had been so superficial. They eventually received this reply: '...*The British High Commission tries to assist the families of bereaved British nationals as best we can by liaising with the local authorities and conveying as much information as possible to the individuals concerned. However, I am afraid that we do not have the authority or jurisdiction (or in any case the resources) to investigate the possible causes of individual cases ourselves. This is done by the local police and judicial authorities.... May I suggest that if you wish to pursue the case, you should write to the Public Prosecutor's office in Windhoek asking that your husband's case be formally reviewed.*'

This, the family decided, was exactly what they would do.

If ever WHO staff were looking and hoping for inspired leadership, it was when this Director General from Norway took office.

Meanwhile, back in Geneva, I was nearing the end of my temporary sojourn. But I was resisting returning to Africa until the Administration had arrived at some conclusion as to who was to blame for the crash. Adding to my disquiet, I was still suffering health problems and I wasn't prepared to compromise on treatment by going to a country with inadequate medical facilities. By April I was still suffering pain and stiffness, so the Joint Medical Services (the body which looks after the health of all international civil servants) referred me to Dr. Jacques Compère, orthopaedic surgeon. His radiological examination showed that the anterior pelvic plate inserted during surgery had broken. This was not an immediate risk however, since the bone had largely healed.

Most of my pain was caused by the widening of the sacro-iliac joint. I had physiotherapy for a month, and the condition improved.

In May 1998 I returned to Baltimore for a consultation with Dr. Michelson at Johns Hopkins. He confirmed that the plate was broken but recommended that it remain in place for the present. He advised WHO that I should continue to do sedentary work only and that I should be assigned to a region where sophisticated medical care was available in case the need arose to remove the plate and to fuse my widened right joint.

By August, when my six months' assignment in Geneva was up, sweeping changes were underway at the WHO headquarters. In July, Dr. Gro Harlem Brundtland, former Prime Minister of Norway, had succeeded Dr. Nakajima as Director General. She was charged with saving the Organization following its drastic decline. She inherited, according to one body of international health experts*, a demoralised staff, and an Organization rife with rumours of corruption and cronyism, and seriously lacking in leadership. Her main challenges, in terms of reclaiming the organization's right to lead the world in the field of health, were:

- Revising WHO's governance structures to give greater voice to new actors on the global stage.
- Developing more effective mechanisms for responding to national needs for capacity strengthening.
- Creating effective coordination between WHO and other agencies.
- Enhancing the Organization's authority in scientific and technical matters.
- Reassessing the relationship between WHO's HQ, regional offices and country offices.
- Revising procedures for the allocation of resources to ensure that they give full weight to the needs of individual nations.
- Ensuring that staff positions are created on the basis of need and filled on the basis of merit.
- Redefining WHO's essential functions.

These were no small tasks, and there was a worldwide wave of support for, and optimism about, the new incumbent.

I was present at the World Health Assembly when Dr. Brundtland gave her first speech, outlining her initial reforms. Her four priority strategies would be, she said, to reduce the burden of disease, particularly in poor countries; to reduce risks to health; to create sustainable health systems; and to develop an *enabling* policy and institutional environment in the health sector.

Dr. Brundtland's most important pledge was to create 'one WHO'. 'We must be able to say,' she proclaimed, 'that WHO is one. Not two, meaning one financed by the regular budget and one financed by extra-budgetary funds. Not seven – meaning Geneva and the six regional offices.'

This promise was hailed by the medical press as being long overdue, since a major criticism was that the regional offices of WHO had become too autonomous. The African Office, in particular, had become notorious for 'doing its own thing'; the Regional Director and the Programme Directors ran their own little empires. One result was that the quality of staff recruited to fill vacant posts was compromised by politics and nepotism. Another was the location of the WHO Regional Office in the Congo – always a hot spot, which is why it was a bad choice. The dispersal of AFRO's staff due to the fighting had been a disaster, especially since Africa's health burden meant they faced a Herculean task, even without disruption. The extent of the catastrophe only became clear to the outside world when, in 1994, WHO's external auditor, Sir John Bourne, was forced to admit to the World Health Assembly that he could give no account whatsoever of how the African region had spent their $122 million budget; nor how they'd handled their assets of $20 million and liabilities of $21 million since he hadn't been able to examine their books for two years! His report caused a furore. The then Regional Director, was accused of being high-handed; it was said that he held the regional body more important than the Member States who paid for it.

On her inauguration day, Dr. Brundtland sent the staff a special address, outlining her planned changes. 'Commitment to the cause of world health is a daunting task,' she wrote, 'but serving WHO is also a privilege. We can make a difference. We can help build healthy communities and populations. We can combat ill-health. We can do our part to combat poverty and suffering. Nothing in life – as I see it has – more meaning.'

Of course, the staff agreed with these stirring sentiments. And WHO staff needed building up, because they are the means to world health; the Organization can only function through their ability to support nations in providing drugs and controlling disease, not through nursing the sick directly. But we waited to see if this Director General would also show concern for our personal hopes and needs, within the context of the Organization and its work. Such genuine people skills have been identified in multiple management texts as the key to building a successful Organization. If employees fulfilment and satisfaction is high, they work with more passion and achieve their goals more effectively. It's only when people feel like cogs in a machine that they become the paper-pushers typical, in the public's mind, of the civil servant mentality. If ever WHO staff were looking and hoping for inspired leadership, it was when this fair-headed lady from Norway took over the reins.

Certainly, that was what I hoped for. You might think that asking the new Director General to address my little matter when she was tasked with such vast problems that it seemed the weight of the world was on her shoulders, was presumptuous indeed. But because WHO was a totally hierarchical Organization it was she, in the end, who set the tone for the entire staff; it was her desk on which the buck stopped. I felt that if no-one else was prepared to answer to me then I must complain through every channel I could, even if it took me to the top. I believed that there was more at stake than simply getting a driver arraigned. If the Organization let its staff down at the level of ordinary human decency; if its people could be killed without anyone being willing to find out why, then staff would know that fundamentally they were insignificant and unappreciated. How could the big picture succeed when those who were supposed to be putting it in place felt so alienated from the leadership?

How could the big picture succeed when those responsible for putting it in place felt so alienated?

Dr. Brundtland's first 100 days passed in a whirlwind of activity. She set in motion a massive upheaval aimed at giving WHO a leaner structure. She reduced fifty programmes to thirty-five departments, and regrouped them into nine clusters, intended to reflect the Organization's new strategic direction. Each of the nine clusters had a Management Support Unit with its Personnel, Finance and Planning sub-units. In effect nine separate administrations were created. The WHO headquarters became Babylon. Perhaps predictably the changes were deeply unpopular with the staff. The main criticism was directed at her new group of advisers – the nine new Executive Directors whom she appointed as heads of clusters – because only two of them were drawn from staff ranks. This wasn't just a question of sour grapes – staff genuinely felt that such senior people needed to have deep understanding of the works and policies of WHO. In addition, the posts of seven Assistant Directors Generals and two Executive Directors were abolished; these highly experienced people were given other posts and excluded from the cabinet. This caused panic among senior staff, whose morale started to plummet. In the end, this bringing of new blood into the Organization by removing top managers whom she did not know probably caused more trouble than it was worth, for the resentment certainly did not help Dr. Brundtland. In less than a year most of the new appointees were found unsatisfactory, and either transferred to the regions or given other responsibilities in Geneva. A few left the Organization in disgust.

Dr. Brundtland thus demolished a structure she did not know and tried to replace it with a new structure which she knew even less resulting in organizational failure both in cost and efficiency.

At the end of August 1998, I appealed to my Regional Director to get my stay in Geneva extended until December, not only for medical reasons but also to enable me to finish the work I'd begun. I was awaiting comments from member countries on the African Ministerial Conference on Health and the Environment; and I was also negotiating with various countries to get an African Centre for Health and Environment off the ground. People such as Dr. Kreisel considered such a centre vital in the pursuit of sustainable development and protecting the environment. To my sadness this initiative eventually became a victim of the political tug of war between Anglophone and Francophile countries. Africa remains to this day the only region in WHO without such a centre. We had a hard time convincing the African Regional Director of its importance, and although the Member States agreed to accept South Africa's offer to host the centre, the Regional Director was eventually unable to mobilize external funds for its operation. Perhaps this was because for him, modern and traditional medicine made more sense than preventive public health.

I asked Dr. Samba to consider my doctor's recommendation that I be posted somewhere where the medical care was 'sophisticated.' This excluded Harare because services there were by this time, in my view, about as sophisticated as a kindergarten. I pointed out that I could no longer be assigned to field trips since 'I cannot climb the hills and mountains of Africa to search for water sources nor cross rivers and streams bare-footed to visit African villages,' I told him, waxing poetical. But, I pointed out, there was a lot I could do without travelling. I could prepare plans, provide technical advice on health, environment and sustainable development issues. I had knowledge and experience in formulating policies and preparing large-scale investment projects. I felt it was important to make the parameters clear, so that I would not be assigned to field work or sent on emergency missions to high-risk countries.

Had Dr. Samba seriously considered my plea, a great deal of time and trouble could have been avoided. I thought it would have been sensible to assign me to South Africa until my retirement six years hence; or to negotiate with the Director General to keep me in Geneva in exchange for someone else being posted to Africa. But Dr. Samba turned a deaf ear. I was told that there was no budget to keep me at Geneva. So then the question arose, what constituted 'sophisticated' medical care? And in which country could it be obtained?

This now became a major bone of contention between myself and the administration. My main question, to which I could get no satisfactory answer, was what would happen in the event of an emergency if I returned to Harare? What if I fell, or a car hit me or I twisted myself into the wrong position somehow? I would need immediate surgery. If the plate broke further and the screws were loosened it would be very painful. Knowing, from official reports, how much medical services in Zimbabwe had deteriorated, I was not sanguine about my chances there.

However, the Director of Joint Medical Service, Dr. Henri Celton, told the administration that in his view the medical facilities in Harare were adequate; they therefore saw no reason to detain me in Geneva.

I began to feel betrayed by the Organization. Their stance that good health includes a positive sense of physical, mental and social well-being, had taught me to expect more from them. Clearly these fine words meant little when it came to their own staff. I felt that I was being exploited, that I was just a number in the overall scheme of things. I was determined to fight this, and began to study the thick volumes of staff rules. I soon discovered that I could seek compensation for the pain, injury and loss I had suffered. I decided that this was one way to force the powers to sit up and take notice of the seriousness of the accident, and perhaps to question why no internal investigation had ever been held to look into it.

So it was that in October 1998 I notified the Director of Joint Medical Services of my claim for compensation. I accepted that I must go back to Harare temporarily, since there seemed no possibility of being reassigned to another country, but I decided to pursue my case from there. In February 1999, that's what I did.

*Al-Mazrou Y, Berkley S., Bloom, B, Chandiwana, SK, Chen L Chimbari M, et al. A vital opportunity for global health. *Lancet* 1997; 350: 750-1

CHAPTER FIFTEEN

NAMIBIA DROPS A BOMBSHELL

The objective of diplomatic immunity is to facilitate the work of international civil servants, especially when there is strife in an unstable country. It was never intended to protect staff from criminal prosecution – nor is it normally used that way. So what was going on in Namibia?

In the absence of any official report from WHO as to how her husband had died, Mrs. Watters wrote to the Namibian Public Prosecutor asking him for the reasons for not pursuing the case. When they received no reply, and in keeping with the advice of the British High Commission, she set private legal wheels in motion and hired a Windhoek lawyer, Mr. E. H. Angula, (later Judge Angula) of the firm Lorentz and Bone, and instructed him to formally apply for the case to be reviewed.

My coordination with Mrs. Watters' actions and my own began a kind of pincer movement, with me trying to extract a response from WHO. I assisted Mr. Angula, the lawyer of Mrs. Watters, when I could and hence, I sent him a full report of what had transpired, concluding: 'I am an engineer by profession and have driven a car for thirty years in Africa, Europe and America without a single accident. I watched the driver... it is difficult to say that this was a genuine accident. As I made clear in all my reports, there was no reason for it to happen. The driver knew what he was doing. It was a clear road – no car in front or behind, no obstacle, no animal or human being crossing, no punctured tyres and no rain or turbulent air flow. The driver was jerking his head in a state of excitement. He turned the wheel violently to the right, going out of his lane and, suddenly changing his mind, turned the wheel to the left, accelerating the car. The car seemed to stabilise for a split second then somersaulted. The driver clung to the wheel while my two friends were thrown out and I was knocked in all directions. The driver knew what he was doing. He protected himself as if he knew what was going to happen. I would have been sympathetic if I'd believed the accident was genuine. Only he, the driver, knows his motive. He should face justice for the death of two innocent hard-working people. It may take time, but the truth will be revealed one day.'

Mr. Angula, however, was skeptical. He asked Mrs. Watters, what exactly she sought? She wrote back *"At the end of the day, my main aim is to have it acknowledged in court that the driver was responsible for my husband's death.* (My italics) Even if you feel that the chances are not good of winning the case, I still wish to pursue the option which you feel is most likely to bring a conviction.'

Her lawyer, however, informed her that in his view, it would be difficult to convince a court that the driver was negligent on the available evidence. 'According to our law,' he wrote, 'in order for the driver to be convicted of culpable homicide, you, as a private prosecutor, have to prove beyond reasonable doubt that the driver acted or drove negligently and his negligence caused the death of the deceased. Negligence has been defined in our law as 'the failure to exercise the degree of care and skill the reasonable man would have exercised in the circumstances'. The standard by which a driver's conduct is to be judged is an objective one. It has been said that a court should not judge the conduct of a driver with hindsight, examining his conduct in the placid atmosphere of the court in the light of after-acquired knowledge. Foresee-ability is the corner stone of negligence. According to this, the reasonable man in the position of the driver would have foreseen the reasonable possibility of his conduct injuring another person. He would have taken reasonable steps to guard against the occurrence, and if he failed to do so, he was, negligent.'

He continued: 'The court assumes the role of the 'reasonable man' and decides what the reasonable man would regard as the just facts of the case. It is the court which decides, based on the direct evidence placed before it, or on the inference which the court can reasonably and justifiably draw from the evidence before it.

'The impression is created by the statement of Mr. Zawide that the driver acted intentionally by abruptly turning the steering wheel to the right, and that there was no reason for him to do so. Frankly, this evidence creates a problem. It implies that the driver intended to kill himself as well as the passengers in the vehicle. Otherwise, one must conclude that the driver knew that even if the vehicle were to roll, only his passengers would be killed or injured and not himself. The driver made the statement that the vehicle started swinging and that he tried to control it but unfortunately 'it just overturn'. He went on to say he suspected the back tyre had burst. In our opinion', concluded Mrs. Watters' lawyer, 'it will be difficult, on the available evidence, to convince the court that the driver was negligent.

Mrs. Watters responded to this by writing: 'Thank you for the documents from the prosecutor's office on the investigation of the accident which took my husband's life,' her letter read, 'on which basis the decision was taken not to take the culpable homicide investigations further. Having studied the documentation I feel however, that a conclusive and plausible explanation for the accident has yet to be established. I appreciate the legal definition of 'negligence,' however there are questions that must be addressed and answers found, regardless of legal terminology. These could in turn lead to a different legal definition as to why the accident occurred, e.g. momentary insanity, to take an extreme example. Such an explanation may not be so far-fetched; certainly there is a need to find an alternative explanation.

Firstly, Mr. Mootu's stated reason for the accident was the 'swinging' motion of the vehicle, which he explains by way of a suspected puncture. However, the police confirmed that the tyres were in order. Furthermore, the WHO office in Windhoek confirmed that the car had only recently received a full inspection. It would therefore be reasonable to conclude that the accident cannot be attributed to the car's condition or a puncture. These facts call into question the credibility of the driver, and his ability and competence as a professional driver. The road was straight and in good condition i.e. made of tar, and dry. (...)

Furthermore there was no other vehicle on the road which could have caused distraction or interfered with the driving.

'Secondly, the car left Windhoek at 13:30 hours, after my husband had had lunch with Mr. Zawide. There is a discrepancy as to when the accident occurred, according to the documents. The stated time varies, according to the source, from approximately 15.15 to 15.45. My husband's time of death is stated as 15.00 hours according to the official certificate issued by the Government mortuary after the post mortem examination. Why do the reports vary so widely? This question needs an answer, since the time of the accident has a material bearing on how fast the driver was driving. The site of the accident is approximately 300 kilometres from Windhoek, so a driver would have had to have been driving at approximately 200 km/hr in order to get there by 15.15, not to mention 15.00 hours as per the autopsy report. Less recklessly perhaps the driver would have been driving at 130 km/hr to have got there by 15.45. We understand that he was asked a number of times to slow down.'

'Moreover, the signed statements are not consistent in their reports of the prevailing weather conditions, i.e. *was* it raining? And was the road consequently wet or dry? All these points I believe indicate the need to investigate more systematically what exactly took place on 11 February just outside Otjiwarongo. I would like your opinion of the reason for the accident and if you, as a lawyer, believe the investigation was conclusive and was carried out thoroughly. If you do, could you please give me your reasons? I personally feel that the best course of action would be for the case to be re-opened, since the message conveyed by the documents you have sent is inconclusive.'

Although this letter represented the human, rather than the legal position, it summarised precisely the issues which I consider the WHO ought to have satisfied themselves of in their own internal inquiry. To answer one of Angula's main objections, one might also have pointed out that from the 'reasonable man's' perspective, since the driver alone was able to wear a seat belt, this reduction in his personal risk might possibly have accounted for his seeming willingness to risk his own life.

As a result of this letter, Mr. Angula took the extremely unusual step of applying, in December to Namibia's Prosecutor General, Advocate J.

L. Heyman SC, for a statutory certificate *'Nolle prosequi'*, which would enable Mrs. Watters to institute a private prosecution.

'The magistrate found,' he explained to the Prosecutor, 'that [Watters' and Damon's] deaths were not brought about by any act or omission *prima facie* involving or amounting to an offence on the part of any person.... Following the said magistrate's ruling, you declined to prosecute any person. Having considered all the available information our client is of the firm belief that the driver of the vehicle, one Niklaas Mootu, drove the vehicle recklessly and/or negligently and was accordingly the cause of the accident. She feels that the driver should have been charged with culpable homicide. We have been instructed to request that you issue a certificate *nolle prosequi* so that our client may institute private prosecution against said driver.'

The Office of the Prosecutor General made a bombshell announcement.

It would appear from the extraordinary legal wrangle that now began, that this decisive and unexpected move by Mrs. Watters set the cat among the pigeons behind the scenes. It was tempting, for the purposes of this book, to plant a mole in Namibia's government offices to find out what was really thought, said and done by the authorities. Such a 'Deep Throat' may well have found some very interesting evidence to explain the extraordinary sequence of events that now followed.

In March the Office of the Prosecutor General made a bombshell announcement. Mr. Angula immediately sent a fax to Mrs. Watters which read: 'We received this morning the accompanying letter from the office of the Prosecutor General. It would appear that instead of giving us the Certificate *Nolle Prosequi*, he has decided to prosecute himself. We have asked him to advise when the prosecution would commence. We shall advise you of the date of the trial...to enable you to attend the hearing.'

On the surface, this appeared to be very good news indeed. The accompanying letter read: 'From the Chief Clerk to the Prosecutor General to the Public Prosecutor at Otjiwarongo.

THE STATE VERSUS NIKLAAS MOOTU

I refer to your Otjiwarongo Inquest no 12/97.

The Prosecutor General instructs that Niklaas MOOTU be arraigned in the Magistrates Court on a charge of CULPABLE HOMICIDE. Alternatively: a contravention of section 138 (1) of ordinance 30 of 1967, reckless or negligent driving (DECEASED: Gregor Watters AND AP DAMON.) The inquest Otjiwarongo Inquest no 12/97 is returned herewith.

Please report the outcome of the proceedings.'

In May Angula informed Mrs. Watters that the trial date had been set for June 3, 1999, and she considered whether to fly to Namibia. I was approached to appear as a witness for the State. However, Angula advised Mrs. Watters that on this, his first appearance at court, Mootu would merely be informed of his rights, and told he was entitled to be legally represented. 'He will immediately be asked to plead to the charge. If he pleads guilty then the matter is dealt with in a summary manner. The Magistrate will question him to make sure that he admits to all the elements of the crime. Then he will be convicted accordingly and sentenced. Should he decide to plead not guilty, the matter will be postponed to a future date for trial, when all the state witnesses will be summoned to give evidence. The defense will also have the right to call witnesses,' Angula wrote.

However, on May 25 came the first clue that the Prosecutor General's firmness of intention might be wavering, and that justice, even now, might be evaded. Angula sent an urgent fax with the news that the trial had been postponed. The police, it seemed, had been unable to track Mootu down in order to serve him with a summons. A second summons had been prepared, a second trial date set. This time, surely, the police would succeed. However, once again their skills seemed unequal to the task, despite knowing precisely where Mootu lived and where he spent the eight hours of his working day. On June 2, a Ms. Visser of the Prosecutor's office blithely announced that they had failed to serve the summons again, and the trial would now be on July 18. But in July Angula reported that the police had still been unable to find the driver, and accordingly the matter had been removed from the roll. Ms. Visser, on behalf of the Prosecutor, was issuing yet another summons. Mootu would now appear on August 31.

By now Mrs. Watters was beginning to suspect that this cat and mouse game was all a ruse to prevent Mootu's ever coming to trial. With admirable restraint Mrs. Watters pointed out to Angula that: 'Since Mr. Mootu is employed by the WHO in Windhoek, where he reports to work daily and is present eight hours a day, it is difficult to understand how it has not been possible for him to be served the court summons. We would like clarification of the following: How many un-served summons can be issued before a case is considered closed? Can this process continue indefinitely? Is there a limit as to how many times a person may evade a summons? Should he continue to avoid them, will he be penalised?'

After the fourth summons withered un-served in the hands of the police, even the impassive Mr. Angula began to get annoyed and wrote to MErs. Watters: 'We registered our strong displeasure with the Prosecutor, whereupon she undertook to remove the docket from the current police officer and hand it over to another whom she thinks is more capable. We also furnished her with the work address of Mr. Mootu. Furthermore, we requested her to ask the police to liaise with us in order for us to assist him wherever we can. A new summons will be issued for the appearance of Mr. Mootu on 5th October.' He had threatened, he added, that if satisfaction wasn't obtained this time, the matter would be taken up at diplomatic level.

Was it possible that mere ineptitude on the part of the police had been the problem all along? I was doubtful and outright suspicious, when I heard the news in Harare. Some complicity, at least, by the WHO staff, seemed certain.

By this time, I too had engaged a lawyer – an American by the name of Edward Flaherty, who practiced in Geneva. I had instructed him to fight the WHO's decision to send me back to Harare. Now, I asked him to raise this matter too. In a letter to the Director General, Flaherty wrote: 'It is our understanding that the Namibian judicial authorities have re-opened the case and are prosecuting the WHO driver for culpable homicide. Incredibly, it appears that although this man continues to work for the WHO, the Namibian authorities have been unable to serve a summons on him. This is apparently due to his efforts to avoid responsibility. I would suggest that such behaviour is directly at odds with the drivers' responsibilities as an international civil servant. Should he continue to pervert the course of justice...we demand that WHO suspend the driver from his post forthwith and withdraw all financial support pending full and final resolution of the matter. Failure to do so would seem to make the WHO an accomplice.'

Both my lawyer and I suspected that WHO was involved in the failure to contact Mootu which seemed to be borne out by the next development, for on October 4, the Organization finally intervened. The Office of the World Health Organization in Geneva sent a *note verbale* to the Ministry of Foreign Affairs in Namibia, requesting that diplomatic immunity be observed for Mr. Mootu until such a time as a formal request for its waiver was received from the Namibian Government by the Director General, and until such time as she granted it. This was the first time that any suggestion had been made that this humble employee of the global body should be considered worthy of the august privilege of being immune from prosecution under the law of his land, for a criminal offence that had nothing whatever to do with diplomacy.

Strangely, WHO asked that the request for Mootu's immunity to be lifted, be accompanied by the findings of the Namibian authorities on which the accusation of culpable homicide was based – strangely, because it was in order to make such findings that Namibia wished Mootu to have his day in court. The conclusion was that the Director General would take it on herself to decide the accused's guilt or otherwise before deciding whether he could be prosecuted. My darkest suspicion was that the Organization was fishing, wanting to find out how much the authorities had against him. Such suspicion might have been judged paranoid – if so, it was WHO's deliberate refusal to open up the case that was making me feel that way.

Because this unexpected intervention was a bombshell as far as I was concerned. It was the first time that the word 'immunity' had raised its ugly head, although it was to become a hot potato. No-one up till now had even considered the possibility that this man, having caused the loss of a very senior member of the Organization, not to mention that of an important government official of a member state, would be considered eligible for such elevated protection from the law of his land. The object of diplomatic immunity is to facilitate the work of the international staff, especially when there is civil strife in an unstable country. It was never intended to protect local staff from criminal prosecution – nor is it used that way normally. What could be the thinking behind it? What was going on?

On October 12 a fifth summons was issued. And on October 14 the Permanent Secretary at the Namibian Ministry of Justice wrote to the Prosecutor General saying that *if* he thought there was a need for requesting a waiver of immunity, to forward such a request to the Ministry of Foreign Affairs as soon as possible.

At last, on October 24 came a fax from Angula announcing that 'it was finally possible to serve the summons on Mr. Mootu and that the trial date has been fixed for November 23 at Otjiwarongo'. This sounded so definite, we relaxed again. However, Angula promptly received a letter from the Office of the Prosecutor General. Headed COURT SUMMONS OF MR. MOOTU, it read: 'I wish to inform you that our Ministry has received a complaint from the Office of the World Health Organization regarding the summons in criminal case no 113/099 for Mr. Niklaas Mootu, an official of the Organization.... Your attention is drawn to the fact that Mr. Mootu is covered by immunity from national court jurisdiction as granted to officials of the Organization in the performance of their functions by the Vienna Conventions. Hence your office is kindly requested to submit such documentation to the Ministry of Foreign Affairs.'

It began to seem, to me at least, that behind the scenes there must be powerful, shadowy puppeteers, determined to prevent the truth from emerging at all costs. Until now, I had ascribed the Administration's strange reluctance to probe the cause of this 'accident' to sloth or indifference. Now, faced with their actions in preventing the case from coming to court, I began to ask whether it was their deliberate intention to protect the driver. Someone, it was clear, seemed determined to prevent the man from standing trial. What were they afraid of? What incriminating evidence did they wish to conceal? Had he simply been driving too fast on a maybe wet road, or was the accident deliberate? And if so, was it because someone instructed Mootu to cause the crash? If so, who – and why?

These questions began to fester like a sore in my mind.

Back to work in Harare – Zimbabwe after two years in USA and Geneva

CHAPTER SIXTEEN

SO LITTLE WISDOM, SO MANY RULES

It was painful – but deeply necessary – for one who had served the Organization for most of his professional life, to appeal against its ill treatment. 'Its Organizational culture is in the tradition of the machine metaphor,' according to a group of Swedish health experts. 'A rigid set of rules limits its professional creativity and subjects the staff to excessive authority. Staff are highly dependent on the decisions of their superiors, making their functions increasingly constrained and unrewarding.'

As we shall see in a later chapter, those individuals who achieved great results in WHO – such as the eradication of small pox – risked their positions by ignoring the hierarchical decision-making process and doing what they felt to be right on the ground.

I say this in order to set in context the bitter, sometimes truculent-sounding, correspondence that flowed for the next 20 months between the Administration and me. Since rules, rather than sensitive, intelligent individuals, still dictated the way decisions were made and the Organization was run, I was forced to quote the regulations *ad nauseam* in order to bring the Administration to book.

Things might have been different had I been given the chance to express my deep anguish and growing anger in a constructive way. Had anyone in personnel taken the trouble to sit down with me and ask what my real problem was, I might have told them that I expected from WHO the same tact, sensitivity and courage that the work had demanded of me over the many years during which I represented the

Organization. Just as I had had to walk a tightrope in my dealings with individual countries, aware that if I mishandled people, an entire programme of reform might go awry, so now I expected to be treated with consideration. My integrity had been a key component in my work; now it was a key component in my outrage. My deep disappointment at the administration for its failure to follow good protocol could not simply be ignored, either by my employers or, more importantly, by myself. It wasn't in my nature to simply roll over and meekly accept that I mustn't ask difficult questions. I felt I was being treated with extreme disrespect.

Had some senior representative of the Organization stepped off their pedestal to become human, and said to me, 'We care about you and the rest of the staff. We apologise for our part in what happened to you. We acknowledge that such a deeply painful, fatal crash has to be dealt with in a humane and just way, so that all concerned can put it behind them,' I would gladly have got on with my life, compromising, cooperating, and doing my best to further environmental health in Africa as I always had. Instead, my time and energy became devoted to a bitter struggle against what I perceived as heartless, irresponsible management which corroded everyone's willingness to give of their best.

The official refusal to account for the crash by holding an enquiry was like a cancer growing in my mind, creating unhappiness and increasing acrimony. As a result, there gradually arose three more areas of dissension between myself and my bosses at WHO. The first concerned the amount of compensation due to me, which rested on the (disputed) degree to which I was permanently injured. Second, arising from this dispute, the need for a medical board to settle it. And third, a posting to a place that would afford me the kind of medical care I needed.

In this maze of bureaucracy, even Ombudsmen must know their place.

It wasn't until October 1998, some eighteen months after the crash, that I accidentally discovered I was entitled to claim for compensation for loss of function, on top of my medical expenses. I was poring over the rule book, trying to discover how to force WHO to investigate, when this rule jumped out of the page at me. Money was never my main objective it is a poor substitute for being treated like a human being. But, seeing a chance to again draw attention to the seriousness of the events, I jumped at it.

Dr. Henri Celton of Joint Medical Services (JMS) evaluated me for the loss of function. He advised me also to consult Dr. Michelson, my original surgeon. If Dr. Michelson considered that no further improvement could be expected, it would fall to him to say what percentage of functioning I had lost, according to the *Guide to the Evaluation of Permanent Impairment*, published by the American Medical Association. Dr. Celton would make his own evaluation, also based on this *Guide*. So, rejoining my family in Baltimore over Christmas, I arranged a consultation with Dr. Michelson. The surgeon confirmed that my work life must henceforth be restricted to sitting at a desk; that I could no longer play sport or keep fit by jogging; and that should the broken pelvic plate deteriorate further, I would need urgent, complex surgery.

To me, this summarised a major change in lifestyle, affecting my daily life and limiting my professional future. Worse still was the effect on my psyche, not least because, adding insult to injury, I was being sent to Zimbabwe – a country reeling under political chaos. In such circumstances one individual's health was apt to matter as little as that of a fly in one's soup.

Having held the WHO in such high esteem for so long, I still couldn't quite believe that they had let the crash at the hands of their driver, and Gregor's death, not to mention that of Andrew Damon, to pass without so much as an official eyebrow being raised. Before leaving Geneva, I had checked it out with WHO's legal office, just to make certain I was not maligning them. What enquiries had they made, I asked, following the eye-witness account I had submitted? 'Nothing on file,' I was told casually. 'No reports from Windhoek or Harare, either.' The only document they had relating to it concerned the Prosecutor General's decision not to arraign Mootu. They advised me to check out the Regional Office to see what they had on file. (Theirs too were conspicuously empty, I subsequently discovered.) My anger mounted, fuelled by my impending reassignment to the Harare hotspot. I decided to lay the whole matter before the Organization's ombudsman.

However, I found that in this maze of bureaucracy, even Ombudsmen have to know their place. The poor fellow tried his best to get the Administration to address my problems, but they wouldn't budge. He told me about the difficult time headquarters' staff were undergoing owing to the 'Brundtland syndrome', which he defined as severe insecurity, uncertainty about the future and frustration. He said that he himself was retiring, since he couldn't take the current level of professional harassment. He suggested I take my case to the Board of Appeal. As he gave me this advice, I felt more than ever abandoned and betrayed; it seemed that neither I nor Greg Watters meant a thing to the Organization we had dedicated our working lives to.

They had reduced the issue to mere money.

Arriving in Harare, I found, as I'd suspected, that medical facilities had gone severely downhill since I'd left eight years before. My old doctor was still there, and he confirmed that the hospitals were badly-equipped, and that many specialists had left the country. Even doctors had had to resort to strikes to reinforce their concerns about impossibly low salaries and non-supply of equipment and drugs. There were admittedly a few good consultants left in private clinics, but my own doctor said he would not recommend surgery because of poor nursing care.

I reported all this to the Committee on Compensation Claims. 'Although the percentage of my partial disability may not be judged very high, I am suffering considerable loss of enjoyment of life,' I wrote. 'Whereas I used to play numerous sports including jogging, squash, and table tennis, I am now confined to a sedentary life. I am also unable to pursue the work for which I was trained . . . notably all field work in the construction of buildings, water supply and sanitation utilities. During my sojourn at HQ I had to consult numerous doctors because of recurring pain.

'I find this situation particularly hard to accept because of the grave negligence which was the cause of the accident,' I continued, giving the Committee a blow-by-blow account of what had happened on the road to Otjiwarongo. I was aware that this had nothing to do with the compensation claim, yet in a sense it had everything, for it affected my entire approach to my job. And how else could I challenge the Administration?

In March 1999 I received the Committee's conclusion. It had 'reviewed a medical report estimating the loss of function in relation to the whole individual at *six percent*,' I was informed. Six percent! An insult! 'The most favourable compensation calculation was according to the accident insurance policy under which you are covered as a staff member (Manual 11.7 Annex C.) The calculation is made as follows: six per cent of three times your annual salary at the time of the accident.'

I was incensed. It seemed to me that the Committee didn't give a damn about my quality of life. Worse, they had completely ignored my mental anguish. The central issue of the crash was not even referred to. Internally I raged at them, that they had reduced the issue to mere money, as if that was all I cared about – irrationally, since that's just what the Committee was mandated to do.

I replied, somewhat haughtily: 'I regret to inform you that I decline to accept the decision of the Advisory Committee...until the following issues are resolved: The conflict of professional medical opinion between my doctors and the Director of JMS; and satisfactory and conclusive explanation of the reason for the accident. Does WHO know what exactly took place on 11 February 1997 just outside Otjiwarongo about 300 km from Windhoek? The driver had been asked a number of times by Mr. Damon to slow down. Was the cause of the accident investigated systematically? What did the driver say about the accident? Why was I not invited or informed when an inquest was held? I am therefore appealing to the Director General of WHO in accordance with paras 28-9 (a-e) of the rules governing compensation to staff members in the event of death, injury or illness attributed to the performance of official duties on behalf of the WHO. Kindly consider my request for establishing a consensus on the medical opinions and the subsequent compensation for loss of enjoyment of life, and a satisfactory and conclusive reason for the accident.'

I had taken an irrevocable step, the first in challenging my employers' right to treat their staff with so little wisdom and so many rules.

Soon I received a response in the form of a memo from the Secretary of the Compensation Board, warning me that I would have to bear the costs of setting up a medical board, should it uphold the original decision. I consented, with the proviso that I was consulted about the composition of the board. I pointed out that six per cent seemed very low considering the accident's impact on my lifestyle and professional future, and that I was still in pain. I reiterated my opinion that my injury and suffering were due solely to driver's negligence – or his deliberate intention. This uncertainty had negatively affected my psycho-social well-being, therefore I should be compensated for that as well.

In reply, the secretary requested a detailed medical report from my treating physician. 'Presumably, she wrote, 'as the Board will be held in Geneva, Dr. Compère will represent you.' 'No way!' was my private reaction. I now distrusted the WHO so deeply, I was not about to have their personal physician sit in judgement on me. 'I wish to emphasise,' I responded angrily, 'that no doctor but Dr. Michelson will represent me on the Medical Board.... He performed the meticulous surgery that saved me from spending the rest of my life in a wheel chair.' In any case, I concluded, I had difficulties in communicating with Dr. Compère due to the language problem.'

I realised however, that my ruse might not work, since a medical board would never be mandated to look into the legal aspects of the case. So, having exhausted the rule book for any other recourse, I finally decided to appeal to the Director General herself – to go to the very top. It felt like playing my last trump, and I had never thought it would get to this. But, in September 1999 – while the farce over serving a summons on Mootu was playing itself out in Namibia – I sat down and addressed an eight-page letter to Dr. Gro Harlem Brundtland. Now, surely, those who had been so lax would be held to account.

I humbly requested Dr. Brundtland to authorise an enquiry to establish the reasons for the tragic car accident. I outlined in detail all the circumstances, including the strange behaviour of the administrator and the WHO representative before the trip began. After describing the crash, I continued: 'What, I have asked myself again and again, made the driver turn his head left and right, then abruptly turn the steering wheel, causing the accident? As an engineer, I would have to say that this is the easiest way of turning a vehicle upside down. The driver has a good knowledge of the behaviour of an object in motion such as the vehicle he was in control of. He told us that he had won awards for safe driving, so what made him cause such an accident on a clear road? His motive will remain unknown until he is adequately investigated and questioned. How can the security and safety of international civil servants be protected when a negligent driver, perhaps with malicious motives, commits such a terrible act, which is then left un-investigated where people of every nationality, race and ethnic background meet and work, such neglect would create a rueful precedent.'

This conclusion was an oblique reference to the many racial tensions that feature among workers in UN Organizations. Hatred, fear and prejudice flourish her as much if not more than in any other workplace. Complaints of discrimination and 'mobbing' (negative social behaviour such as verbal aggression, rumuor-mongering, physical aggression, attacking the victim's private life, social isolation, and forcing somebody to carry out tasks affecting his/her self-consciousness) were so deep-seated and common that they were the subject of several official reports. Bitter individuals often ended up taking their grievances to the ultimate authority: the Tribunal of the International Labour Organization. Yet another reason to marvel that WHO's management saw fit not to introduce any training in the way of team-building that would address these issues head-on.

'Dying and suffering in the service of humanity,' I continued in my letter, 'is an honour to WHO staff. Many of my colleagues have met their end proudly in the service of the Organization. But death or injury caused by negligence, possibly even malice, threatens all international civil servants. I could have accepted this tragedy if it were genuinely an accident. We who work in hardship areas are used to taking risks. But it is incredible that a licensed driver employed by WHO could make such a tragic blunder and not even be questioned by the Administration. Worse, this man has been allowed to continue driving, with the prospect of another crash a distinct possibility.'

I reminded Dr. Brundtland of what she had said in her inspiring inaugural speech: 'Making a difference will demand all our dedication and commitment. It will demand that WHO works as one Organization, as a team with a strong spirit – turning our diversity into our strength. To succeed we will need the contribution of each and every one of us at every of the organization.' That was a great rallying cry, I said, but to transform it into action required care and compassion.

I concluded with my reservations about the medical board, finishing, in what I hoped was a suitably restrained tone, 'WHO is an international advocate for the health rights of all mankind on planet earth. This does not exclude its staff members.'

It was perhaps too much to hope that Dr. Brundtland would respond promptly and sympathetically, apologising and acknowledging that a mistake had been made, although I couldn't help thinking this would be appropriate. Of course, she did have one or two other million little problems on her mind – but then she also had assistants to whom to delegate staff matters, which were a not unimportant part of her brief. But as weeks went by, and I received not so much as an acknowledgement, I became even more disillusioned. Eventually I enlisted the help of my lawyer, Ed Flaherty, in requesting the courtesy of a reply. Even he was forced to write twice before getting any response.

It took four months. Finally, a letter arrived from one Ms. Renée Lopez, the coordinator, Department of Human Resources, apologising for the delay. 'Please rest assured that a complete response to your letters will be sent shortly.' This was followed by yet another month of silence. Flaherty wrote again, saying 'I must once again ask for your intervention. I understand that large bureaucracies move rather slowly, but given the degradation of Mr. Zawide's health...such ongoing delay is becoming indefensible.' He backed this with a medical report by Dr. Michelson, recommending 'that Mr. Zawide's assignments be restricted to those areas of the world where he would have access to good medical care since he has an ongoing issue with not only the broken hardware but also the degenerative change in the sacroiliac joint.' Flaherty requested Dr. Brundtland to transfer me immediately from Harare. Also, that a medical board be constituted forthwith, since a year had now passed since I had objected to the amount of compensation.

Three weeks later, Ms. Lopez finally got her act together to reply on behalf of Dr. Brundtland. 'Dr. Celton of JMS,' she said, 'was familiar with Mr. Zawide's case and has not advised the Administration that Mr. Zawide is not fit for duty in Harare. Unless and until we receive such advice, we do not intend to seek his reassignment.' As for a medical board, she blamed Dr. Michelson for the delay in constituting it. He had now been asked for his evaluation of loss of function. 'If no agreement between director JMS and Dr. Michelson is reached, arrangements will be made to fix a suitable date for the medical board or a teleconference.'

To my amazed disappointment, she made no reference whatsoever to the main thrust of my letter, the need to look into the crash. For a man seeking evidence that the Organization which supposedly cared deeply about the poor of the world, took the welfare of its own staff just as seriously, this was doubtful evidence indeed.

*_The Future of Global Health Cooperation: Designing a new World Health Organization_. Forss, Kim, Stenson, Bo and Sterky, Goran. Division of International Health Care Research, Karolinska Institute, Sweden. Current Issues in Public Health 1996, 2, p138-142

Presentation at an international conference in
Pretoria, South Africa

CHAPTER SEVENTEEN

A HEARING, AT LAST

'When I use a word,' *Humpty Dumpty continued thoughtfully, 'I use it to mean just what I choose it to mean.' It is tempting to believe the WHO bureaucrats had studied this text in depth. Except that if they could use ten words to obfuscate the issue, so much the better.*

To return to Namibia, the conferment of diplomatic immunity on Niklaas Mootu raised him above the status of ordinary mortals, who are held accountable for breaking the law and expected to pay for their transgressions. Why did he qualify? Such protection was not normally conferred on local staff, especially when facing criminal charges.

It's no good looking to official communications for an answer, for they seem to enter Alice-in-Wonderland territory. The Administration's language, while appearing to say one thing, always resulted, strangely, in something quite other. We have already seen how the words, 'The Prosecutor General instructs that Niklaas Mootu be arraigned in the magistrates' court on a charge of culpable homicide' meant, in reality 'If the police are unable or unwilling, for reasons known only to themselves, to arraign a person, he remains unarraigned, in court or anywhere else'. To quote *Through the Looking Glass*: 'When I use a word,' Humpty Dumpty continued thoughtfully, 'I use it to mean just what I *choose* it to mean.' It is tempting to believe the WHO bureaucrats had studied this text in depth. Except that if they could use ten words to obfuscate the issue, so much the better. The humble observer might be forgiven for wondering if the entire attempt to bring a public prosecution wasn't simply a charade, a convenient way of preventing Mrs. Watters from prosecuting Mootu.

Of course, it may have been sheer coincidence that by the time the police succeeded, on their sixth attempt, in serving a summons on the man, the WHO had already intervened to protect him. But although their efforts were effective in preventing Mootu from being questioned in court, they didn't actually refuse to waive his immunity. They simply used a delaying tactic – i.e., that the Director General *might* lift his immunity; she just hadn't made up her mind yet. For so decisive a woman, you'd think three years would have been enough.

Some said that in Dr. Samba's view, those who appealed against his administration needed psychiatric treatment.

The number of words that now spewed forth from the vast multi-storeyed complex in Geneva, attempting to explain who had said what to whom, and why it delayed them, are not only tedious and boring but seem to confuse rather than clarify. Longfellow's dictum that 'It takes less time to do a thing right than to explain why you did it wrong,' comes to mind. For example, the matter of convening a medical board to settle how much my life had been permanently altered by my injuries. The busy Dr. Michelson, in demand all over the world, had agreed to represent me – that much was undisputed. But as the months went by, the Administration blamed him for lack of progress, claiming that faxes and letters had gone unacknowledged or ignored. It's possible they were right, Dr. Michelson having by now left Johns Hopkins. But when the same excuse is applied to too many people, it arouses suspicion.

When my lawyer asked Dr. Michelson for his response to the accusation, he replied somewhat testily, 'I have no idea what is the reason for the delay in the constitution of Mr. Zawide's medical board which he has been trying to get done since May of 1999. I have said and written that I would be available ... ever since it was requested.'

In August 2000, by now thoroughly exasperated, I complained again to Ms. Lopez, pointing out that inadequate care in Harare had forced me to travel four times to America for treatment in the past two years at my own expense. Plus: "The WHO has completely closed its ears to my request for a transparent investigation into the cause of the accident. My report has not been given the least consideration.'

Unable to contain my feelings I broke out of conventional language, quoting Shakespeare: 'He hath laughed at my losses, mocked at my gains, scorned my nation, thwarted my bargains, cooled my friends, heated my enemies.' Could this obduracy be, I suggested, as in Shylock's case, due to racism? 'I was raised in an environment where human dignity is highly respected,' I continued. 'The two colleagues... were human beings. They left loving families with broken hearts, and yet WHO denies them justice...I have a moral and ethical responsibility towards them. I joined WHO to serve humanity and not to make a fortune; I was a successful consultant running a private engineering firm. I am proud of my achievements. I wait for justice to be served.'

Underlying my words was a sense of being treated as though I was worthless or not good enough, such as inevitably arises when deeply personal issues and requests are treated as irrelevant by those we work with. When mutual respect is lacking, we tend to look in a different light on sacrifices made willingly at the time. It now seemed to me that every success I had achieved while working for WHO was forgotten. In treating me as if I didn't matter, or as if they didn't trust me, WHO's bureaucracy was dismissing me as a human being. As a cog in a machine, this was not supposed to matter. But, being of flesh and blood, matter it most certainly did. *'The deepest principle of human nature is the craving to be appreciated.'*

And so events moved painfully and ponderously towards the only recourse available to me: a hearing by the Headquarters Board of Appeal (HBA), the body that arbitrates between the WHO and its staff when there is a deadlock. Accordingly on October 10, I gave my Regional Director, Dr. Samba, notice of my intention to appeal. I was not alone in protesting at his management style – in fact in 2000 the whole Congolese General service staff, who were temporarily reassigned from Brazzaville to Harare, appealed against his administration. Eventually they took their case to the International Labour Organization Administration (ILOAT). Some said that in Dr. Samba's view, those who appealed against his administration needed psychiatric treatment.

The HBA is made up of five members, the chairman, two people appointed by the Director General and two by the staff panel. The Appellant can object to any of them if he so chooses – I didn't. Their job is to summarise the essential facts, give the Board's findings and conclusions, and end with its recommendations. It is left to the Director General to decide what action to take. Accordingly, I made a 13-page statement, summarising everything that had happened. These are some of the points I emphasised:

'When the local authorities first looked into the matter, the Appellant was not even called as a witness…. The driver was re-integrated into his post…. The cause of the accident is highly suspect, or at the least inexplicable…There has been no investigation by WHO.' My lawyer added: 'Aside from the driver, the Appellant is the only witness to the accident and events immediately preceding it…Appellant's recollection is presently the only recitation of the facts available, and must be taken as true, unless shown otherwise.'

There followed a list of letters and memos pertaining to the medical board, or the lack of one, every scrap of paper being included as annexures. Section III dealt with Receivability, that is, whether the case fell within the parameters of the Board as defined by the WHO Manual. This usually relates to whether the correct time limits had been observed. I, perhaps anticipating trouble, held that 'a more than reasonable time had passed' for WHO to set up the medical board, so the fact that they had not done so, plus their failure to investigate the accident or to relocate me to a different duty station added up to a refusal to do so.

A whole page was devoted to the failure to investigate, pointing out that I would suffer the effects of the crash for the rest of my life. Since no other vehicle was involved, the cause had to have been either driver-related or mechanical. 'It appears that the driver's actions were outrageous, negligent, perhaps even to the point of being deranged or intentional,' I continued. Only an investigation could ascertain which.

I went over the Administration's view that this was a matter solely for the Namibian police. 'Such a position is untenable and inexplicable. An internal investigation is a matter of respect for Appellant, who is a long-time WHO employee and has suffered…. It is undisputed that international law calls for respect by the employer Organization for the dignity of the employee. Refusing to conduct an investigation when so much wrong and damage has occurred is a denial of such right.'

I held that the Administration's view that it was up to local authorities to prosecute was all the more untenable because they and they alone had raised the question of immunity. If the driver was found guilty of reckless driving, WHO was failing in its duty by allowing him to continue driving other dignitaries. Had this been a case of financial misconduct, an internal investigation would have been automatic, and there were even stronger reasons for making it mandatory in this case. According to section 11.7; 310.2. 'In connection with processing a claim for compensation for injuries, a report from the staff member's supervisor or from Personnel on the circumstances should be provided. Although this section concerns verification of the claims of the injured staff member, it also calls for a report on the circumstances of the accident.' In short, there was no question that the WHO should look into the matter and apply proper disciplinary procedures if called for.

Regarding the Administration's failure to constitute a medical board, I had found the offer of only six per cent compensation quite shocking. I said plaintively, reaffirming the Alice-in-Wonderland effect, 'Although it appears in reading the letters going back and forth that the parties are in agreement as to the fact that such a board should be constituted, Appellant has been requesting the same since May 1999...' (i.e, for a year and a half!)

When mutual respect is lacking, we tend to look differently on sacrifices made willingly.

Finally, I addressed the failure to transfer me to a duty station where sophisticated medical care was available. 'There are two possible implications to the Administration's position that I am not at risk,' I wrote. 'Either it believes that Harare does have sophisticated medical care, or it does not believe that I need immediate access to the same on an ongoing basis, as recommended by my doctor.' To refute the former, I pointed out that doctors and medical services in Harare had all gone on strike for a month recently, and that political and civil unrest were contributing to plummeting healthcare standards.

On December 6, WHO retorted by objecting to the Appeal's 'receivability,' or legality. Renée Lopez, the coordinator, Human Resources, based this on the fact that the investigation 'was definitively refused in the letter from Director, Human Resources (Mr. Slater) dated September 6. This letter had stated, 'As to your request that WHO investigate the accident in question...we must confirm that this is a matter for the Namibian police and judicial authorities.' Lopez tried to suggest that the Board's only function was to deal with matters relating to staff's appointment status. Her next statement astonished me with its effrontery. A criminal investigation or formal enquiry into the cause...is clearly not within the purview or competence of WHO.'

I wondered what other organization in the world would continue to employ a possibly dangerous driver without even troubling to establish the facts? Or informing the families of deceased staff members of the results? It was, as Alice said, 'curiouser and curiouser.'

Lopez added that, as to the medical board, there had never been a decision *not* to convene one. 'Therefore, the Administration must object to the receivability of this issue other than the alleged delay.'

Luckily the Board disagreed; it met on December 22 and decided to proceed with the appeal in all its aspects. 'Discussions concerning receivability are now closed,' they announced in a letter. Matters should then have proceeded smoothly to the hearing on January 30. But even then, the Administration tried to wriggle out of it. It was as if they were determined to do their own thing, and were contemptuous of the Board. For at the very last minute, on January 29, another letter came from Renée Lopez to the Chairman: 'The Administration reiterates its view that these issues are irreceivable. In particular...decisions concerning a staff member's immunity are the Organization's prerogative, affecting as they do its relations with Member States. The exercise of this prerogative falls outside the competence of the HBA. The Appellant's claim in this regard is thus irreceivable. However, the Board should also note that no decision on waiver of immunity has yet been taken. A communication from the Namibian Ministry of Foreign Affairs has been received, which is understood as a request for waiver of immunity. The Director General intends to take a decision promptly upon receiving such additional information as has been requested.'

The rest of this communication suggested to me that there had been frantic activity behind the scenes, designed to avoid the appeal procedure, for it revealed that, unbeknownst to me, a telephonic medical board had been hurriedly convened on January 11. 'Their report will be conveyed to the Advisory Committee on Compensation Claims...then transmitted to the Director General to make the final determination,' Ms. Lopez wrote. 'The Regional office for Africa has informed us that arrangements are underway to reassign Mr. Zawide to a duty station in South Africa, where his duties will be sedentary. In the light of these developments,' Lopez continued smoothly, 'a suspension is requested to allow for the completion of the relevant administrative procedures as their final outcomes will have a direct impact on the appeal and may lead to a mutually acceptable solution.' She concluded: 'The Organization understands any distress the Appellant may feel about his situation and this information should dispel any doubt about the Organization's desire to resolve those substantive issues that are within its authority and capacity to resolve.'

Far from dispelling my doubts, however, this missive deepened my suspicions. The telephone conference I had been demanding for 20 months had proved easy to organise when push came to shove – Dr. Celton had casually delegated his counterpart in Washington DC to liaise with Dr. Michelson. And as to finding a mutually acceptable solution, I would have been considerate had the Administration contacted me, but they hadn't. So, I assumed that this was yet another ploy.

The argument that my whole case was 'not receivable' meant that yet another hearing had to be held – a special hearing to decide whether to hold a hearing! This happened on 30 January 2001, and I flew all the way to Geneva from Harare to attend it, protesting vigorously that it was 'frivolous'. I was so incensed that I demanded reimbursement of my travel costs, and a *per diem* allowance while in Geneva, which was later granted by the Director General. Its source was no doubt aid money that could have been put to much better use in poverty-stricken Africa.

Edward Flaherty, on my behalf, presented my case. It was based on three things: 1) Incomplete consideration of the facts; 2) failure to observe or apply correctly the provisions of the Staff Regulations (those all-important regulations!) or the terms of my contract; and 3) personal prejudice on the part of responsible officials. Failure to investigate the driver's alleged misconduct amounted to 'incomplete consideration of the facts', he said. And since it had impacted my ability to carry out my duties, it without doubt affected my appointment status. 'Moreover, the Administration's inexplicable refusal to undertake an investigation, or to constitute the required medical board, may also be deemed to have resulted from prejudice. He added, 'It is the Appellant's belief that the WHO Administration has interfered with the efforts of the Namibian public prosecutor by refusing to lift the functional immunity without explanation.'

As to Lopez's contention that there had never been a decision *not* to convene a medical board, this was rejected with derision. Eighteen months had passed since one had been requested, Flaherty pointed out, a delay which was tantamount to denial.

The lawyer put several questions to the Administration, represented by Renée Lopez and Ms. A. Ankrah-Ntambwe. 'Who, behind the scenes,' he asked, 'made the decisions to challenge receivability? And before that, not to hold an investigation?' They promised that answers would be forthcoming in their written response.

Having heard their arguments, the Board again decided receivability was not an issue: it would proceed with the appeal in every aspect. 'No further arguments should be presented on this subject,' its secretary reaffirmed. 'However, in view of recent developments, the Board has decided...to allow the appellant to submit a written supplement to his Statement.' Following my vehement protest, they also rejected the Administration's suggestion that the time limit of 90 days allowed for completion of an appeal be suspended. I breathed a sigh of relief. At last, it seemed, somebody was standing up to the bureaucrats on my behalf. And surely, once the Board had considered the facts, they could only decide in my favour?

CHAPTER EIGHTEEN

LOOKING GLASS LOGIC

'...if it was so, it might be; and if it were so, it would be; but as it isn't, it ain't.' That's logic.

My language was emotive and angry in the supplementary statement the Board allowed me, in contrast to the restraint I'd shown until now. I referred to 'the bad faith and disdain which the Administration has repeatedly shown for the past two years'. I described their representations as 'hollow' and 'blatantly false'. I accused them of trying at all costs to avoid this hearing with their pretense of last-minute attempts to resolve things. I apologised for wasting the Board's time with the Administration's frivolous objections; I hoped they would realise I had exhausted all other avenues beforehand. It would be easy to blame the delays on bureaucratic hiccups, but I put them down to 'callous or incompetent' administrators.

Since the Administration had promised to name, in their formal reply, those who had made the crucial decisions, I asked the Board to keep them to this. Failure to do it, I said, would be further evidence of their bad faith. As to the medical board, 20 months' delay in convening it was grounds enough for an enquiry, despite the last-ditch attempts. I refuted outright the accusation that the delay was caused by Dr. Michelson. With regard to my new South African posting, I pointed out that I had neither been informed nor consulted. And if I accepted the offer 'it does not erase the fact that the Administration refused for some 20 months to take the complaints seriously'. This inexplicable indifference should be evidence enough for the Board to make a conclusion.

As to Mootu's immunity, by now nearly four years had passed since the crash – time enough for a decision to be made! I concluded that all this 'must be sternly dealt with by the HBA... to ensure that no other WHO staff member is ever again forced to endure such disrespectful and disdainful treatment'.

The hearing of my case – Number 476 – finally began on March 20 in Geneva. Mrs. Watters was called as a witness, which caused a flutter of anxiety in the Watters household.

Although Mrs. Watters wished to support me, her daughter, however, was concerned about the treatment she might receive by the HBA, which as it turned out was sympathetic and understanding.

Mrs. Watters was asked to go over the events from her point of view. She explained how the Organization had failed completely in providing her with a proper report on the accident. She recounted the circumstances as she knew them, but pointed out that her only source of information was the autopsy report. She confirmed that the Namibian authorities had taken up the case again following her application to the court via a private law firm; and that they had asked WHO to raise the driver's immunity in December 2000. It was now March and as far as she was aware, no response had been made.

Mr. A T Slater should have been the next witness, having been Director of Human Resources at the time, but he declined to appear on the grounds that 'his involvement in the case was not personal and to his recollection had only been to reiterate, on behalf of HRS as its then Director, a position that had previously been communicated by the staff member responsible'. This, to me, was just another case of evasion. My third witness was Dr. Celton., who went over the medical records.

Renée Lopez had drawn up an 11-page rebuttal of my arguments. At the risk of boring the reader, here is a selection of the main points made by the World Health Organization. They give a sense of their tone, and where the Organization was coming from:

- While the Organization understands any distress the Appellant may feel about this tragic car accident, his arguments are mistaken.
- On the issue of the investigation the Appellant suspects that the driver's actions were 'outrageous, negligent, perhaps to the

point of being deranged or intentional'. Clearly however the Organization had neither the means nor the authority to carry out in Namibia the sort of investigation that the allegations made by the Appellant would call for.

- The Namibian authorities did conduct an investigation in 1997... an official inquest was held... affidavits admitted. The public prosecutor decided not to prosecute. Therefore there was no basis for the Organization to conclude that the driver's action were 'outrageous' etc. No basis either to discipline him for 'being guilty of serious misconduct'. In any event, initiating disciplinary proceedings against the driver is not a claim that can be entertained by the HBA.

- Until the Public Prosecutor's decision was communicated to the WHO, Mr. Mootu's duties were severely restricted. Immediately after Mr. Mootu recovered from his injuries and reported back to duty the WHO representative restricted him to office-related tasks and driving for short distances in and around Windhoek. This was despite the fact that Mr. Mootu had been considered as being reliable; that he had served as the personal driver of several WHO Representatives in Namibia, and that only five days before the accident he qualified for a safe driving bonus for not having any accidents in the previous year. Nonetheless it was only after it was confirmed by the Namibian authorities that the police had declined to prosecute, that Mr. Mootu was able to undertake the full range of his responsibilities again.

- While a summons to appear before the Namibian courts was delivered to Mr. Mootu last year, the Appellant's claim that 'it is outrageous that WHO refuses to lift the driver's privileges and immunities' is mistaken. In fact no such decision has been taken by the Director General.

- Because Mr. Mootu was immune from legal process (see note 3 below), the delivery of a summons required a prior request for waiver of his immunity and the Director General's decision to waive it. Since no such request had been received, let alone agreed to, the delivery of a summons was in breach of Mr. Mootu's immunity. The Organization therefore immediately sought the assistance of the Ministry of Foreign Affairs of

Namibia to ensure observance of Mr. Mootu's immunity by the Court – this being without prejudice to whatever decision the Director General might take in the event that a formal request for waiver of immunity was made. The following day the Ministry expressed its regret and informed the Organization that it had advised the Court to adhere to the established channels.

[Note 3 reads: This immunity arises from Sect 19 of the Convention on Privileges and Immunities of the Specialised Agencies which Namibia has agreed to apply to WHO and its officials by reason of Article V of the Basic Agreement for the Establishment of Technical Advisory Cooperation Relations concluded between Namibia and the Organization on 12 April 1990. Section 19 provides that officials of the specialised agencies shall a) be immune from legal process in respect of words spoken or written and all acts performed by them in their official capacity'.]

- Only at the end of last year did the Ministry inform the Organization that following consultations, it had been concluded that Mr. Mootu should be prosecuted. Understanding this communication as a request for waiver of immunity from legal process, and in following on its earlier communication, the Organization requested such documentation as may be available. This was keeping in mind that no explanation for a change of decision concerning prosecution had been received. As indicated to the Ministry, upon receipt of such documentation the Director General will advise without delay of her decision concerning Mr. Mootu's immunity.

- In summary the Organization asserted Mr. Mootu's immunity from legal process because the summons he received took no account of it. In so doing the Organization made an entirely proper exercise of its authority. Observance of the privileges and immunities of the Organization and its officials by Member States is of utmost importance to the Organization under any circumstances. Furthermore, no decision on waiver of immunity has yet been taken, but, now that a communication which is understood as a request for waiver has been received, the Director General intends to take a decision promptly upon receiving such information as may be available.

- It should be borne in mind that decisions concerning a staff member's immunity are the Organization's prerogative, affecting as they do its relations with Member States. The exercise of this prerogative falls outside the competence of the HBA. Any Appellant's claim in this regard is thus irreceivable. Without prejudice to this strongly-held view, the above summary should dispel any doubt cast by the Appellant on the Organization's desire to give this matter its utmost attention.

With regard to the Medical Board, the Administration contended that 'The Appellant's arguments are incorrect.... Firstly, there is no conflict of medical opinion between the Appellant's doctor (Dr. Michelson) and JMS regarding the percentage of loss of function. JMS submitted the latter evaluation to Dr. Michelson for his comments and/or agreement, to which he never formally responded, either positively or negatively.

Secondly the length of time it took to convene the medical board cannot be attributed to any decision by the Organization not to do so. No such decision was ever made. In fact, a medical board was convened on 11 January 2001.'

Several memos were itemised. The fact that medical care in Harare was insufficient was disputed: the Director of Joint Medical Services had done a tour of inspection of eight types of facilities there in 1999, they said. His conclusion was that 'most diagnostic and therapeutic procedures were easily available, and could be implemented by the physicians and specialists of excellent quality available in Harare'. The city had since been made a regional health referral centre for all UN staff. As for political unrest causing a negative effect, Mr. Zawide's opinion 'does not match the Administration's assessment of the situation'.

Ironically, Zimbabwe's health delivery system was ranked by the World Health Organization the worst in the world later that same year, 2001. It came last out of 191 countries, according to the August 11 issue of the *British Medical Journal*, performing even worse than the Democratic Republic of the Congo (DRC). It seemed that there were different assessments for different purposes.

The following paragraph is long and tedious but its self-righteous tone is quite revealing. It refers to the accusation that I had been treated disrespectfully and with disdain. This is not borne out by the facts, and negates the efforts of those many staff members who were well aware of the tragic accident and who did their utmost to respond to his needs. Thus, the Appellant was assigned to Geneva for an extended period, despite the fact that his expertise was sorely needed at the regional level. Upon return to Harare, he was confined to sedentary work in view of his condition. When re-organization resulted in a change in the structure of the Regional Office, a suitable position was identified for him at the WHO Collaborating Centre. A medical board was convened and great effort was made to ensure the participation of his chosen medical representative. Finally, there has been a willingness to cooperate with the Namibian authorities, bearing in mind the rule governing WHO's relations with its Member States. All these actions exhibit an awareness of the Appellant's particular circumstances, and a respect for the Appellant who is a valued staff member of the Organization.'

As for this 'valued' staff member's demand to know who had made the decisions that so upset his peace of mind, the Administration retorted 'the Appellant is already in possession of numerous signed correspondences in relation to the decisions... the Administration draws his attention, they almost sneered, 'to the information provided therein should he require further details.'

In conclusion: The Administration has demonstrated that is has addressed the specific needs and concerns of the Appellant further to the accident in 1997 as has been either appropriate or possible. Thus, the Director General's intent to carefully consider whether a staff member's immunity from prosecution should be waived has been indicated...' 'Contrariwise,' continued Tweedledee, 'if it was so, it might be; and if it were so, it would be; but as it isn't, it ain't. "That's logic'.

CHAPTER NINETEEN

IN WHICH THE MURKY
IS MADE MURKIER

'The Board noted that the objective of diplomatic immunity was .... not to allow individuals to break the law with impunity.... The Organization must carry out its own internal Administrative enquiry into the circumstances of any accident in which a WHO vehicle was involved...'

While the players in this saga waited patiently for the Board's report, I prepared to start my new job in Cape Town. Had all things been equal I would have been delighted, for South Africa at this time was an exciting place to be. It certainly had good medical services – its famous Groote Schuur Hospital was the first in the world to boast a heart transplant, carried out in 1967 by Dr. Christian Barnard. And South Africa's Truth and Reconciliation Commission, set up to expose the atrocities committed under the apartheid regime and lay the ghosts to rest, had just completed its work. That painful process of putting the past behind it, which had taken two and a half years, had afforded thousands of people affected by the wicked deeds of apartheid, the opportunity to tell their tale. Based on the premise that 'not even God forgives before it is asked,' and that 'We needed to know what lay behind us before we could go forward', it had brought many unpalatable truths into the open. No wonder I resonated with it! This was all that I asked for myself, in order to make a transition and a new beginning.

I was to be based at the WHO's Collaborative Centre for Urban Health Development, a centre of excellence located at South Africa's

Medical Research Council (MRC). By now, relations between myself and the WHO Administration had reached such a low ebb that nothing seemed to go smoothly. In my view, the posting was nothing but a hastily-arranged, last-ditch effort to wriggle out of the embarrassment my appeal was causing. The job was sprung on me out of the blue, without prior consultation. The Administration denied this, saying that not only had it been discussed with me, but that a letter had been sent to me the previous November. If this was so I never received it.

Whatever the truth behind this bickering, it was clear from the moment I started my new job on 28 March 2001 that no-one had thought the matter through. Not even a UN employee can take up a job in a new country without red tape, and the WHO bureaucrats, with all their experience, were fully aware of the formalities that must be gone through. Yet no-one had sorted out the formal documentation. At the end of April, the Administrator in the WHO office in Pretoria complained to the Regional Office that *'We are finding it difficult to get accreditation for [Mr. Zawide's] residence in South Africa - i.e., registration at the Ministry of Foreign Affairs and the usual enjoyment of diplomatic privileges, such as duty-free importation of personal effects, issue of ID cards etc. According to the Ministry of Foreign Affairs they were supposed to have received a motivation for the creation of a new post, as well as a brief description of the duties to be performed by Mr. Zawide. We are therefore requesting an urgent regularisation of his situation in South Africa, in particular an application to the Government for the establishment of his post at the MRC.'*

Meanwhile, I was unable to get on with any work, and it was difficult, in the absence of ID documents, to sort out routine matters such as bank accounts and rental accommodation. So I decided to take home leave for two months, and went to Ethiopia and America.

According to the all-pervasive Rules, Dr. Brundtland was supposed to give her decision about the Board's findings, and release their report, at the end of May. However, true to form, May came and went with no word. Once again Flaherty was forced to request the courtesy of a reply. On June 18, he wrote to her 'As you may be aware, under WHO staff rule 1230.3.1 you had 60 days from receipt of the Board's report to take your decision. Mr. Zawide has still not received your decision nor the courtesy of an explanation for the delay. Moreover, it appears that the alleged transfer of Mr. Zawide to Cape Town (a ruse blatantly fabricated... presented to the HBA in an apparent, last-minute attempt to mitigate Mr. Zawide's claim]... has been revealed to be the fiction Mr. Zawide believed it to be when first presented to him. Several of the HBA members aggressively complained to the WHO representative at the hearing about its habitual dilatory tactics in appeals in general and Mr. Zawide's case in particular.'

On July 3 Dr. Brundtland finally forwarded the Board's 12-page report, together with her response.

The report itself was a model of clarity, and its plain speaking was a relief to read after all the confusing, obfuscating language that characterised the correspondence from WHO. The Board's five members, Dr. HM Kahssay, the Chairman, (appointed by the Director General); Dr. D Buriot and Mr. G Presthus, also appointed by her, and Mr. M. Szczeniowski and Dr. R. Gray, from the staff panel, had obviously listened carefully to the witnesses and studied every document. They had cut out all the waffle as if with a scalpel.

The first nine pages summarised the events, issues, and arguments. The next three presented the Board's thinking, conclusions and recommendations. Since they go to the heart of this book, I hope the reader will forgive me for reproducing them verbatim. They give the same meagre facts, but not from my subjective point of view. The italics are my own.

(1) Considerations Of The Board Of Appeal

'The Board took note that WHO was not in a position to carry out a criminal investigation, and agreed that such an investigation was the responsibility of the local authorities. In the light of the contradictory statements made by the various parties involved, e.g. concerning weather conditions and the state of the road, and the gravity of the accident in which two people died and a third was seriously injured, the Board considered that *such an enquiry was essential.*

In this context the Board noted that the objective of diplomatic immunity was to facilitate the work of WHO's international staff, *not to allow individuals to break the law with impunity.* They considered that *WHO should do everything in its power to facilitate an investigation into the accident by the Namibian authorities,* and to ensure that justice was done.

The Board members agreed that the Administration was correct in requesting information from the Namibian authorities concerning their reasons for re-opening the case. However, they also agreed that the Administration should request the WHO representative in Namibia to do everything possible to ensure that the information was provided quickly to enable the Director General to take a reasoned decision on raising the driver's diplomatic immunity, in order to facilitate the investigation and, if appropriate, his prosecution.

The Board further noted that it was not even clear from the information provided what the state of the WHO vehicle was prior to the accident and whether or not it was properly equipped with seat belts. The Board emphasised that it was the responsibility of the Administration to ensure that all official vehicles were properly equipped and in good working order. The Board considered that *in the case of an accident involving a WHO vehicle, the first duty of the Organization was to ensure that the vehicle in question was in good condition, had been correctly serviced and maintained and was properly equipped.*

This implied that the *Organization must carry out its own internal Administrative enquiry into the circumstances of any accident in which a WHO vehicle was involved.* Only thus could the Administration be in a position to ensure that all possible precautions were taken throughout the Organization to prevent anything similar happening again.

The Administration had been specifically requested to provide copies for the Board of all documentation concerning the accident. The only documents provided were the form WHO 417 submitted by Mr. Zawide. Reference was made to [Dr. Rojas'] oral report, but no evidence of it was presented. As stated in the Board's memorandum to the Administration dated 21 March 2001 requesting the Administration to release all the documentation it had in its possession, the Members concluded that no other documentation existed and noted that there was nothing which indicated that any form of internal enquiry into the accident had been carried out.

(2) Convening of the Medical Review Board

The Administration said that the delay in convening the medical review board was the result of the failure of Dr. Michelson, the Appellant's doctor, to respond to correspondence from Director, JMS, concerning the evaluation of the Appellant's disability.

The Board members studied the documentation provided by the Administration and listened carefully to the detailed explanations provided by the Director, JMS, in the course of his testimony. They understood that Director JMS had made the convening of the medical review board conditional on receipt of a response from Dr. Michelson, the doctor appointed by the Appellant to represent his interests, concerning agreement on the percentage of his disability. However, the HBA had found nothing in the Rules and Regulations governing the medical review procedures to justify such a pre-condition. Furthermore, the HBA noted that once a staff member had requested a medical review, the Administration was under an obligation to implement the procedures within a reasonable period of time.

The Appellant having requested a medical review, it should have been carried out with due expediency. The Board noted that on 21 December 1999, Dr. Michelson requested the Director, JMS to contact his secretary to coordinate a telephone conference. The conference did not take place until 11 January 2001. *The Board considered that a delay of more than a year to organise a telephone conference between three members of a medical review board, all of whom were located the in the USA, was unacceptable.* The Board noted that it took JMS a total of seven months to send two reminders to Dr. Michelson, which they also considered to be unacceptable.

(3) Reassignment to another duty station

The Board noted that the Appellant had requested transfer to a duty station where more sophisticated medical care was available. However, the Board members noted that the reports presented by Director JMS on the medical facilities available in Harare in 1999, indicated that they were sufficient to cater for the needs of the Appellant, and they were not in a position to dispute those findings. The Board noted that in an emergency, the Appellant could rapidly be evacuated, in the same way as any other staff members who needed special medical care.

The Board considered that the type of job the Appellant was asked to perform was at least as important as the medical facilities available in his duty station. His condition required a sedentary job, and this the Organization had provided.

The Board noted that in January 2001, transfer had been arranged to Cape Town, where the Administration said he would continue to perform sedentary tasks. However, the Board considered that the lack of prior consultation and the extremely terse way in which *the transfer had been notified to the Appellant,* constituted an example of *the extremely poor style of communication adopted by the Administration towards the Appellant.* The Board members felt that this lack of empathy was particularly regrettable in view of the physical and psychological trauma which they considered to be inevitable following an accident of this kind, in which two of his colleagues had lost their lives, and the Appellant himself had been seriously injured.

(4) Conclusions of the HBA

The Board concluded that the *Organization was in a position to carry out an internal administrative enquiry into the state of the WHO vehicle prior to the accident and surrounding circumstances, and should have done so immediately and on the spot.*

The Board further concluded that the Organization should do everything in its power to facilitate investigation by the Namibian authorities, and to ensure that justice was done as quickly as possible. They agreed that a decision concerning the lifting of diplomatic immunity could have far-reaching consequences for other WHO staff throughout the world, and could not be taken lightly. Nevertheless, *it was also important to avoid giving the impression that a WHO staff member would be allowed to break the law with impunity if involved in a criminal act.*

The Board concluded that *the delay of nearly 20 months in the convening of the medical review board from the date on which the Appellant confirmed his request that a review be carried out, was unjustified and warranted compensation.*

The Board concluded that the Administration, in locating the Appellant in Geneva following his return to work after the accident and then in providing him with a sedentary job in Harare, his normal duty station, had acted in accordance with his needs and with the advice of his medical practitioners. Nevertheless, the Board considered that the poor communication style and lack of humanity shown by the Administration in its dealing with the Appellant deserved censure.

(5) Recommendations of the Board

The Board recommended that the Organization follow up the matter of investigation and eventual prosecution with the Namibian authorities, and take immediate steps to ensure that they provide the information required to allow the Director General to take a decision concerning the diplomatic immunity of the driver involved in the accident as quickly as possible. *As a matter of courtesy and respect, the Board further recommended that the families of all the victims of the accident including the Appellant, be contacted by the Administration, provided with a full explanation and kept up to date on this issue.*

The Board recommended the payment of US $ 30,000 as compensation for the failure of the Organization to convene a Medical Review Board within a reasonable time, the refusal of the Organization to conduct an internal investigation into the accident in spite of the conflicting statement of the Appellant and the driver concerning the state of the WHO vehicle, weather conditions at the time of the accident, etc., and the failure of the Administration to treat him with due consideration and respect.

The Board further recommended the reimbursement of legal costs up to a maximum of US$ 7500 on presentation of receipted bills. The Board recommended the reimbursement of travel costs and payment of per diem at normal WHO rates in connection with his two appearances before the Board in Geneva.

The Board recommended no further redress.

(6) Additional recommendation

The Board condemned the disregard for WHO rules and Regulations and the HBA Rules of Procedure shown by Mr. AT Slater, ex-Director HRS, in his refusal to appear as a witness before the Board. *The Members recommended that the disrespect he had shown towards the Board be reprimanded.'*

And so, as Edward Flaherty had predicted, the Board of Appeal came down heavily in favour of myself – of David as opposed to Goliath, in this struggle. But the perceptive reader will have smelled a rat over one particular paragraph, and found it as hard to swallow as I did! This was the Administration's claim that not a single piece of paper had passed between the various offices regarding this incident, and that the only documentation on file was the report submitted by myself. This defies belief, and makes a mockery of the proceedings. Not even a written report from the driver? Or the Administrator (who'd told me herself that she had submitted one)? Or Dr. Rojas? And was there no insurance claim relating to the vehicle? On whom was the blame laid in *that* document? Even if the families were considered too insignificant to merit an official report on the deaths of their loved ones, after the increasingly-distressed letters from both me and Mrs. Watters, and their suggestions of a cover up, one suspected a mountain of internal memos existed and had been hidden away. To me it meant that despite the expensive and intensive investigation, the true facts were as murky as ever and I could not lay the matter to rest.

It doesn't take the skill of a Poirot to conclude that the WHO Administration was concealing something. Especially since the one man who might have thrown light on the events, Anthony Slater, the ex-Director of Human Resources, had refused to appear and be answerable. The puppeteers behind the scenes – perhaps with the blessing of Dr. Brundtland – clearly had scant respect for the Appeal process. The Board, like the Ombudsman, must know its place, it seemed.

The only question remaining was, what would the Director General do about this report? The process was the only one open to staff for the resolution of disputes, and unless she was an utter despot, she could hardly ignore the report since it was intelligent, fair and balanced. It presented a chance for her to show herself in a good light, by offering leadership her staff would respect and respond to. For rest assured, I was not the only one who had followed the proceedings and been interested in the outcome. Was the 'Brundtland Syndrome' mere paranoia, or did WHO staff, from top to bottom, have good reason for the feelings the ombudsman had described: 'severe insecurity, uncertainty about the future and frustration'? In no organization has that mixture ever been found to produce good work.

CHAPTER TWENTY

DINOSAUR MANAGEMENT

'*Conscious Organizations are committed to learning, growing and being more aware, more responsible, and more aligned with their stated values. Organizations which do not provide such thriving growing grounds for workers will be forced to employ those who are slower to wake up – living and working less consciously. Like the prehistoric dinosaurs, eventually these Organizations will die.' John Renesh, futurist and social commentator.*

So, the staff awaited the Director General's response to case number 476 with interest. Would she demonstrate that she cared, what happened to her staff, exposed as they were to risks all over the world? Would she stand by the fine words of her inaugural speech, when she had promised to 'create an Organizational structure not driven by bureaucratic rules but one that promotes performance and results'? Or would she prove that red tape and expediency mattered, in the end, more than solving the mystery surrounding the death of one of her own people?

Three months after a response *should* have been received, according to the infamous Rules – and then only after prompting from my lawyer – I at last received my answer. This was what Dr. Brundtland wrote:

'The HBA report on your appeal, a copy of which is enclosed, has been received. In reviewing this report, I have noticed that one element of the appeal was non-transfer to a duty station where adequate medical care is available. I note, however the Board's conclusion that the Administration, in locating you in Geneva following your return to work after the accident and then in providing you with sedentary work in Harare, acted properly. I endorse this conclusion. I note, in any event, that you have been transferred to the WHO Collaboration Centre in Cape Town, South Africa, which is also clearly a satisfactory duty station.

I am also aware that a medical board was convened in January 2001, and I am pleased that your request in this regard has already been met.

I have also noted your request and the Board's considerations regarding an investigation into the accident and the initiation of disciplinary proceedings against Mr. Mootu. Nonetheless, it is for the local authorities and not the Organization, to carry out investigations into the causes of motor-vehicle accidents. I am, therefore, not in agreement with the Board's recommendation that steps be taken by the Administration to pursue this matter or the investigation and possible prosecution of parties involved in the accident. Furthermore, I note that the status of the matter has been explained in detail in the HBA proceedings. Taking this into account, I am unable to agree to the Board's recommendation that the Administration should contact you or the families of all persons affected and provide you with a full explanation and further details on this issue. I also note that this was not part of your claims.

With respect to the second paragraph of part 8 of the report, I cannot accept the reasoning of the Board nor its recommendation to pay you US $ 30,000. Nevertheless, I acknowledge that the time taken to convene the medical board may have added to your distress, even if it was due to circumstances largely beyond the Organization's control. Furthermore, I am struck by the circumstances of your case, including your pain and suffering. Taking these considerations into account, I have decided that you should receive payment of US $35,000.

With respect to the Board's recommendations concerning the payment of legal costs and expenses related to your appearance before the Board, I agree that your legal costs be reimbursed up to US $2000 upon receipt of an itemised invoice.

I hope that you will accept this decision as final. However, should you feel unable to do so, you have the right to appeal to the Administrative Tribunal of the International Labour Organization in accordance with Staff rule 1240. To be receivable by the Tribunal a complaint must be filed within ninety days after notification of the decision impugned as provided in the Statutes of the Tribunal.

Yours sincerely

Gro Harlem Brundtland MD, MPH

Dr. Brundtland had added insult to injury

It should be immediately clear that this official – not to mention officious – response did not a thing in terms of putting my mind at rest. To me, if anything, Dr. Brundtland had added insult to injury, because she patronisingly professed herself unable to accept the reasoning of the Board – even though they, not she, had heard the evidence, and had been appointed to advise her – yet nonetheless, she upped its recommended recompense to the tune of $5,000! Did she really think that money was what it was all about? Was I now supposed to sit down and shut up, like a greedy child given an ice cream?

What grated even more was her queenly tone – she was granting me this huge sum, presumably out of precious funds ear-marked for important aid work, not because she believed her organization to be at fault, but because she had been 'struck by the circumstances of the case'. And it seemed to me nothing short of breathtaking hypocrisy to express her concern for my pain and suffering, without making the slightest effort to end it. She could have done so at the stroke of a pen, by following the recommendation of her Board to lift Mootu's immunity and at last allow Namibian justice to take its course.

Where the Board's logic was irrefutable in pointing out for instance that the purpose of immunity was *not* to protect staff from the effects of their wrongdoing – she simply ignored it, which amounted to an abuse of power. The fact that a highly-respected WHO official and a senior Government representative from a Member State had been killed without so much as one internal memorandum on the subject, did not, apparently concern her. Whether human error or a deliberate attempt of assassination was involved clearly weighed far less heavily on her mind than the WHO's rights to diplomatic immunity. "The status of the matter has been explained in detail in the HBA proceedings', she purred, as if to imply that the Board, in their simple way, had somehow not been able to comprehend the explanation!

Dr. Brundtland didn't even refer to the criticisms of her staff, such as the *'extremely poor style of communication adopted by the Administration'*, and *'the unacceptable delay of more than a year to organise a telephone conference'. And she totally ignored the observation that 'the Organization was in a position to carry out an internal administrative enquiry into the state of the WHO vehicle... and should have done so immediately and on the spot'.*

To me the whole exercise was a thoroughly unsatisfactory waste of time. I consoled myself that at least it had not been a waste of money too, since Dr. Brundtland had agreed to pay me more than the Board had recommended, and thrown in my legal and travel costs to boot. However, monetary gain was never my main objective, and to be offered it with total disregard for the deeper human issues, seemed a Pyrrhic victory. Far from giving me the peace of mind that comes from telling one's story and being heard, as in South Africa's Truth and Reconciliation Commission, the result plunged me deeper into anger and depression.

The extraordinary elevation and protection bestowed upon this humble Namibian driver, the unquestionable author of the whole catastrophe, could be explained only in two ways to my mind: either the Administration desperately sought to exonerate itself from blame in order to avoid being sued (the lack of seat belts making insurance cover doubtful); or there had indeed been foul play, emanating from the Regional or Namibian Office. This was my suspicion. With racism and ethnic intolerance rife among a very insecure staff, it is not beyond the bounds of possibility to imagine this. Only the following year, in 2001, the WHO Representative in Burundi Dr. Kassy Manlan of Ivory Coast was murdered in his house, his body being found later by fishermen on the shores of Lake Tanganyika. In 2005 four former senior police officers were sentenced to death for the crime; three more were given life imprisonment; two received 20-year sentences, and four guards were jailed for two years for assisting in the murder. According to lawyers, Manlan was killed to prevent his investigating the embezzlement of funds intended to buy malaria medicine. No WHO staff were implicated, but the case proves that the WHO Administration is keen to seek justice when it suits them. Was it, I wonder, because Dr. Manlan was a political appointee that his murder was so thoroughly investigated, while Dr. Greg Watters and Mr. Damon were mere professionals, so their deaths did not merit even internal analysis?

What did Dr. Brundtland's response say about her leadership skills? Much has been written about the soft stuff of people management that is the lever to high performance. 'It is based on a clear and compelling vision and a supporting set of values demonstrated in behaviour,' Daniel Goleman explained in his best-seller, *Emotional Intelligence*. 'Organizations that genuinely understand the power of corporate EQ harness the emotional potential and commitment of individuals towards a greater purpose,' he wrote. By confining her reply to the self-serving aims of the Administration, Dr. Gro Harlem Brundtland probably did more damage than she was aware.

At this point it seems relevant to examine the verdict of experts on Dr. Brundtland's overall tenure at Geneva, brief though it was. Critics have suggested that she tried to run the WHO as she had Norway in her three terms as prime minister – 'insulated by a close-knit cabinet of advisers who try to muzzle internal dissent in order to stick to a strong party line,' according to Britain's *Economist*. She was highly successful in some areas, for instance in gaining a massive 40 per cent more extra-budgetary funding. And there's no doubt she moved both health and the WHO centre stage in terms of global development. But her staff relations were abysmal. She was a 'data-oriented person' according to one senior man. When she made the shock announcement that she would not be standing for a second term, there was widespread speculation that one reason for her departure was dislocation from her staff. 'There was a feeling that while she boosted staff morale when she took office, she squandered their initial enthusiasm by becoming increasingly isolated, uncommunicative and hidden behind her cabinet,' wrote Gavin Yamey, in the *British Medical Journal*.

'WHO's Director General has many constituencies, including governments, the media and staff, Gavin Yamey continued. 'Many of those I interviewed said that Dr.Brundtland has been a great leader on the world stage, but a poor leader of the Organization. Staff at high levels said she gave them great freedom and support to develop their programmes, but many staff at lower levels feel disenchanted by her management. She boosted their morale on arrival, by being highly visible and promising a new era of openness and communication, but there was a large gap between rhetoric and action. Her increasing isolation from them was matched by their falling enthusiasm.... In a 2001 survey of 637 WHO staff, 40 percent rated their morale as bad or very bad.'

'Leaders are dealers in hope,' Napoleon rightly said. A work force that doesn't understand what is going on becomes discontented, unhappy and demotivated. Under the machine paradigm, the aim of controlling staff rather than inspiring them made sense. But with today's growing recognition that human beings prefer self-regulation, as do all other forms of life, attempts to control them through rigidity is suicide, destroying individuality and collective vitality. Much could have been done if our Director Generals and Regional Directors had taken this into account. For Dr. Ibrahim Samba was even worse than Dr. Brundtland when it came to staff communications. Known as a 'slave driver' and 'an unguided missile' by his senior advisers, he also put more emphasis on mobilizing extra-budgetary funds and increasing the quantity of staff rather than the quality. Dr. Samba was seen as a strong Regional Director by the African Ministers of Health, due to his tremendous achievement in increasing WHO activities in country health projects. The down side was that money rather than health development was the main preoccupation of most meetings. Samba was indeed good in managing the budget – until 2003, that is, when the office ran out of funds even to pay staff salaries due to unplanned expenditure on the return of the Regional Office to Brazzaville and the depreciation of the US dollar. He had to request an advance of US $ 7.5 million from the headquarters administrative support funds. To Samba's credit however is his earlier successful onchocerciasis control project; although it too succeeded partly due to massive mobilization of donor funds.

Jim Collins, author of *Good to Great*, a study of how certain good organizations moved into the 'great' category, cited a direct relationship between the absence of celebrity and the presence of great results. 'When you have a high IQ celebrity as CEO, the company turns into a situation of the one genius with 1,000 helpers', he wrote.

For the world's poor – the millions dying of disease and ignorance – such ill-informed leadership is bad news indeed. It is also deeply depressing for people of the developed world who, confronted with daily TV shots of disease-ridden children and extreme third-world misery, console themselves with the belief that at least WHO is looking after them in a noble way.

Where did Dr. Brundtland's reply leave me and Mrs. Watters? Denied closure by the wavering about the waiver, we were also denied access to the normal legal channels that govern individual countries because we were international citizens. So, there was only one place left to turn to – the International Labour Organization.

It was never my intention to appeal to this body. Its Tribunal was considered by international civil servants to favour the Administration. However the Director General's refusal to conduct an internal investigation or to remove Mootu's immunity, put me in a difficult position. Convinced that the Administration had something to hide, I sat down and replied to Dr. Brundtland. The date was September 11, 2001 – that fateful day which has become synonymous in all our minds with a terror from which the world has never recovered. The UN's failure either to avert the tragedy of the Twin Towers or to be effective in handling its aftermath was, say some, symptomatic of a deeper malaise to do with lack of funding and commitment to global governance and control of terrorism. The World Health Organization had had its budget frozen for 13 years due to such lack of support, which was no doubt one reason for its appalling lack of management training.

This tiny case in a tiny country which was allowed to blow up out of all proportion, costing thousands of dollars, because it wasn't dealt with properly at source, was perhaps symptomatic of that. The WHO's failure to run itself effectively, or to show compassion to its staff, or to allocate money to the development of management skills and team building, are all related. The shortage of cash and of world support affected it in a myriad of ways over its entire global structure, greatly undermining its effectiveness.

In my response to Dr. Brundtland I expressed my satisfaction with the Board's conclusions, and, by contrast, my dissatisfaction with her decision. 'The inexplicable refusal of the Administration to carry out an internal enquiry and the Board's finding that no documentation exists... reinforces my assertion that the accident [was] suspicious, 'I wrote. 'The Board's recommendation that the families of the victims be contacted... was humane and just, and would have helped heal the wounds and dry the tears of those who lost their beloved ones.

'The main purpose of my appeal was *not* for monetary gain,' I pointed out. She had ignored the Board's recommendation that Mr. Slater be reprimanded for the disrespect he showed in refusing to appear. Additionally, I suggested she reprimand Ms. Rene Lopez for her frivolity in objecting to the receivability of my appeal.

Of course, it was wishful thinking that the DG would act on my suggestion when she had ignored her own Board of Enquiry. The reply – received many months later, though dated 1 November – came from one Enid Steward-Goffman, Director Human Resources, which returned to Tweedledee country with the statement: 'In the Director General's letter of 3 July... she explained the reasons why an internal investigation... was not undertaken. We are aware that you have received this letter and therefore you may wish to refer to it again.' The observant reader will note that she had explained no such thing.

The next big thing

The International Labour Organization aims to increase productive labour, improve working conditions and raise living standards all over the world. It sets minimum international labour standards through drafting international conventions. Its Tribunal (referred to as ILOAT) was established in 1946 to hear complaints by UN officials about their employment terms and conditions, and to settle disputes about workers' compensation. Its jurisdiction is recognised by forty international Organizations ranging from the European Patents Office, The European Organization for Nuclear Research (CERN), the International Federation of the Red Cross and Red Crescent, to

UN bodies such as the Food and Agricultural Organization (FAO), the Industrial Development Organization and last but not least, WHO. The ILOAT thus serves as the final arbiter of employment issues for some 35,000 international civil servants, deprived by their occupation of recourse to domestic employment law either in their own country or (because of their employer's immunity) of the country in which they reside and work.

It was to this august body I now turned.

In a note to my lawyer, Ed Flaherty, I wrote 'This is our last legal fight and I am fed up with WHO's atrocious behaviour. So let us finalise this case as soon as possible.'

I rejected all the compensation offered, even though, following the medical board's report, the final amount had been upped from six per cent to nine. I decided to include in my appeal to the ILOAT a claim for a whopping $250,000, to make up for all the prevarication. In Flaherty's view, any American corporation found guilty of causing such distress, would have been fined millions.

CHAPTER TWENTY-ONE

A BLATANT LIE

The appeal to the ILOAT occupied many working days by many highly-paid people who could have been far more usefully employed.

My appeal to the International Labour Organization covered 24 written pages, plus annexures; the WHO's Response took 33 pages; my Rejoinder took another 17 pages; and the Surrejoinder to the Rejoinder, a final 16. An outstanding illustration of the maxim that 'It takes less time to do a thing right than to explain why you did it wrong'! The appeal process lasted almost a year, because it all had to be done via the written word – no personal hearings were allowed. This is a source of niggling criticism of the ILOAT.

The Tribunal judges certainly required patience, for many of the documents were repetitive and tedious. But we ask the reader's indulgence for going over some of the ground, for it sheds further light on the thinking of WHO bureaucrats, and by contrast, on the feelings of the real people who were their protagonists.

It is easy to lose sight of the hurt feelings at the heart of the matter. Behind all the pompous official language there are no doubt unquestioned assumptions about keeping a stiff upper lip and suffering nobly when your masters treat you badly. If this is so, how about the tradition of justice and fair play that stems from the same cultural source? Was it beneath WHO's dignity to enquire why two people had been killed on a straight road with no obstacle in sight? Or did they simply not care, since there was no publicity surrounding the case?

From our side we sought to put the trauma behind us through finding out the truth. But there were wider implications as well. Our many friends and colleagues in the international civil service also needed to know if this seemingly callous disregard for staff really represented the leadership's approach. In an Organization supposed to embody the world's compassion, it was a shocking idea.

What had started out originally as perhaps nothing more than a routine case of utterly incompetent driving, had been blown up by insensitive, uncaring staff management into an international court case that brought into question the WHO's entire values and culture. But then the driving, far from being incompetent, could have been a highly-skilled manoeuvre intended to kill someone. Perhaps the regional and country offices knew more about it than they were prepared to admit; it certainly seemed that the faceless bureaucrats at headquarters were doing all they could to avoid the truth coming out while appearing to be playing by the rules. These were questions we hoped this clumsy, long-winded procedure would settle.

It was possible of course that while most members of the Organization were caring and supportive, the career bureaucrats and legal advisers were pragmatists, anxious to avoid the large claims for damages that might ensue if they conceded that the driver was to blame. Compared with this risk, what did the feelings of a mere handful of people matter? Were they too blinkered, and lacking in wise leadership, to consider the wider implications?

While the appeal ground on, events in Namibia seemed to confirm WHO's iron determination to avoid having the driver questioned. The Namibian judiciary were now contesting Mootu's diplomatic immunity in the highest court of the land. The WHO hired an expensive lawyer to argue for the driver, and spewed out yet more reams of paper to substantiate his position. Arguably the whole exercise cost them more than any claim would have. We shall return to this fight in due course.

If Dr. Brundtland hadn't made up her mind by now, she never would.

I focused on three issues in my appeal: first, the WHO's failure to carry out even a rudimentary enquiry, and their obstruction of justice in allowing Namibia to do so through waiving Mootu's diplomatic immunity. Second, the ignoring of my request for a medical review board for nearly two years, which I felt had been glossed over in the Director General's reply; and third, my assignment to an inadequate duty station for two years, plus the atrocious handling of my eventual reassignment, which I considered amounted to harassment. Each issue was argued, replied to, counter-argued and awarded the final rejoinder by the WHO. And at each stage it got progressively nastier.

Having reviewed the facts, I started by claiming that I had suffered 'malicious and insufferable treatment' at the Administration's hands, accentuated by the Director General's refusal to accept the objective recommendations of the Board of Appeal. I also cited a complete lack of consideration in communicating with me throughout', and accused my seniors of 'ill-will, bias, prejudice and bad faith'.

The WHO responded with hurt surprise, referring to this sentence several times. For instance, 'Since the Complainant raises legal issues the Organization is compelled to respond in kind. However this is not intended to minimise in anyway the distress expressed by him as a result of the accident. The Organization observes that the Complainant's arguments rest on the premise that 'he has not received the slightest consideration from the WHO Administration'. This is incorrect. On the contrary it has shown consideration throughout.'

'The Organization disagrees with the Complainant's presentation of events. E.g. he presents decisions taken in good faith as 'malicious'. WHO will address some of his incorrect allegation in the course of its reply, but it will not seek to rebut them all, preferring instead to focus on the legal issues.'

The investigation

My main contention was that the failure to investigate constituted disrespect towards me and the late Greg Watters. Also, that the findings might have made it necessary to discipline the driver. Without establishing the facts, the WHO could be endangering this man's passengers today. 'The ILOAT has held that an Organization owes a duty of protection to its staff and must do its utmost to afford them such protection. Failure to perform this duty constitutes an abuse of authority.'

I was still suffering stress from suspecting I had been the victim of an assassination attempt. For this reason alone, I said, WHO had a moral obligation to clarify matters. The Organization should lift the driver's diplomatic immunity immediately to allow the judiciary to hear his explanation. I derided WHO's contradictory stance that on one hand it was the duty of the Namibian Authorities, not the WHO, to hold a criminal investigation, while on the other, the Director General was obstructing them from investigating, by not waiving immunity. It seemed to me that if Dr. Brundtland hadn't made up her mind by now, she never would. To me it all implied that the WHO had something to hide. I agreed that immunity was a serious political issue – 'but so is the loss of lives at the hands of the Organization'.

First, I outlined the facts: that at the time of the accident it was not raining, and visibility was clear; that there were no other vehicles in sight, nor any animals, people or other obstructions. There was photographic proof that no tyre had burst or been punctured. The only causative factors appeared to be excessive speed, the driver's agitated state, and his totally unprovoked actions, which alone caused the car to veer and roll so violently.

I enlarged on Mootu's 'agitated state'. 'He was acting strange', I said. 'He had refused to slow down after being asked to several times; he was not focusing on the road, but looking to left and right and shaking his head. For no apparent reason, he glanced back, and it was then that he swung the steering wheel to the right, causing the car to roll'. 'The Complainant is not unconvinced that the driver intended to cause the crash, or at the very least acted negligently and recklessly. Indeed, the Namibian authorities have found enough evidence to reopen the case. Surely the WHO has a stake in seeing if its own employee was to blame?'

I went on to say that, to my chagrin, the driver had been reinstated immediately after the accident. The WHO claimed ingenuously that they had no reason to do otherwise since his license had not been taken away neither had any restriction been placed on him. However now the Namibian authorities had found reason to prosecute, and Mootu was still an official driver.

No attempt was made either, unless lies had been told, to ascertain whether perhaps mechanical failure was to blame. And to add insult to injury, the Director General had completely ignored the opinion of her Board of Enquiry that 'It was the responsibility of the Administration to ensure that all official vehicles were properly equipped and in good working order,' and that 'in the case of an accident involving a WHO vehicle, the first duty of the Organization was to ensure that the vehicle in question was in good condition, had been correctly serviced and maintained and was properly equipped'.

They claimed that Dr. Rojas had made an oral report, obviating the need for further enquiry. But no evidence of this was offered, and the Board was forced to conclude that the event had not been thought worthy of recording by the regional office – not even, in my words, 'to preserve the dignity of its staff members'. Aware that the rules-bound Administration would find this concept easy to dismiss, I quoted case law from previous hearings: The ILOAT has held that such a principle of law exists and that it must be taken seriously. It so stated in *Gusten...* (ILOAT Judgement no. 1496), ... wherein an Organization must heed its staff member's dignity and good name and not cause him unnecessary hardship. In the case of Sita Ram vs WHO (ILOAT Judgment no 67) the ILO Tribunal addressed the issue of respect and moral injury, and held that: "Just as it is implicit in every contract of service that the staff member shall be loyal, shall treat his superiors with due respect and shall guard the reputation of the Organization, so it is implicit that the Administration in its treatment of the staff shall have a care for their dignity and reputation and shall not cause them unnecessary personal distress. Often distress and disappointment cannot be avoided, but where it can, it should." (ILOAT Judgement no 67.)

In summary, I concluded, the WHO is abusing its discretion and authority.

The WHO responded by stating that an investigation *had* taken place – that of the judicial authorities, which had led to a decision not to prosecute. In relying on the Namibian authorities the Organization had acted reasonably, it held, since it lacked the means, the expertise and the authority to carry out the kind of investigation called for by my allegations. In the light of the Prosecutor's decision, there was no basis for the Organization to conclude that driver had acted 'negligently and recklessly', possibly with intent to cause the crash, as I claimed. In any case, my request that Mootu be disciplined fell outside the Tribunal's remit.

Regarding Mootu's continued driving duties, they said that pending the inquest, he had been restricted to office-related driving for short distances around Windhoek. In a footnote they added 'This is not to suggest that he had a poor driving record: he did not.' [A strangely obstinate observation, totally overlooking that part of his record that presumably recorded he had caused two deaths.]

In answer to the accusation that their driver might, to this day, be putting passengers at risk, they said, 'It is noted that he has been assigned the duties of logistic officer, which allows him to drive, but only on deliveries within the City of Windhoek.' This position seems defiantly illogical. Firstly, if the man was going to kill people, what difference did it make if they were on the streets of Windhoek? Secondly, they had employed Mootu as a senior driver, therefore a driver was presumably what they needed for their three vehicles. How many deliveries did this small office have? They accepted that he might not be a fit person to do the job, despite being unwilling to test the hypothesis in court, and despite, presumably, great inconvenience. Why?

When they continued, 'over three years later, the Namibian authorities informed the Organization that the driver should be prosecuted, no explanation was given for this reversal.' This point was heavily laboured several times, as if to imply that the delay alone made all other argument unnecessary. 'The Director General has not been provided with the information she needs to make a decision regarding whether or not to waive the immunity which Mr. Mootu enjoys as a WHO official. Since she has made no decision, the Complainant's plea against the Organization's alleged refusal to lift immunity is mistaken.'

This claimed ignorance of the facts, again laboured throughout, is ingenuous. Clearly the Director General had all the information she needed. The involvement of Mrs. Watters in getting the case re-opened, plus my oft-repeated account of the events, were well-known to her. And as is clear from every sentence of their response, the case had been gone over with a fine tooth comb.

'The Namibian Government' held an inquest, continued the WHO, 'to determine whether the accident involved reckless or negligent driving. Various affidavits, including one from the complainant, had been provided. And although WHO felt strongly that the demand for them to carry out an investigation ignored the practicalities, they also felt constrained to point out that 'The Complainant's description of the accident does not quite reconcile with the information... the Organization has. For instance, while the Complainant states that Mr. Mootu was driving at excessive speed, that he was told by Mr. Damon to slow down several times and that he ignored these requests, the report filed by him at the time with the Organization made no mention of this. Nor did the Complainant's sworn statement of 28 Feb 1997, in which he said: 'The driver was driving about 120-130km/h, not very fast'.

'Likewise no mention was made... of his conviction that the driver intended to cause the crash, as he now alleges. On the contrary he stated then that the driver tried to control the vehicle.'

'As to the weather and the condition of the road – elements which are in dispute – a police report at the time mentioned that it was raining and the road was very wet.'

WHO concluded: 'While the Organization understands the complainant's distress... his argument that the accident and its cause is an internal affair which must be investigated by WHO ignores the practical limitations.'

This seemed to me patronising and willfully dense, since I had stated repeatedly beforehand, and specifically under paragraph 49 of this appeal: 'At no point had the Complainant requested that the WHO conduct a criminal investigation. Rather, it asked the Administration to carry out an internal or administrative one. Considering the severity of the accident, this was hardly an extraordinary demand.'

As to my dignity, the Organization was dismissive, if not scornful. 'Turning now to the Complainant's request for... disciplinary action against Mootu "in order to maintain his dignity", WHO notes...that the judgements cited by the Complainant on protection of staff members' dignity were issued in circumstances which bear no resemblance to the case at hand.'

Lastly, regarding seat belts, the Organization noted the allegation that except for the driver's seat, the vehicle was not equipped with seat belts, despite the fact that Greg Watters had written to personnel alerting them the absence of safety belts in the WHO field vehicles, which he had written in response to a circular instruction from personnel, warning staff that they would not be covered by the accident insurance for travel inside a WHO vehicle if they were not wearing a safety belt at the time of the accident. 'The Organization is not aware of [such] a communication having been received from Dr. Watters,' they announced. 'At the same time it underscores that since 1995 all WHO vehicles have been purchased with seat belts.' This was no guarantee. I thought, since safety belts get stolen or removed, and their re-instalment required constant vigilance by the Administrators at the field level. 'Finally WHO notes that in many countries, like Namibia, seat belts were not required for passengers. However close attention has been and continues to be given by WHO to the matter.'

But Mrs. Watters remembered well Gregor's response to a relevant staff circular about damages not being covered by their insurers in the event that passengers involved in a WHO-car-accident were not strapped in. Strangely or predictably, when Mrs. Watters asked Greg's Watters secretary to trace this memo for them, it had disappeared without trace.

Rejoinder

Given my chance to rebut these arguments, I retorted that the judicial investigation held in Namibia was flawed and incomplete. As to my sworn affidavit, it had been dictated hurriedly just two hours before my flight, and only after repeated requests to speak to the police. I had told the Administrator and the WHO Representative that the cause of the crash was the abrupt turning of the steering wheel, and that I suspected foul play. I repeated this to the Permanent Secretary of the Ministry of Health and the UNDP representative when they visited me in hospital. They agreed the matter should be investigated.

For the first time in an official document, I now mentioned the other things I found suspicious: the unnecessary field trips; the strange behaviour of the Administrator; the hour's delay for our appointment with the Minister of Health; the assigning of an old, ill-equipped vehicle when later models were available.

'After the accident WHO lobbied to close the case and when the Namibian Government decided to prosecute, the Organization appointed an attorney to protect the driver. Surely these facts warrant further investigation? Surely if nothing was irregular the WHO would have lifted Niklaas Mootu's immunity to allow the authorities to proceed?' I demanded.

My language became more heated in my frustration and impotence. 'Why would someone allow a person who had just caused a wreck that claimed the lives of two people, to continue driving? If the driver's actions weren't outrageous and potentially criminal, the Organization's were.'

'The Organization seems to think that because the Namibian authorities decided not to prosecute, that the driver's actions were not negligent or that it had no reason to think so,' I said. 'One reason the government took so long to reopen the case was because I was hospitalised for one year, unaware of what had happened in my absence. Then Mrs. Watters and I began pursuing the case with the Public Prosecutor, at which point the Government realised conflicting information had been given, and took steps to prosecute the driver. They subpoenaed [me] and would have prosecuted if the WHO had not intervened. 'As for my omission of key facts in my original reports, I retorted: ' Probably there were a number of issues that were not mentioned in the report, either because they were forgotten amid the upset of the accident or only recalled later.'

'The Organization selectively cites a sworn statement... to show that there is a discrepancy between [my] rendition of the facts and that of the Organization,' I went on. 'If this is so, a full and fair investigation must be conducted in order to rationalise such discrepancies. However, a closer reading of the same report reveals that there was something amiss with the way Mr. Mootu was driving.' And I quoted: 'He was unable to control the car since it was accelerating at high speed.' And, further on, 'The cause of the accident was the sudden turning of the steering wheel.'

There was also the evidence, I reminded the Tribunal, of the photos and of sketches showing the route taken by the Landcruiser as it somersaulted into the air and crashed so violently that it rolled over seven times, covering 30 meters. This indicates the high speed at which it was travelling, also suggested by its condition afterwards. 'Such evidence cannot be ignored and must be brought to light in court,' I said.

In explaining my silence about my suspicions at the time, I recalled the terror I'd felt while recuperating in Windhoek. '[My] primary concern... was staying alive,' I reported. Perhaps, as one who'd lived through the Red Terror, the threat seemed more real to me, whereas to WHO it probably sounded melodramatic. It was only when I'd had time to think more calmly, I explained, that aspects of the crash began to strike me as strange.

As for WHO's comments about seat belts: 'Regardless of whether WHO vehicles have been purchased with seat belts since 1995... apart from the drivers seat there were no belts in the car. The WHO also points out that seat belts were not required for passengers in Namibia at that time. But all cars must be equipped with them regardless of whether or not passengers are required to wear them. The WHO has an obligation to make sure its vehicles are properly equipped.' As to the case law, I'd quoted it to make the point that an international Organization should not act in any way that would offend or harm a staff member's dignity. 'Indeed', I wrote scornfully, 'the Complainant would be hard-pressed to find a case similar to his where a WHO staff member caused the deaths and injuries of other staff members and failed to be investigated or disciplined.'

Either these forms were deliberately destroyed or the WHO had been caught out in a blatant lie.

Surrejoinder

The World Health Organization was given the last word, although it is clear from their 'Surrejoinder', which contained another eight annexures, that many more words could have, and would have been said, but for this cumbersome process of having to write everything down. Major issues were now being discussed for the first time. Had the key players been cross-examined, my weighty accusations and the WHO's evasions could perhaps have been settled more satisfactorily.

The first four paragraphs of the surrejoinder reiterated the official view, already stated. The following 22 paragraphs deal with the immunity issue.

The Organization repeated its contention that it had acted reasonably in relying on the Namibian judiciary's conclusion, without making any of its own concerning the deaths of these two valuable men. They ignored those of my claims to which they had no answer, but took up the following: (i) That the investigation was insufficient and flawed; ii) that WHO had lobbied to close the case and iii) that the re-opening of the case proved that there was something amiss in the circumstances surrounding it.

To (i) they said that the evidence included photographs and sketches taken at the scene, confirming that an investigation did take place, the thoroughness and reliability of which the Organization had no reason to question.

To (ii) they replied: 'WHO did not lobby to close the case, as the Complainant speculates without offering a shred of evidence. It awaited the outcome of the investigation.'

And to (iii): 'The Complainant maintains that the decision was reversed *three and a half years later* (their italics) because he and Mrs. Watters 'started pursuing the case with the Public Prosecutor, at which point the Government realised there had been conflicting reports'. To what reports he refers is unclear, but the Organization notes, in any event, that neither his affidavit nor the report he sent to the Organization made any mention of reckless driving, let alone intent to cause the crash. Neither did he make any mention of foul play or excessive speed. On the contrary, he said the car was going 'not very fast'.

The Organization noted that considerable time had elapsed before I became involved with the public prosecutor. Even more elapsed before I formally raised the issue of investigation within the Organization. They said that it was not until late 1999 (over two and a half years later) that I formally requested an investigation in a letter to the Director General.

'If he had reason to believe that the driver had acted in a manner which he now describes, he had ample opportunity to raise the issue earlier.'

'WHO notes for instance that the Complainant sent a long letter dated 15 Sept 1998 to his Regional Director in which he describes the accident without ever mentioning 'foul play'. In any event the Namibian authorities' belated decision to prosecute doesn't alter the fact that they decided not to prosecute [in the first place]. Nor does it alter the Organization's view that it acted reasonably.'

WHO claimed there were discrepancies in my testimony, such as: 'allegations that do not reconcile with the information WHO has, or even with the Complainant's own statements made elsewhere. Specifically, the unnecessary field trips, and the delay of the mission by an hour.'

'In his letter to the Director General of 29 Sept 1999 the Complainant made no mention of unnecessary field trips or any delay in the mission. On the contrary he gave details of his involvement in planning the mission, and explained that the driver reported on time to pick them up from the hotel.' Here, clearly, was one of those misunderstandings which, in a courtroom situation, would have been cleared up instantly, since the delay had occurred the day before. As to the quality of the vehicle, the Organization said that the mission was assigned one of two official vehicles normally used and 'considered suitable'. 'The Organization strongly denies the allegation that [Mr. Zawide] was "treated abominably", claiming it had shown concern throughout. It quoted a letter from Aster Gashaw, now married and going by the surname Beza.:

'Dr. Rojas, who was in close contact with AFRO, HQ, and the physician, assisted Mr. Zawide both professionally and personally from the date of the accident until his departure to the States. He managed to get Professor Oosthuizen, the best reputable physician in the country, who attended him regularly and who went out of his way to accelerate his evacuation to the US based on Dr. Rojas' personal concern. Dr. Rojas visited Mr. Zawide at least three times a day including weekends and out of office hours. He also telephoned him regularly while in the States.'

A footnote adds that Mrs. Gashaw Beza denies various allegations made by Zawide, in particular that he mentioned foul play to her. She says she didn't even know about the all-important meeting with the Minister of Health. (How could she expect anyone to believe this when, in her own words, her duty as Administrator was 'to contribute to the success of the mission by providing logistical and administrative support'?)

Aster's full statement was reproduced in annexure 2, and contains one hugely significant statement to which the WHO, unsurprisingly, did not draw attention. She stated unequivocally: 'Immediately after the traffic accident, which was a shocking experience for all of us, the *necessary WHO forms were completed and sent to Afro HQ*. I remember Mr. Zawide mentioning that the driver was not driving carefully.... I advised him to report to Dr. Rojas.' This confirms that I told Aster about the driver's reckless behaviour, and that he caused the accident. It also infers that Dr. Rojas was given the same account. Strange that he kept silent! Strange that these 'necessary WHO forms' never surfaced at the Board of Enquiry!

Either they were deliberately destroyed or the WHO had been caught out in a blatant lie. Such was the inadequacy of the Tribunal, however, that I was never given the opportunity to question the statement.

CHAPTER TWENTY–TWO

NOTHING LESS THAN DESPICABLE

*I*mmense difficulties in achieving good staff relations face any Organization *that spans the world, considering how easily misunderstandings occur, even when people share the same language and culture. Disputes often arise between staff of different nationalities. Conspiracies to eliminate those who do not suit supervisors, Regional Directors or even Director Generals are common, and often badly handled or not handled at all; individuals then suffer acute distress, to the extent of committing suicide or becoming a mental case.*

It could be argued that staff management must perforce be a low priority for Organizations such as WHO, under constant pressure to lower their budget. Within these constraints staff are expected to contain disastrous new diseases such as SARS at the drop of a hat, end killer plagues such as AIDS and cure all other ills mankind is heir to. WHO staff are held in such high esteem that few people seem to realise that they need enormous support, even more than most. Good staff management demands time and effort, but it's been shown to pay huge dividends in the corporate and all other worlds. Why not at WHO? It would make their work – and their budget – infinitely more effective.

My case illustrates how quickly people become de-motivated when channels of communication are poor, when there is a good grievance procedure which is ignored, and when staff are angry. When, in my 1999 letter to the Director General I'd said 'Dying and suffering in the service of humanity is an honour to WHO staff,' I had been quite sincere, believing that this spirit of dedication imbued the entire Organization. Now, despite the generous medical care I'd been given, and the many individuals who'd been kind, I was contemptuous of the Organization's leadership. I noted the bureaucrats' insistence that, far from treating me with disdain, I had been given what most Organizations would consider generous treatment, including my (paid) flight to America with my sister-in law, when it would have been cheaper to send me to London, alone; arranging for an ambulance to take us straight to Johns Hopkins; paying me in full during my long absence from duty. And finally relocating me to Geneva, where I received a good 'per diem' allowance on top of my salary, and where many people were kind to me while I reoriented myself.

However, seen through the eyes of a man who'd experienced a horrific and totally uncalled-for crash; who'd lost a close friend and narrowly escaped death himself, at the hands of that same Administration; and then received nothing by way of official explanation or apology, it all looked very different. Perhaps I could be forgiven for, at times, believing that everything that happened was part of a sinister plot. Even to this day I cannot be sure that it was not.

We haven't finished yet with the ILOAT hearing! The following excerpts relate to the section on my treatment after the crash, as WHO had attempted to show that I was most unreasonable to complain. My rejoinder stated:

'The Organization attempts to exhibit its magnanimity and self-sacrifice by stating that it dispatched a doctor to the scene. It was proper for the WHO representative to come to the scene of this one considering it involved WHO staff members on a WHO mission. That the doctor visited the Complainant in hospital the same day cannot be considered some unprecedented act of good will – rather part of the ordinary course of his work.

Prudence rather than humanitarianism was exercised.

Unless there is a practice of allowing people who can't walk due to broken pelvises to rent their own taxi cabs, the Complainant is not struck by the Administration's bequest of an ambulance.

Considering [my] injuries were sustained during a work assignment and but for the accident, I would never have incurred the medical and travel costs, the endorsement of compensation should not be portrayed, as the Administration attempted to do, as an act of benevolence.

The Administration points out how generous it was in allowing the Complainant to work in Geneva with *'per diem'* remuneration, but my services were actually important and useful, as proven by the fact that the Executive Director of EOS invited me to stay in Geneva until the end of 1998.'

And so on. All this was a preamble to the saga of the delayed medical board, which the WHO, in some exasperation, insisted had been dealt with and should be dismissed. In deciding to pay me compensation the Director General took into account that the time taken to convene the board may have added to my distress, even if it was due to circumstances beyond the Organization's control. That part enraged me, knowing that they hadn't actually tried to reach Dr. Michelson – they waited a year after he had agreed to sit on the board.

The WHO's inexplicable animosity toward the Complainant was further evidenced by its failure to officially inform me that the Board had been empanelled, or tell me of its findings afterwards. And 'the fact that it didn't inform me of its decision until a full 15 months after it had met, only exacerbates the issue. I still hadn't been provided with a copy of the full report of the medical board, I'd requested. And I had declined to accept the nine percent compensation until the cause of the accident had been investigated.

In their final rejoinder, WHO were at pains to describe the considerable 'good-faith' efforts they had gone with regard to the Board of Appeal, supplying copies of memos and letters. 'The delay did not reflect lack of willingness on the Organization's part, they assured the Tribunal. The compensation of nine percent was above and beyond the US$ 35,000 Dr. Brundtland had conferred to make up for the delay. They felt I had no cause for complaint.

The Immunity Issue

Readers of the above may find themselves in sympathy with both sides of the dispute at times. However, the real issue was the immunity question, and when answering those charges, the administration's tone subtly changed to one of lofty boredom, as if this was really beneath them to explain again. They devoted many paragraphs to it, spelling out their position as if to a child. There was an element of boxing with shadows, things being insinuated without being spelled out, and 'difficult' issues, such as the purpose of immunity, being evaded altogether.

I batted first, claiming that the refusal of the Administration to let the driver have his day in court amounted to an abuse of discretionary power. I described the cat and mouse game played out in serving Mootu with a summons, with the apparent complicity of the WHO's Namibian office. I reminded the Tribunal of the HBA's common-sense observation that immunity was never intended to protect staff who'd committed criminal offences. 'Surely it cannot be the goal of the WHO to harbour possible criminals?'

WHO stuck to the oft-repeated position that the Namibian Government owed them an explanation for deciding to prosecute after all, which had apparently paralysed the normally decisive Director General. 'Since she has made no decision, the complainant's plea against the Organization's alleged refusal to lift Mr. Mootu's immunity is mistaken.'

'In any event,' they continued, 'decisions regarding a staff member's immunity are Organizational matters which fall outside the scope of actions or decisions that a staff member may appeal under the staff rules. Therefore, the request for an order that WHO waive his immunity is irreceivable for this reason alone. (This strange word 'irreceivable' seems to be one the WHO is particularly fond of.) For the umpteenth time, they dwelt on the long gap before Namibian judiciary had changed its mind. Then, conveniently ignoring the substance of my plea, they trotted out the legal position. 'As a WHO official Mr. Mootu was immune from legal process for any and all acts performed by him in his official capacity unless an express decision had been taken by the Director General to waive his immunity. This arises from Section 19 of the *Convention on Privileges and Immunities of the Specialised Agencies, which Namibia has agreed should include WHO and its officials by reason of Article V of the Basic Agreement for the Establishment of Technical Advisory Cooperation Relations* concluded between Namibia and the Organization on 12 April 1990.'

'Accordingly, a delivery of a summons to Mr. Mootu required a prior request for a waiver of his immunity. Since no such request had been received, let alone agreed to, the delivery of a summons was in breach of the Namibian Government's undertakings. The Organization therefore was constrained to insist on the immunity of its staff member... and to seek the assistance of the Ministry of Foreign Affairs of Namibia in ensuring that the Court be made aware of Mr. Mootu's immunity.'

'By official communication of 7 October 1999 the Organization informed the Ministry of Foreign Affairs of Namibia accordingly. At the same time, it underscored that its request for assistance in ensuring observance of Mr. Mootu's immunity was without prejudice to whatever decision the Director General might make in the event that a formal request for waiver of immunity were received. WHO added that in the event of a formal request, it would wish to receive such documentation as was available concerning the findings on which the accusation of culpable homicide was based. The next day the Ministry expressed its regret and informed the Organization that it had advised the Court to adhere to the established channels. Over a year later on 13 November the Ministry informed the Organization that, following consultations, it had been concluded that Mootu should be prosecuted. The Organization understood this communication as a request for waiver. However before being in a position to agree to it, the Organization had to be satisfied that the request was prompted by no consideration other than pursuit of justice. It would be improper for instance, for a prosecution to be pursued for political or extra-judicial reasons. Ensuring that a prosecution is properly motivated is a matter which the Organization has a duty to scrupulously verify. WHO notes as well that proper adherence to the concept of privileges and immunities of international civil servants and the modalities for seeking and considering their waiver has implications for the UN system as a whole.'

'In this case no explanation had been provided to WHO for the Namibian authorities' reversal of decision more than three years after WHO had been informed of their decision not to prosecute the driver. First in June 1997, WHO is informed that Mr. Mootu will not be prosecuted. Then in November 2000 it is informed that he will be prosecuted.' [Just in case the Tribunal hadn't got that!] 'The unexplained reversal was of course a cause for concern... aggravated by the absence of accompanying documentation as had been requested from the Namibian Government earlier, in the event that a request for waiver of immunity were made.'

'Taking the above into consideration, the Organization reiterated the request that it be provided by the Government with such documentation as may be available concerning the findings on which the accusation of culpable homicide was based. At the same time it made it clear that without delay upon receipt of such documentation the Director General would be in a position to advise the Ministry of her decision.'

'To this date the Organization has not received documentation from the Ministry, even though, by official communication of 11 Sept 2001, WHO reiterated that upon receipt of the documentation requested, the Director General would be in a position to advise the Ministry without delay of the Director General's decision. This being the case, continuation of the proceedings was in breach of the aforementioned convention which the Namibian Government had expressly undertaken to apply vis à vis WHO and its staff. Consequently – and without any prejudice to the substance of the case – the Organization has been compelled to assert its staff member's jurisdictional immunity. The issue is under consideration by the Namibian courts.'

There is much more of this in the same vein. While it is all no doubt legally accurate, it seemed to me ponderous, pompous and self-righteous. Surely a phone call or two would have sufficed to make clear what was required, had they really been willing to cooperate? Did WHO care more about observing the correct protocol than about getting at the truth?

In my rejoinder, I drew attention to an obscure footnote to Section 19 of Article V of the *Convention on Privileges and Immunities of the Specialised Agencies*, which seemed to imply that this agreement did not apply to Niklaas Mootu. It read: 'with the exception of those who are recruited locally and are assigned to hourly rates. To best of my knowledge, Mr. Mootu was both recruited locally and paid an hourly rate. I also pointed out that there was nothing in the document to indicate that entities seeking to have immunity lifted were required to provide certain information.

The WHO's insinuation that this was 'the pursuit of prosecution for political or extra-judicial reasons' puzzled me; I pointed out that. 'There was nothing to indicate that the Namibian Government's decision to prosecute was irregular. In the absence of any evidence to the contrary, immunity should have been granted immediately.' I asked the Tribunal to consider whether WHO was not attempting to use immunity to veil unethical practices. There is often hostility among staff due to differences in political opinion, culture, ethnic origin, language, gender etc. Personal prejudices and jealousies regularly lead to non-renewal of contracts, poor performance evaluation reports and failure to rise in the hierarchy. It is not impossible that staff hostility could manifest in acts of revenge.'

'As to the Organization's statement that lifting immunity "has implications for the UN system as a whole" I can only reiterate the conclusion of the HBA that even if Mr. Mootu is protected by diplomatic immunity, its purpose is to facilitate the work of the Organization, not to create barriers to the pursuit of justice.'

In their final rejoinder, the WHO had very little new to add, other than to say that Mootu was *not* paid at an hourly rate, so the *Convention* did apply to him. They insisted that their stance did not demonstrate bad faith, nor was it an attempt to hide anything. 'The Organization acted responsibly throughout' was their lofty conclusion.

The Reassignment Debate

The Director General was mistaken when she said that my new job in Cape Town cancelled out the gripe about my two years in Harare. I'd been forced to travel to the United States for treatment several times at my own expense because of the inadequate medical facilities, and I considered the abrupt transfer had been cooked up as a way of evading blame. This time it was the WHO who retorted 'Nonsense!', only in more diplomatic terms. They'd seen no necessity to transfer me, they said, because everything I needed was in Harare, as the Director of JMS had informed me. I was not in imminent need of surgery, and if an emergency had arisen, I could easily have been evacuated. (Tacit acknowledgement of inadequacy!)

WHO said that a comprehensive review of the facilities had been made in 1999 by Dr. Celton, to establish their suitability for making the city a referral centre for medical evacuations of all UN regional staff. He had visited hospitals, clinics, emergency rooms etc. and had concluded that excellent private physicians could provide most diagnostic and therapeutic procedures. Harare did, in fact, subsequently become the regional referral centre.

I wholeheartedly disagreed – as did many experts, including some in the WHO itself. I quoted the *Wall Street Journal:* "The main hospital in Harare, once one of the best in Africa, is now regarded as little more than a death trap." And the *Financial Gazette*, writing about a trust established to rescue Zimbabwean hospitals, had said they lacked everything from money to basic equipment such as latex gloves and blood pressure kits. 'Zimbabwe's health system has recently been ranked last out of 191 countries in a study by WHO to determine their ability to turn expenditure into health,' it reported. True enough, the World Health Report 2000 lists Zimbabwe in the lower echelon of all categories. 'It is therefore curious that the WHO can argue that the healthcare facilities in Zimbabwe come close to even the most rudimentary level of health care, let alone being adequate to assist the Complainant with his complicated injuries and recovery,' I commented, continuing, 'No thought whatsoever seems to have been given by the WHO to coming up with a solution to more closely match the Complainant's interests, despite my age, work experience and seniority. This constituted an abuse of discretion by the WHO Administration, which adds to the evidence of prejudice. The Tribunal is asked to recognise this.'

WHO responded that in compiling their World Health Report, they'd had countries, not individuals, in mind. The ranking was based on factors such as the population's life expectancy, how health care was funded, planned and stewarded etc. As a WHO staff member, I'd had access to the top quality physicians available in Harare, all paid for by WHO. If I chose to fly to America for treatment, that was my choice – it wasn't necessary. I begged to differ.

Reassignment to Cape Town

Accusations about the handling of my reassignment were also strongly rebutted. The transfer had never been discussed with me, I pointed out, violating the principle that the Administration should consult with its staff first, and give them proper notice. I described the Administrative confusion that arose because the post had not been established; there was no memo of understanding about it between the WHO and South Africa's Medical Research Council, and no funding for the project. AFRO had not applied to the South African Government for accreditation of the post. I had written several letters asking the Administration to clear up the problems, but for three months they did not communicate with me at all. To this day no funding had been received. Their treatment throughout the transfer was nothing less than despicable,' I said.

WHO, however, said 'this claim is surprising', and painted a very different picture. Despite their view that since my claims were not part of my HBA appeal, they were not receivable, they said, they were responding because the claims were incorrect,. 'The Complainant was transferred to Cape Town for programmatic reasons in the context of a restructuring of which all AFRO staff had been informed in March 2000. When the new Organization was approved that October, he had sent a memo giving his comments. His transfer to the WHO Collaborating Centre for Urban Health had been discussed with its head, Professor John Seager, in October 2000. He had been formally told of the decision in a letter dated 29 January. All his queries had been answered promptly.

In short, he had been treated with the utmost dignity! In support of this claim the WHO quoted my second-level supervisor, the Director, Division of Healthy Environments in Sustainable Development (DES), who said: 'When Mr. Zawide was formally informed of his reassignment he appeared very happy. During the weekly meeting of the staff of the Division, he gave two main reasons for being happy. One was the opportunity to work with highly competent people and two, because the health facilities in Cape Town are better than in Harare, according to him.'

'Mr. Zawide made a pre-visit to the MRC. We had a briefing session after he returned to Harare. I went myself to Cape Town in July

2001 and met Dr. John Seager to discuss the practical modalities of Mr. Zawide's position. We are now in close relationship with the MRC for common areas of work. The equipment Mr. Zawide requested was provided. The sticker-number for the funds planned for the research activities and publication of bulletins in 2002 was already transmitted. We received a few weeks ago from Mr. Zawide some leaflets for distribution to countries, this is done. We are requesting a staff member from MRC to help us.'

'We all in AFRO gave and continue to give a lot of consideration and respect to Mr. Zawide.'

I responded that I'd been upset by the insulting way in which the transfer was carried out. A terse three-line memorandum had informed me that I was to be transferred and that a detailed letter would follow. I only received this three months later, after I had been forced to go home on leave because none of the documentation regarding my post had been completed. Even then I lacked funding, and I kept sending reminders about this. In the meantime, I was forced to use funds from the host institution, on the understanding that AFRO would reimburse them. This treatment was not only 'horrendous', it was incompetent, I said.

About the reminders over funds, WHO commented: 'My supervisor in AFRO found no trace of having received the Complainant's correspondence, despite a daily recording procedure for incoming mail. In any event as soon as it was possible to do so, taking into account internal requirements for the disbursement of funds, the amount of US$50,000 was transferred. In the meantime, there had been discussions about funding between the directors of the two establishments, and there was no problem in advancing the money, knowing that these things took time, and that it would be reimbursed by AFRO.'

The final rejoinder ends, 'The Organization requests the dismissal of the Complaint in its entirety, and of all claims requested.'

Now it was down to the Tribunal.

CHAPTER TWENTY-THREE

INCOMPREHENSIBLE!

*T*he fact that the Namibian authorities opened their own enquiry *could not in any way exempt the Organization from ascertaining whether the condition of the vehicle, the preparation of the mission and more generally, the circumstances of the accident revealed any administrative failure, the consequences of which it would have a duty to bear...' ILOAT's Judgement number 2190.*

On November 5, 2002, the International Labour Organization Administrative Tribunal made its final judgement, number 2190, in the case of Zawide vs the World Health Organization.

The judges, having examined the written submissions, began with a lengthy summary of the facts, which, you will be relieved to hear, we do not intend to repeat! Among the things I sought in redress were US$250,000 in moral damages, plus costs arising from the proceedings, 'and interest on all amounts claimed'.

Before responding, the Tribunal considered my request for a large number of documents and other items of information to be produced, and for the hearing of witnesses. 'The Tribunal considers that it is not necessary to grant these requests since the file contains all the information it requires to render its judgement,' they loftily pronounced.

'Regarding enquiry into the circumstances of the accident and the Organization's position on the lifting of the driver's immunity from legal process,' they continued, 'to justify the fact that it has not conducted an enquiry into the circumstances and causes of the accident, the Organization states that the Namibian authorities conducted a judicial enquiry and that the public prosecutor decided initially not to prosecute...the Organization asked to be provided with documents enabling it to assess whether the immunity of its employee should be lifted. Having not received the requested documents, the Director General considers that she is still not in a position to take a decision on lifting the driver's immunity.'

'The Tribunal accepts the defendant's position on the issue of lifting the immunity... that the employee does belong to the category of staff members who have immunity, and the Organization has a discretion to assess, in the context of its relations with a Member State, which are beyond the jurisdiction of the Tribunal, whether it is appropriate to lift the immunity from legal process of its employees. (See in this respect judgements 933 and 1543.) Similarly, the Tribunal can only reject the claims concerning disciplinary proceedings against the driver, since such proceedings are likewise at the discretion of the Organization, as stated by the Tribunal in several of its judgements.

Nevertheless, it is *incomprehensible* that no internal administrative investigation was conducted following an accident which involved a WHO vehicle driven by an employee of the Organization in the context of an official mission, and which caused the death of two passengers, one of whom was a WHO staff member, as well as the serious injuries suffered by the complainant. The fact that the Namibian authorities opened their own enquiry *could not in any way exempt the Organization* from ascertaining whether the condition of the vehicle, the preparation of the mission and more generally, the circumstances of the accident revealed any administrative failure, the consequences of which it would have a duty to bear. As noted by the Board of Appeal, there is no evidence to suggest that any internal enquiry whatsoever was conducted in connection with this accident. This failure caused the complainant an injury which the Tribunal considers to be equitably compensated by an award of US $5,000 dollars.'

The belated convening of the medical board

'On this issue the Director General acknowledged that the time taken to convene the medical board may have added to the Complainant's distress, and she took this into account in determining the sum of US$35,000 granted to him. Thus, contrary to the Complainant's assertions, all measures were taken to inform him of the convening of the medical board and of the follow-up to it. Whilst the delay...though not entirely attributable to the Organization, remains difficult to explain, there is no evidence that the Organization showed bad faith or reluctance, and the award of compensation granted...in the impugned decision ought to have put an end to any criticism by him on this issue. The Organization cannot be considered to have failed to notify the Complainant in due time of the decisions taken on the basis of the medical board's recommendations.'

The Complainant's successive assignments

'Regarding Harare...the evidence on files shows that the medical facilities of that city afforded the Complainant suitable medical care; that he could have been evacuated in the event of an emergency; and that the surgeon treating him in the US had simply recommended that his duty stations be confined to regions where satisfactory 'sophisticated medical support systems' are available, which did not exclude Harare. No abuse of procedure has been established and there is no evidence to suggest that the Complainant's return to Harare, which was decided on after consultation with the head of the Joint Medical Services, caused any deterioration of his condition or any injury warranting compensation beyond that which was awarded to him in the impugned decision. The same applies to his transfer to Cape Town.

'The Complainant's claim that the Tribunal should order the Organization to undertake disciplinary investigations into the actions of the Director of the Joint Medical Service [in point of fact, the man in question was the Director of Human Resources] who allegedly refused to appear before the HQ Board of Appeal, and of the staff member who allegedly entered a 'frivolous and dilatory' plea of irrecevability before the board, clearly cannot be allowed by the Tribunal, which has not jurisdiction to issue injunctions against international Organizations, let alone to cast judgement on the means of defense used on behalf of such Organizations in the context of internal appeal proceedings of litigation.

'Consequently, the Tribunal only partially allows the Complainant's claims and awards him compensation of US$ 5000 for the reasons stated.... The arguments put forward in support of his claim for interest are rejected, given that for the most part, the sums which the Organization has agreed to pay...have already been paid or have been offered under proposals which the Complainant was unwilling to accept at the time. Similarly, there is no need to reconsider the evaluation of expenses incurred before the Board of Appeal nor the reimbursement of any other expenses since the sums awarded in the impugned decision must be considered as compensation for all losses claimed by the Complainant.

'He is entitled to an award of costs, which is set at US$ 2000.'

Decision

For the above reasons

1. The WHO shall pay the Complainant in addition to the compensation it has agreed to pay him, the sum of 5,000 United States dollars.

2. It shall pay US 2,000 dollars in costs.

3. The Complainant's remaining claims are dismissed.

In witness of this document... Mr. Michel Gentot, President of the Tribunal, Mr. Seydou Ba, judge, and Mr. James K Hugessen, Judge, sign below, as do I, Catherine Comtet, Registrar.

Delivered in public in Geneva on 3 February 2003.

So, what I referred to as 'my terrible experience with the WHO' was over. I had no-one else to turn to. And while I was pleased to have it acknowledged by this high authority that the WHO's actions had indeed been 'inconceivable', I still felt deeply that justice had not been served. This had been my final recourse in terms of trying to get my case heard, and it had proved a woefully inadequate way to try to get to the bottom of what, for all anyone knew, was almost an assassination. In terms of human rights, the limits of the Tribunal were narrow indeed.

It was of little consolation to me to know that I was in the minority in getting any satisfaction whatsoever out of the UN's alternative system of justice. Only 29 per cent of those who, deprived of the fundamental right to protect themselves in a national court of law, take this route, get a judgement even partially in their favour. 'The Tribunal is less an unbiased forum and more a rubber stamp for the international Organizations that subscribe to it,' is the view of lawyer Edward Flaherty.

That the system is seriously flawed was confirmed recently by an eminent British legal expert, Geoffrey Robertson Q.C., who was asked by the ILO Staff Union to advise them as to whether the ILOAT conforms to international human rights law. He found it did not. 'In principle,' he wrote, 'a tribunal of this potency and importance must operate, and be seen to operate, to the highest standards of transparency and fair play. In particular, it must exhibit basic judicial guarantees of independence and impartiality and afford to complainants fair and public hearings consistent with the concepts of natural justice (or 'due process') under domestic legal systems. These principles are fundamental and universal. International civil servants, deprived of the access to domestic employment law guaranteed to other workers, must in lieu be afforded comparable rights by ILOAT if unjust discrimination is to be avoided. The international Organizations which patronise ILOAT are all committed, in one way or another, to uphold international law, which includes...human rights. *It would be indefensible hypocrisy to deny their own employees the protections required by that law.* The mission of the ILO is to ensure respect for the basic rights of workers, including the right to a fair system of adjudicating disputes with employees. It behoves the Organization to ensure that its system of adjudicating disputes with its own workers is beyond reproach. The ILOAT statute and rules have undergone few changes since 1946. It is only to be expected that any thorough contemporary analysis will suggest a number of improvements.

There are two fundamental ways in which ILOAT fails to conform to the requirements for a judicial body, and in certain other respects it denies to complainants rights that are becoming recognised as essential to due process. This finding – that it lacks the necessary qualities of independence and transparency – does not mean that its decisions have necessarily been biased in favour of employers. What can be said is that the deficiencies in compliance with human rights standards have produced a *perception* of injustice, and have denied to unsuccessful complainants a proper opportunity to press their case to a more satisfactory conclusion. These consequences are serious enough to require urgent rectification.

The Tribunal statute has this basic defect: Article III (2) provides that the seven judges 'shall be appointed for a period of three years by the Conference of the ILO' – and there is no prohibition on re-appointment for further three-year terms. For example, the current President was appointed in 1992, and obtained further three-year appointments in 1995, 1998 and 2001. *In other words, the Tribunal members are 'contract judges', whose well-remunerated employment is contingent upon the regular approval of the very body which is a defending party to their proceedings.* * This position is plainly incompatible with the rule that requires the judiciary to be independent, and which is breached by any arrangement which offers an inducement to the judges to decide cases in ways which will not upset the re-appointing body. There are many decisions of national and international courts to the effect that, in principle, judges on two or three year renewable contracts lack the essential requirement of independence, because they do not have security of tenure.

To secure independence and impartiality, judges should be appointed for one term only, perhaps of five or seven years. Moreover, since the statute is surprisingly silent about their qualifications and contains no provision permitting their dismissal for incapacity, these *lacunae* should be filled, by provisions which *inter alia* require them to be lawyers of distinction in the employment field (with some experience in human rights), appointed before the age of sixty-five, and subject to regular health checks. Best practice would indicate that they should be appointed, not by the international labour conference itself but by an independent appointments commission. *Until these changes are affected, ILOAT will not fully satisfy the requirement of an independent and impartial tribunal.*

The other fundamental defect – its failure to provide a fair and public hearing – arises from ILOAT's regular practice, rather than from its statute. Article V provides: 'The Tribunal shall decide in each case whether the oral proceedings before it or any part of them shall be public or in camera.'

This statute plainly and properly presumes that there *will* be oral proceedings, and requires the Tribunal to decide whether circumstances (for example, considerations of protecting personal privacy or national security) may require any part of them to be held behind closed doors. Moreover, the ILOAT Rules ... provide by Article 12 that parties applying for hearings should indicate the issues and the witnesses; that they may make oral submissions and call evidence; that the Tribunal shall determine the conduct of hearing; and that witnesses and experts shall take a form of solemn declaration before giving evidence. *In other words, the Statute and Rules contemplate in the clearest terms that there shall be full and fair adversary hearings, if these are requested by either party.* There is no express power for the Tribunal to refuse a hearing (other, of course, than under Article 7 of the Rules, which provides for summary dismissal of frivolous or irreceivable complaints). If the Tribunal were to take the step of refusing an application for a hearing, under what might possibly be attributed to an inherent power, it would have to provide very good reasons.

I was astonished to be informed that ILOAT routinely and invariably denies all applications for oral hearings, since such a practice would contravene its Statute and Rules. But I have examined its recent decisions, and have found no case in which a hearing application has been granted. Instead, in the Preamble to every judgement in cases where such application has been made, there is the routine recital:

Having examined the matter under submission and decided not to allow the complainants' application for hearings.

By this formula, it appears on the face of these judgements; the Tribunal invariably decides that it shall not afford oral hearings. I am told that *between 1995 and 2001, oral hearings were requested in over two hundred cases, and refused in every instance.* This practice in effect renders otiose Article V of the Statute and Article 12 of its Rules. It is not, in my view, a practice that is permitted by the Statute: *it is ultra vires* and unlawful.

That said, it has undoubtedly had serious consequences for complainants who have been deprived of their presumptive rights of oral challenge to the written case prevented by the employer. The adversary system presupposes that oral testimony and argument can transform, or critically affect, the judicial approach to both facts and law. It is likely that some of the decisions rendered against employees would instead have been decided in their favour had they enjoyed the right (that the Statute and Rules are designed to afford them) of calling witnesses and experts, and availing themselves of the additional hearing rights referred to in Article 11 of the Rules. The unlawful practice adopted by ILOAT has deprived them both of an oral hearing – obviously vital in itself – and of having that hearing in public, which has additional advantages for justice in that it conduces to honesty on both sides and enables public scrutiny of the fairness of the Tribunal's process.

This is why, of course, all human rights treaties require a 'fair and public hearing' for disputes concerning civil obligations: *a fortiori* they are breached by a Tribunal which offers no hearings at all. There may be cases where the facts are not in dispute and the legal issues can be satisfactorily adumbrated on paper, and there may be cases where the use of personally sensitive data calls for *in camera* measures. But to deprive all complainants of a hearing to which they are presumptively entitled cannot be justified. The very fact that ILOAT has adopted a 'blanket refusal' policy in respect of hearing applications, thereby contravening the spirit of its statute and rules, demonstrates the need for a new written rule which makes pellucidly clear that any party is *entitled* to an oral hearing on request, which may only be refused in limited and defined circumstances and with a reasoned decision that such circumstances exist.

The existence of this (at least arguably) unlawful practice draws attention to another defect in the ILOAT structure: *there is no provision for appeal* (see Article VI: 'judgements shall be final and without appeal'). The necessity for adequate appellate review has been emphasised by the European Court of Human Rights in its case law on Article 6. There are a number of ways in which the requirement could be satisfied without undue expense: for example, first instance hearings could be conducted before one or three judges, whose decision could be appealed on 'judicial review' principles, without any re-hearing of evidence, to a chamber of five or seven judges. There must, at any event, be some avenue of appeal to an independent body.

I have identified in the preceding paragraphs several breaches of fundamental human rights principles in the way ILOAT is constituted and operated. There are other aspects of its structure and operation which do not conform to the best due process practice, such as:

- Lack of 'equality of arms' between employer and complainant, in particular because there is inadequate power to obtain disclosure of the employer's documents;
- The Tribunal's over-strict interpretation of Article II(6) to deny staff associations the right to complain on behalf of members, or to permit 'class' complaints, or even to allow staff associations to file amicus curiae briefs;
- The Tribunal's failure to draw up rules of evidence (consistently with its unlawful refusal to countenance oral hearings).'

To sum up, this eminent lawyer makes it quite clear that the ILOAT, this all-important last port of call for the many international civil servants who fall foul of the U.N. system for one reason or another, is deeply flawed and does not represent justice. But it's a great deal better than nothing. I count myself lucky in that at least part of my complaint was upheld. That one word used to describe the Administration's behaviour, *incomprehensible*, says it all, and has been the universal response from people everywhere to my story. But – and it's a big but – in the final analyses all the ILOAT could do was demand that more money be offered me – and money, as I have said all along, was not my main objective. The system has no teeth to insist that justice not only be done, it be seen to be done. I had no other recourse but to draw attention to the fact that all these bodies are a law unto themselves, and sometimes get away with actions that are totally unacceptable in normal society, by writing this book.

*Emphasis added

CHAPTER TWENTY-FOUR

THE NAMIBIAN FARCE PLAYS OUT

'The attempt to immune a Namibian citizen from the operation of the general laws in the country on account of him being a driver of a UN Organization may be viewed as an abuse of the privileges accorded to such organization by the host country...' Attorney General Pendukeni Ivulu-Ithan in a memorandum to Advocate Heymann and the Ministries of Justice and Foreign Affairs, September 2001.

All this time, a big struggle had been going on between the Namibian Government and WHO to get the case against Mootu into court.

It started in October 1999 following another summons for Mootu. This led to a somewhat strained exchange between WHO's Namibian Office (now headed by Dr. Martin Mandara) and the Ministry of Foreign Affairs, *Information and Broadcasting*.

'The Organization will be grateful to receive such documentation as is available concerning the findings by the appropriate Namibian authorities on which the charge of culpable homicide against Mr. Mootu is based. Upon receipt of such documentation, the Organization will be in a position to advise the Ministry without delay of the Director General's decision regarding its request to waive Mr. Mootu's immunity from national court jurisdiction.'

If ever there was a Catch 22 situation, this was it: the point of putting the driver on the stand was to question him properly and put right the mistake that had been made at the flawed inquest. *Then* there would be documentation. At present all they had was Mootu's appallingly inadequate statement, 'Unfortunately it just overturned' and the two grim death certificates.

So, to the Namibian authorities, the basis of these charges seemed self-explanatory. 'It was obvious he'd been careless or reckless – two people were dead!' Advocate Heyman, the Attorney General said with some exasperation. In December 1999 there was an exchange of letters between Dr. A. Kawana, Permanent Secretary of Namibia's Ministry of Justice, and E.E. Coetzee, a Senior Legal Officer in the Office of the Attorney-General, asking for a legal opinion as to whether Mootu could be arraigned notwithstanding Dr. Brundtland's prevarication. After due deliberation, Coetzee replied: 'The crux of the matter is whether Mr. Niklaas Mootu is covered by immunity from national courts' jurisdiction. Section 18 of Article VI of the Convention on the Privileges and Immunity of the Specialised Agencies 1947 provides :

'Each specialized agency will specify the categories of officials to which the provisions of this article shall apply and of article VIII shall apply. It shall communicate them to the Governments of all States parties to this Convention in respect of that agency, and to the Secretary General of the United Nations. The names of the officials included in these categories shall from time to time be made known to the above-mentioned Governments'.

Section 19 of Article VI of the same Convention provides that:

'Officials of the specialized agencies shall: a) be immune from legal process in respect of words, spoken or written, and all acts performed by them in their official capacity. This presupposed, said Coetzee, that a list of such officials must be sent to the Ministry of Foreign Affairs, and kept by them. This is confirmed by section 4 of the Diplomatic Privileges Act, 1951(Act No. 71 of 1951.), which states:

'The Minister shall cause a register to be kept in which there shall be registered the names of all persons who shall be immune under section 2 or the recognised principles of international law or an agreement contemplated in section 2A....from the civil or criminal jurisdiction of the court of the territory and every such registration shall be cancelled upon the person concerned ceasing to be so immune.'

However, Coetzee noted that in Namibia "The Ministry of Foreign Affairs unfortunately does not keep such a register.'

The only list they had been able to locate was one detailing diplomatic agents – people such as Ambassadors, high commissioners, and representatives of the UN agencies such as WHO, UNDP, and UNESCO. Nothing so lowly as a driver – which, of course, makes the utmost sense. Diplomatic immunity was not designed for drivers.

At this point the legal argument becomes a little difficult to follow, for Coetzee continued somewhat lugubriously. 'Section 10 of the Act provides that the immunities, privileges and exemptions provided for in the Act shall not apply to or be extended to Namibian citizens. Provided if the Government of Namibia has by agreement with a United Nations Organization or institution undertook [sic] to extend any immunities privileges or exemptions to Namibian citizens who are representatives of another Government.'

He continued 'Section 1 of Article V of the Basic Agreement for the Establishment of the Technical Advisory Cooperation Relations concluded between Namibia and the WHO provides that: *"The government, insofar as it is not already bound to do so, shall apply to the Organization, its staff, funds, properties and assets the appropriate provisions of the Convention on the Privileges and Immunities of the Specialized agencies."*

'In my opinion,' Coetzee concluded, 'when immunity is granted to the agency by the host nation, such immunity is not automatically conferred on all the staff of the agency. The agency elects which officials are afforded immunity. In section 1 of article V of the agreement 'staff' is unfortunately not defined. Compare this with the agreement between Namibia and the UNDP, where locally recruited staff are specifically excluded from immunity.'

The logical inference, he said, was that all staff, from the head of the agency to the driver, provided *they are not Namibian nationals*, were entitled to immunity from criminal jurisdiction. 'Mr. Mootu is a Namibian national and, in terms of section 10 of ACT 71 of 1955, is *not* entitled to such immunity.'

'Given the clear provisions of the act in this regard it is immaterial that the word 'staff' is not defined in the WHO agreement, or that the locally recruited staff are not specifically excluded as in the case of the UNDP agreement,' he wrote, finishing with a triumphant flourish,

'Consequently there is no need to apply for waiver of immunity. It follows Mr. Mootu is liable to be prosecuted in terms of our laws.'

The Namibian government therefore decided to call the WHO's bluff and go ahead with a prosecution.

The Attorney General gets tough

Nevertheless, the case languished for another 20 months, until the Namibian Attorney General, who rejoiced in the wonderful name of Pendukeni Ivula-Ithan, lost patience. Her frustration was clearly expressed in a memorandum sent to Advocate Heymann in September 2001, and copied to the Ministries of Justice and Foreign Affairs.

'It is indeed incomprehensible,' she wrote, 'how and why this case has to drag on for so long when an advice was given by my office as far back as December 1999. Further to our advice, it is trite law with universal application that no citizen is above the law of his or her country. For those nationals on whom the law of their countries do not have to apply, a special law to immune them is specifically enacted. This category of nationals is restricted to heads of state and or government. The attempt to immune [sic] a Namibian citizen from the operation of the general laws in the country on account of him being a driver of a UN Organization may be viewed as an abuse of the privileges accorded to such an organization by the host country. By this memo I wish, in my capacity as the Attorney General of this country, under the power vested in me under Article 87 c of the Namibian Constitution, to draw your attention to our advisory opinion of December 20, 1999. Any attempt to ignore such advice is tantamount to subverting the letter and spirit of the Namibian Constitution.'

Subsequent to this defiant statement, Mootu's lawyers were curtly informed, in a letter of 19 October 2001, *'that it is the view of the Attorney General that Niklaas Mootu does not enjoy diplomatic immunity. Furthermore, you are advised that... a warrant for the arrest of Mr. Mootu was issued.'*

So, in November 2001 Mootu faced a criminal trial in Otjiwarongo. Metcalfe and Associates, who represented him (for which lengthy task they were no doubt paid princely sums by the WHO) immediately sought to block the proceedings. Mr. Metcalfe began by stating, that as an employee of the Organization, the driver enjoyed diplomatic immunity notwithstanding the fact that he was a citizen of the Republic of Namibia, in terms of both the Convention and the Act already referred to.

The magistrate, a Mr. Nanhele, then summed up events thus far. He described the many attempts to serve a summons, apparently blocked by staff WHO's Windhoek office concealing Mootu. He outlined the parts of the Constitution and Act quoted by both parties to support their position. A key point, he said, was that WHO had not complied with these documents because they had not submitted a list of staff to the Ministry of Foreign Affairs. '*The accused is not immune from the jurisdiction of the National Court,*' he summed up. 'The matter can proceed before this court. The plea and trial was set for March 6, 2002. Round one to Namibia, it seemed.

At last matters were coming to a head. Mrs. Wattes accompanied by her son, also a lawyer prepared once again to travel to Namibia to testify. Her lawyer, Mr.Angula, wrote: 'The Prosecutor told us that the matter will proceed, even though the lawyer for Mootu has indicated that he will take the point of immunity again.'

But Mrs. Watters was still worried that the case might yet fizzle out. and wrote to Mr. Angula to which he replied, a little ambiguously, that he had spoken to Mr. Metcalfe, Mootu's lawyer, and 'All that WHO wants, which the Namibian Government appears not to have done, is a formal request to WHO to lift the immunity. It appears that there are still discussions between the Office of the Attorney General and WHO over the immunity matter.'

On February 21, 2002, I was subpoenaed to appear at the trial as a State witness. Earlier I had appointed my own Namibian lawyer, a Mr. Aggenbach of Koep & Company, to represent me in the legal process in Namibia. So I made travel plans with a feeling of relief that we were approaching the last fence.

However, yet again we faced disappointment. Two days before my departure I received a fax from the office of the Prosecutor General informing me that yet again, the trial had been postponed. The defence had produced, like a rabbit out of a hat, a key piece of new evidence: a flimsy bit of paper which, they claimed, had been submitted to the

Ministry of Foreign Affairs four months before the accident. It was a list of WHO staff – and there on page 2, was the name Niklaas Mootu.

In case the obdurate Namibians were not convinced, however, Metcalfe rammed home his arguments in a long document entitled 'Objection in Limine – Heads of Argument'. ('*In limine*' comes from the Latin 'on the threshold' and means, in this context, a preliminary objection.) Metcalfe summed up Magistrate Nanhele's response at the previous trial, then said that WHO Administrative assistant Mrs. Irma Naanda would confirm in person that 'the requisite list has been presented to the Ministry of Foreign Affairs annually, and specifically for 1997'. This is strange – what, one wonders, had the Ministry of Foreign Affairs, Information and Broadcasting, done with the list all these years? Could the staff have filed it straight into the waste paper basket? It would seem a disrespectful place to put communiqués from so august a body.

Metcalfe pointed out that even though locally-recruited staff were specifically disallowed diplomatic immunity in the UNDP agreement with Namibia, such exclusion had not been made in the WHO agreement. Article V specifically stated that all WHO staff members 'shall be deemed to be officials within the meaning of the Convention'. The Ministry of Foreign Affairs was obliged by these legalities to recognize Mootu's immunity. The correct procedure would be to formally request a waiver from WHO. 'WHO would not wish,' Metcalfe blandly informed the court, 'to protect its staff and members from prosecution, and where the prosecuting authorities are of the opinion that a prima facie case can be made out against an accused person who enjoys such immunity, such immunity ought to be waived.'

Diplomatic *immunity was not designed for* drivers.

It seemed that the WHO lawyer was worried that the validity of this newly-discovered list might be called into question however, for he continued. 'The Ministry of Foreign Affairs does not comply with its own legislative requirements as per section 4 of the diplomatic Privileges Act 71 of 1951'...He then launched into a lengthy account of a legal precedent.'S v. Penrose 1966 (1) (SA5 (NPD) at 9E-H per Harcourt J.) which dated back to 1962 when Namibia, then called SWA, was under the jurisdiction of South Africa. A lawyer by the name of Didcott defended a Mr. B C Penrose, Colombia's Johannesburg Consul. What crime Penrose was supposed to have committed we are not told: the point was he too had fought not to be prosecuted. Didcott had argued that even if Penrose was not registered in terms of the Act, it did automatically bar him from claiming immunity.' Errors in registration and publication thereof could not rob a person, who was legally entitled to be registered, of the right to immunity', he said. 'The provisions relating to registration and publication were of prime importance only in regard to desirable publicity to enable persons contemplating bringing proceedings readily to avoid the penal sanctions of section 11. An error in publication might well excuse, or at lowest diminish the responsibility of (and therefore the punishment to be imposed upon) someone bringing proceedings against one entitled to immunity but who had not been registered and whose name had not been published in the Gazette.' Mr. Didcott backed this up with a reference to English case law (Halsbury P274-5). His triumphal conclusion was that 'inclusion or omission from official lists was not conclusive of the status of the accused.'

'The WHO has thus complied with the legal requirements expected of itself and the failure of the State to comply with its obligations cannot ergo rob the accused of immunity, Mr. Metcalfe said sternly.

However, he hadn't finished yet. 'The State prosecutor [in the Penrose case] argued against this claim to immunity and contended that section 4 of the Act required that a register of persons entitled to immunity had to be kept and that such registration had to be published periodically in the *Government Gazette*. He produced the relevant gazettes to the Court and pointed out that the name of the appellant did not appear therein. '*The magistrate then decided, particularly because of the substantial penal consequences provide Section 11 of the Act for the bringing of any proceedings against persons entitled to immunity,* (our italics) to adjourn the case.'

In other words, list or no list, the WHO demanded immunity. But despite this formidable barrage of legal rectitude, including its threatening reference to 'section 11', the magistrate, a woman by the name of A. Mutilitha, made one last attempt at asserting Namibian independence. Refusing to listen to or read the heads of argument, she declined the application. Ignoring the agreement between WHO and the Namibian Government, and dismissing the elusive list of staff, Mutilitha grandly declared herself to be *functus officio*. This, in legal parlance means 'a person who has discharged his duty, or whose authority has come to an end.' According to *the Oxford Companion to Law*, *functus officio* applies to 'an arbitrator or judge to whom further resort is incompetent, his function being exhausted'.

The question as to whether or not Mootu was immune, she said, had been decided, and was not capable of being further considered by her. Her attitude seemed to be: the criminal trial is going ahead whatever you say, and enough of this nonsense!

The saga ends

However, the WHO was not going to be dictated to by a minor magistrate, whatever her *functus*. The legal boffins withdrew into their corner until June, only to emerge with a knock-out blow: a court summons by Metcalfe on behalf of Niklaas Mootu against three respondents, Magistrate Mutilitha, the Prosecutor General and the Government of the Republic of Namibia.

In July the respondents gave notice of their intention to oppose this action. The case was heard in the High Court, in January 2003. Mootu's notice of motion consisted of three pages, outlining events up to Mutilitha's refusal to allow further discussion of the immunity issue, 'despite the uncontested fact that my name appeared on the diplomatic list thus handed in'. 'This is the decision which is sought to be reviewed and set aside.'

The motion was backed up by 17 annexures. They included correspondence dating back to 1997: the statements made after the accident by Mootu and myself; copies of *'notes verbale'* between the various dignitaries; the full text of the relevant Agreement and Convention; transcripts of all the various court proceedings, and an affidavit by Dr. Mandara, the swearing that all was 'true and correct'.

When it came to the recalcitrant Mutilitha, the motion read, 'It is submitted that the first respondent misdirected herself in failing to consider the question of diplomatic immunity when the relevant facts, germane to the earlier finding which had been the basis of declining immunity, had been placed before court. This would then have brought any proceedings to an end, instead of which, the applicant would be obliged to go through an entire criminal trial and run the risk of conviction and incarceration before the matter could be determined by this Honourable Court on Appeal.'

Well yes, that had probably been the plan...

The motion continued: 'It is respectfully submitted that the first respondent failed to properly exercise the discretion vested in her or to apply her mind to those considerations in declining the renewed application on the basis of being *functus officio*'.

Even if ...[Mutilitha's] ruling that she was *functus officio* is not to be set aside, it is submitted that this would be an appropriate case for this honourable court to grant the declaratory relief sought which would then bring an end to the criminal proceedings in the exercise of its inherent jurisdiction and in particular where the administration of justice would be served by making a declaratory order of such a nature at this stage.'

Though this sounds like gobbledegook to this uninitiated, its intention is quite clear. And it was underscored by reference to even more obscure legal precedents regarding 'international proceedings in a magistrate's court' (Wahlhause v. Additional magistrate, Johannesburg 1959 (3) SA113 (A). Mootu, alias Metcalfe, continued, "The administration of justice would furthermore be served by such an order by not proceeding with a trial which would essentially be an exercise in futility and could result in grave injustice.' Two more cases were quoted: Hendricks & others. Attorney-General and two others (unreported High Court 20/8/2002 and NANSO v. Speaker of National Assembly and Others 1990(1) SA 617 (SWA).

Whatever was confusing about this in-depth defence, one thing was certain: the lawyers were determined to keep Mootu out of the witness box. They had done their work thoroughly and at a great expense. In the event, the honourable Justice Mtambnengwe, having heard the case and ploughed through the thick pile of paper, had little choice but to cave in. 'It is ordered,' he decreed, 'that the decision of the first respondent (Mutilitha) taken on 6th March 2002 in which she found that she would not consider the question as to whether the applicant was immune from prosecution by virtue of the provision of Act 71 of 1951, is hereby reviewed, corrected and set aside. And 2, That the applicant enjoys diplomatic immunity by virtue of the provisions of the Act 71 of 1951.'

Greg Watters and Andrew Damon could still not rest in peace, then.

The Prosecutor General in the person of Advocate M. Imalawa wrote on 16 February 2004 to Mrs. Watters referring to this long outstanding case, the State versus Nikllas Mootu: *Kindly be informed that the accused Mr. Mootu, approached the High Court of Namibia for relief after being charged in the Magistrate's Court with Culpable Homicide. The high Court ruled in favour of Mr. Mootu, namely that he enjoyed diplomatic immunity from prosecution and can not be charged criminally with regard to the accident which claimed the life of your husband. Kindly accept the assurance of this office's highest consideration at all times.'*

Far more outrageous things have happened and been kept out of the public gaze.

My own feeling is that this was not a victory for WHO; it confirmed only that the accused enjoys diplomatic immunity, despite being a Namibian citizen. It did not clear him of the crime of culpable homicide of which he still stands accused. The door remains open for the Prosecutor General to proceed with the initial proposal made by the Ministry of Justice, to request WHO's Director General to waive Mr. Mootu's immunity and allow justice to be served. That's where the case stands at the moment. This is a challenge both to WHO and the Prosecutor General: WHO has a moral duty to waive his immunity to prove to the world that it is not abusing the privileges of diplomatic immunity given to its international civil servants; the Prosecutor General should proceed with the formal request through the Ministry of Foreign Affairs to prove that his country is a land of justice whether Mootu is found guilty or not.

'Something is very wrong when people such as Mr. Zawide, who risk their lives working for a humanitarian Organization, are treated so badly,' lawyer Edward Flaherty commented. But he wasn't really surprised. His extensive experience in fighting on behalf of international civil servants, has given him insight – and a degree of cynicism – regarding the UN system of justice.

'Civil servants' immunity from prosecution is based on the assumption that the UN and its offshoots have an alternative legal system which meets the minimum standards of due process. In fact, they have no such thing. And because no-one, ultimately, can be held accountable, this kind of botched up 'investigation' happens again and again. If such a cover up was attempted in a big American company, its senior officials would not only be sued, they'd be subject to criminal charges for gross negligence. It is interesting, and probably extremely relevant, that since 1997/98 the UN has taken out insurance on staff who suffer death or injury arising from their work. It pays out up to $500,000 on a death of a staff member – unless the death was caused by gross negligence, as in this case.'

'Such small-scale accidents are easy to hush up or ignore in bodies which operate on a global scale, and have a sense of their own sovereign power, because so few people are affected,' Flaherty points out. 'Far more outrageous things have happened and been kept out of the public gaze. Each one plunges the general morale of UN staff down a few degrees.'

He cited the case of three civil servants murdered in West Timor in September 2000. 'There was an uprising in the country, and a breakdown of law and order. A mob of para-militaries was advancing through the bush towards a town where the UN High Commission for Refugees (UNHCR) had a sub-office. Parked outside this office were four shiny, new, four-wheel drive vehicles, worth 60,000 US dollars each. The senior UNHCR official got into a panic and issued an order for these trucks to be driven away and hidden so that the mob would not destroy them. He left with them, instructing the three remaining staff to man the office in the face of the advancing horde. One of them sent an e-mail: 'We are waiting for the enemy, we sit here like bait, unarmed, waiting for the wave.... I will draft the agenda for the meeting tomorrow at Kapang. The aim of the meeting: to examine how we are going to continue this operation. I have to go now. I hear screaming outside.' It was the last message he ever sent. All three attempted to flee on foot, but were brutally macheted to death in front of the office, their bodies immolated with gasoline and set alight.

'Although the families of these men would normally have been entitled to collect on the Malicious Acts Insurance that covers every UN staff member with a contract of one year or more, the insurance company refused to pay out on account of the gross negligence of the UNHCR management in contributing to the deaths of the three staff members. So the UNHCR had to pay $1.4m to the families of the three victims; they paid the divorced father and the mother of the American $350,000 each, because they didn't want them to make a big fuss about it. All this money came out of the regular UNHCR budget,' Flaherty recounts.

'In Mr. Zawide's case, the ILO couldn't ignore the fact that he had been badly treated,' he continues, 'so they decided, Okay, it's worth $5000. But that's an insult. If a private company had treated a staff member like that, it probably would have cost them $15 million in damages. As for Mrs. Watters, I think the special clause the WHO forced her to sign regarding the insurance pay out was illegal. It probably wasn't enforceable because they had an absolute right to be paid the benefit without signing anything.'

But despite his general contempt for the ILOAT, Flaherty instances some cases in which the bureaucratic bungling of Organizations such as WHO was so bad that the Tribunal found in favour of the appellants. Millions of dollars of donors' money was paid out to settle such claims. We shall explore these missing millions in the next chapter.

Attending a regional workshop on environmental health in
Africa in Harare, Zimbabwe

CHAPTER TWENTY-FIVE

FOOD FOR GOLIATH'S LAWYERS

*S*ince all countries are forced, as was Namibia, to subordinate their own legislation to that of lordly UN bodies such as the WHO, it may be instructive to enquire further into this internal UN system of justice.

So, what happened next? Since all countries are forced, as was Namibia, to subordinate their own legal system to that of lordly UN bodies it's worth questioning what internal the UN system of justice consists of. Does the ILOAT make UN bodies accountable for their actions? What reparations are demanded for mistakes, and who insists that these mistakes are rectified, and not repeated?

Since 1946, the Statute governing ILOAT has been amended four times. Article II states that '[It] shall be competent to hear complaints alleging non-observance, in substance or in form, of the terms of appointment of officials of the International Labour Office, and of such provisions of the Staff Regulations as are applicable to the case. The Tribunal shall be competent to settle any dispute concerning the compensation provided for in cases of invalidity, injury, or disease incurred by an official in the course of his employment, and to fix finally the amount of compensation, if any, which is to be paid.'

Article VIII states 'In cases falling under Article II, the Tribunal, if satisfied that the complaint was well-founded, shall order the rescinding of the decision impugned or the performance of the obligation relied upon. If such rescinding... is not possible or advisable, the Tribunal shall award the complainant compensation.' The Tribunal's judgments are final and without appeal. They may be reviewed only in exceptional circumstances and on strictly limited grounds. These include: failure to take account of some material facts; a material error that involves no exercise of judgment; an omission to rule on a claim, or the discovery of some new essential fact that the complainant was unable to benefit from in the original proceedings. The plea must be such as to affect the original ruling. Pleas of a mistake of law, failure to admit evidence, misinterpretation of the facts or omission to rule on a plea, are not grounds for review.

Indications are that they fail to learn from their mistakes.

Any compensation awarded shall be borne by the international organization concerned. However, since no budgetary provision is made for such awards, the legal costs and compensation have to be paid from the organization's regular budget. Sometimes millions of dollars are involved, yet this money may not appear on any published statement of accounts, and no particular official appears to be accountable for paying it.

There is no evidence that international organizations are required to reassess their modus operandi when they are found guilty by the ILOAT of some grave misdemeanour. Indications are rather that they fail to learn from their mistakes, since appeal cases continue to be won and compensations paid for similar problems. Not only do those who are to blame go unpunished, there is also a suspicion among international civil servants, that it is those who complain who are punished indirectly. There appears to be a blacklist of appellants, whether written or not. Staff who have gone so far as to lodge an appeal say they are unlikely to be promoted or even to get a job with any other UN organization, no matter what their 'rights' under the Tribunal Statute.

From October 1946 to November 2004, the Tribunal examined some 2,374 appeals made by international civil servants within and outside the United Nations system. The annual number of appeals brought to the Tribunal has increased from less than ten in the early years, to almost a hundred per year recently. Analysis of 500 ILOAT cases from January 1990-February 1996 reveals that there were more appeals against the World Health Organization, than any other body. Next on the list were cases against the Food and Agricultural Organization (FAO); the International Labour Organization (ILO), the United Nations Educational, Scientific and Cultural Organization (UNESCO); the World Intellectual Property Organization (WIPO) and a few cases against the United Nations Industrial Development Organization (UNIDO). The remaining cases involved bodies outside the U.N system.

Of the 500 cases examined in total, the causes were diverse. Most WHO appeals concerned the termination of appointment, harassment in various forms, serious misconduct and unsatisfactory job performance.

Staff Regulations embody the conditions of service and the basic rights, duties and obligations of the World Health Organization secretariat. The Rules implement the Staff Regulations, which are promulgated by the World Health Assembly. The Staff Rules are established by the Director-General, subject to confirmation by the Executive Board. The immunities and privileges attaching to the WHO by virtue of Article 67 of the Constitution are conferred in the interest of the Organization. They furnish no excuse for non-performance of private obligations, or for failure to observe the laws of the country in which staff are stationed. The decision to waive any privileges or immunities, as we have seen, rests with the Director General.

Staff are enjoined to 'neither seek nor accept instructions from any government or from any authority external to the Organization' in the performance of their duties. This puts staff assigned to countries in a difficult situation, since that country's own authorities also have to be satisfied with their performance in relation to the country concerned. The Organization extends or terminates their contracts based on appraisal reports, one criterion of which is 'working relationship with national counterparts.' If any government official complains about a staff member, the Organization may terminate his or her contract, or reassign the person elsewhere. It follows that international civil servants have to walk a tightrope in order to satisfy both their own superiors and the host government. No Director-General or Regional Director wants to act against the interests of a particular government since, in the final analysis, it is those governments which decide on their reappointment.

During this period, several appeals were lodged against organizations which had either terminated appointments or reassigned staff to another duty station without their consent, simply because they had not satisfied their host governments. Most appeals relating to employment contracts end up being dismissed by ILOAT. This is because renewal of contracts of whatever kind falls within the discretionary authority of the head of the Organization. The Tribunal will not interfere with such a decision unless for the following reasons: it was taken without authority; or it violated a rule of form or procedure; or it was based on an error of fact or of law; or essential facts were not taken into consideration; or it was tainted with abuse of authority; or, finally, a clearly-mistaken conclusion was drawn from the facts. The Tribunal has consistently followed these principles.

Another cause of disciplinary action or termination of employment is 'improper action by a staff member in his official duties, or indeed, any conduct that brings the Organization into disrepute, whether connected with official duties or not'. There's no denying that diplomatic rights make it both tempting and possible to get away with crimes such as illegal trade in duty-free goods; or using the diplomatic pouch for sending foreign currency abroad; or exchanging currency on the black market above the official rate; or presenting false medical and educational claims; or forging documents and signatures. All these have led, at times, to retribution.

Then there are the usual crimes of employees everywhere – alleged dereliction of duty; acting without authority; failure to get on with supervisors, colleagues or national authorities; bypassing the line of command; insubordination, and breach of confidentiality. The WHO is neither better nor worse than any other organization in this regard.

The appointment of staff is at the discretion of the Director General and the Regional Director. It is not for the Tribunal to compare the merits of the candidates. In the event of discrimination or favouritism, the most the Tribunal can do is order compensation for moral damage and legal costs. The main causes of appeal are administrative flaws in the process of staff selection, promotion, reassignment, and termination of appointment on the grounds of abolishing a post.

There's no denying that diplomatic rights make it both tempting and possible to get away with crimes.

Although the Tribunal may not interfere with staff selection, it sees that applicants are considered in good faith and in keeping with the rules of fair and open competition, since in any international organization there is rivalry between different ethnic groups. When a post is filled by competition it must comply with the general precepts of case law. The Director General should have due regard for wide geographical representation, as well as efficiency and technical competence. He or she may not, for instance, give preference to colleagues from his or her country of origin.

During Dr. Gro Harlem Brundtland's tenure in Geneva, and Dr. Samba's in Africa, the number of appeals to the Tribunal increased. Not for nothing was she dubbed the 'Thatcher of the United Nations', and Dr. Samba, a 'slave driver.' The Director General slashed long-term contracts, replacing them with short-term ones. In her term, the notion of having a career appointment in WHO became a pipe-dream. As of December 2001, it was reported that there were 3,608 long-term contracts, mostly fixed term of 2-5 years compared to 4,746 short term contracts of 1 to 11 months. Some short-term contracts were renewed five times or more. This benefited the Organization as short-term employees performed the work of fixed-term staff without getting full benefits or emoluments. Not surprisingly, Dr. Brundtland's restructuring and new policy was met with marked lack of enthusiasm by the staff. According to Professor Jean-Loup Motchane of the University of Paris, who carried out a survey of WHO staff in Geneva in May 2001, the morale of 70 percent of the staff was low, very low or average.

A few cases serve to illustrate the type of appeal lodged against WHO, the result of similar bad management to my own, and which have costed the Organization millions of wasted dollars in compensation.

WHO versus GPA staff: ILOAT case 1624.

In 1994, the Economic and Social Council of the United Nations approved the establishment of a joint, co-sponsored programme on HIV/AIDS (UNAIDS). In 1995, the 48th. World Health Assembly endorsed the establishment of UNAIDS. WHO was to provide its administrative framework; however, the Assembly's resolution on the matter did not mention that this would entail the abolition of existing posts in the Organization's Global Programme on AIDS (GPA). Since employment in the Organization is governed by individual contracts of appointment, a legitimate reason to abolish each post was necessary.

UNAIDS became operational in January 1996, and all 242 GPA posts – 131 of them in Geneva – ceased to exist from this date. The Personnel Division advised each person in advance on their contractual position; UNAIDS absorbed a few; some were reassigned and others offered early retirement or separation by mutual agreement. Some obtained employment elsewhere. But there remained quite a number without work, who'd had long-term appointments. According to Staff Rule 1050.6, amended in January 1989, 'posts of indefinite duration comprise those that continue in existence unless and until an express decision is taken to abolish them...' The application of the reduction-in-force procedure is required when such posts are abolished. On the other hand, temporary appointments for posts of limited duration may be terminated prior to expiration date if the post is abolished.

The reduction-in-force procedure does not apply to a post of limited duration. According to this, a staff member's appointment shall not be terminated before he has been made a reasonable offer of reassignment if such offer is immediately possible. Staff members holding career service appointments shall be given priority for retention. Under these circumstances WHO granted all former GPA staff a terminal indemnity equivalent to at least three months pay, whether or not they were entitled to it. They failed to offer reassignment to some former GPA staff. As a result some 229 former GPA staff lodged an appeal to the ILOAT, and won their case. The ILOAT decided that all those who held posts of indefinite duration, and career service appointments, had to be reinstated, paid salaries and other benefits from the date of the closure of GPA until they were properly terminated or transferred. No-one within WHO will ever admit how much this cost, but it must have been from US $15 - 25 million.

Interestingly, WHO is now doing more work on AIDS than UN-AIDS, which constitutes a seriously wasteful duplication of effort.

Personal Prejudice: ILOAT Case 1342

This case refers to a colleague, WHO sanitary engineer of Indian origin who served WHO for 15 years in Kenya, Ghana and Uganda. While in Uganda, he was notified that his appointment would be terminated in 1988 due to a funding problem. He alleged that the real reason was prejudice, which he had experienced ever since taking up duty there. His supervisors, having sought in vain to replace him, waged a campaign to discredit him, even going so far as to accuse him of complicity in crime. He had angered one supervisor by pointing out errors of judgment, and roused the resentment of WHO officials by making constructive criticism at a regional meeting. He claimed that several government officials were also prejudiced against him.

The upshot was the abolition of his post. He produced evidence that the Ugandan government had never indicated that it wanted his post abolished. The WHO Ugandan representative had agreed to fund the programme for another two years at least, and the government had asked to have his appointment extended. His supervisors and the Regional Director had claimed budgetary constraints in order to have his post struck from the programme.

In November 1988 he lodged an appeal with the Regional Board on the grounds of personal prejudice. In July 1990 the Board rejected his appeal as being devoid of merit. In May 1991 he appealed against this decision to the Headquarters Board of Appeal, which found that officials of the Ugandan Government, AFRO and his supervisors had all agreed that he was a competent and experienced sanitary engineer, and had shown appreciation for his services. The Board therefore concluded that although there was no proof of personal or racial prejudice, this was the most likely cause. They recommended reinstating him.

The Director General, however, rejected the Board's recommendation, so the complainant appealed to the Tribunal in September 1993. The ILOAT could not but agree with the HBA that funding was not the problem. In the absence of any other reason for not renewing the contract, the 'patently untenable' grounds for doing so made it 'more probable than not' that the decision was actuated by personal prejudice. The complainant therefore was entitled to the reduction-in-force procedure before terminating his contract. Not being the outcome of a valid procedure, the termination was invalid, and he was entitled to reinstatement. However, it was too late to do this since the complainant was due to retire within a few months, so the Tribunal awarded him full compensation including salary, allowances and benefits that would have been due to him from the date of his separation in October 1988 to the date on which he turned 60, October 1994, less any earnings in the meantime.

Furthermore, since the termination had been tainted with personal prejudice he had also suffered moral injury, for which the Tribunal awarded him US$4000 in damages. In total WHO was forced to pay out US $ 204,120 in salary, plus the $4000 moral damages and an additional US$105,492.28 by way of reimbursement of all taxes payable by the complainant in the United States since he had established permanent residency in USA. And no-one was made accountable for the loss of this massive amount!

Personal Prejudice: HQ Board of Appeal Case

This case concerned a highly qualified and experienced woman doctor from the Philippines, who worked for the WHO in various regions, including Headquarters, for 16 years. She was forced to leave her job at the WHO Regional Office for Africa in July 1996. Her background included a five-year spell with the Pan American Health Organization, WHO America, as a member of a primary health care team, a project which was terminated when a new Regional Director was elected. Subsequently she worked as a consultant at WHO/HQ in Geneva for about a year, joining AFRO in August 1986, initially as a Technical Officer (TO) in Health System Management in Harare. A year later, she was reassigned as TO on Health Research with the same duty station. In 1990, she was reassigned as a Regional Adviser in Health Research in the Regional Office located in Brazzaville. She was also assigned other tasks, but at all times she continued to hold the regular and statutory Health Research budget post of unlimited duration. Her fixed-term contract was renewed for three successive terms of two years. Her last contract expired in July 1996, when her services were summarily ended, without resort to a reduction-in-force (RIF) exercise.

In October 1995, the Personnel Officer confirmed in writing that her post was to be abolished, offering her separation by mutual agreement with a choice of continuing until either February or July 1996, with relevant indemnities. Negotiations on the terms continued without success until February, when the doctor offered to separate on terms suitable to her. This was rejected by the Administration and she opted for separation at the end of her contract, July 1996. Her request for inclusion in the RIF procedure was rejected by the Administration. In July she withdrew her agreement to separate since her claim for inclusion in a RIF procedure had been ignored, and requested immediate reinstatement. She filed an appeal with the Regional Board of Appeal in September 1996 against the Administration's decision to terminate her appointment without submitting it to a RIF procedure, also citing WHO's failure to reassign her, or give a valid reason for non-renewal of her post.

She claimed that the Administration had failed to follow its own rules and procedures, by transferring her and then using her apparent lack of work as a justification for abolishing the post. Her claims seemed confirmed by the fact that the Administration subsequently hired a retired former staff member as Short Term Professional or (STP) to perform most of her duties; he was a personal friend of the new Regional Director and had strongly supported his election; rumour had it, this was his reward.

At any event, the abolition of the doctor's post was illusory, since her tasks were redistributed. The Administration had advised her that its offer of separation by mutual agreement was without prejudice to her right to a RIF exercise. However, this remained a hypothetical agreement and the Administration could not prove that she had been included in a RIF procedure, despite the fact that it was mandatory. So the lady held that her dismissal was due to discrimination on the basis of gender and place of origin.

I myself worked with this lady, and can testify that she made a significant contribution to health system research in Africa, where she was respected for her competence and hard work. She was highly qualified, holding a PhD from one of the best American universities with considerable experience in community nutrition and integrated health and socio-economic development. The RBA tried twice, within a year, to examine her case, but due to the complexity surrounding it, decided to ask the HBA in Geneva to take over the appeal.

After a thorough review the HBA concluded that the appellant was entitled to a RIF procedure, and that her decision to leave the Organization at the end of her contract did not constitute a waiver of that right. The HBA noted the strong similarities between her situation and that of the Global Programme on AIDS staff. They recommended that she be reinstated with full back payment of salary, allowances and benefits, less any indemnity or earnings since she was terminated. In addition, she was to receive interest at eight percent and SF 2000.00 in legal costs.

Yet again WHO had to fork out a large amount of money which should have been spent on aid, and no-one was held accountable. The doctor was reinstated in May 1999, almost three years after her dismissal, with retroactive payment as directed. She soon discovered that her former post had never been abolished, and had been filled all along, despite the excuse of cost containment.' This was a blatant example of abuse of power and manipulation. The story does not end there, however. As might be expected, the doctor's reinstatement was not popular, and the Administration sought revenge in petty ways. The lady was not paid regularly, and received no monthly salary statements. She was reduced to seeking salary advances from the Finance Officer. It took over six months for the funds to be transferred to the UN Joint Staff Pension Fund.

In 2001 this doctor retired, having reached the statutory age. Her financial affairs were still in disarray, there being considerable confusion as to how to calculate the eight percent interest. Two years later, she was still chasing this up, with much difficulty. Finally, after three and a half years, she was informed that a mistake had been made in the amount she had been reimbursed, and that she now owed the Administration money. She therefore filed a second case against WHO in 2003, appealing against two decisions: their refusal to reimburse her for the interest she was owed; and their demand for reimbursement of the alleged overpayment.

The Administration admitted the mistakes, and the HBA recommended the immediate payment of the interest due, together with an apology from the Organization for the long delay. They also recommended that the request for reimbursement should be cancelled, and her legal fees paid. However, by the time this second case was decided by the HBA, another Director General had been elected, and he saw fit to override the HBA's recommendation. Four years later this lady is still struggling, as she is not in a position to repay the Organization, and feels no legal obligation to do so.

Sexual harassment: ILOAT case 1376/1504

A lady of German citizen who joined WHO in 1987 on a short-term contract as an associate expert, grade 2. worked on several programmes in headquarters until May 1989 when she started a two-year appointment as technical officer with the Global Programme on AIDS (GPA), in Luanda, Angola. In her first-year performance report since transfer to Angola, her supervisor, the WHO's Representative in that country, described her work as 'satisfactory'. At the beginning of her second year, in 1990, a new WHO Representative took up duty. In August 1990 she informed the Director of the National Programme on AIDS at the Angolan Ministry of Health that she intended taking 30 days' home leave in September, if the authorities did not object. She then went on leave as there was no formal objection to her request. In late September the Director of Public Health asked the WHO Representative to have this lady recalled from leave, alleging that she was incompetent and discourteous and in dereliction of duty, because she went on holiday without permission from the Director of the National Programme on AIDS.

While this lady was in Germany the Director of the National Programme on AIDS alleged in a letter of 2 October to the Director of Public Health that she was to blame for a break in the supply of reagents needed for medical tests and for lack of responsibility and respect. The Director of Public Health appended the letter of 2 October to one dated 3 October in which he asked the WHO Representative to have the reagents sent from Headquarters in Geneva directly to him. The lady reported back to Luanda for duty on 22 October.

On 31 October the Chief of the Office of Cooperation with National Programme on Aids sent a telex from Geneva to the WHO Representative in Luanda asking him to discuss with this lady the letter of October 2 and seek written comments from her, and if necessary arrange for her to come to Geneva for consultation. He did not discuss the charge against her. Instead, the lady went to Geneva on 17 November and learnt there of the charges contained in the letter of 2 October, which she denied. The Administration referred her report to an ad hoc commission, and in January the Chief of the Office of Cooperation with National Programme on AIDS informed her supervisor, the WHO Representative, that she was returning to Luanda to settle her affairs and asked him to give her full support. Before she left Geneva, she received a letter dated 28 January1991 from the Chief of Contract Administration, giving her three months' notice, on the grounds of the Angolan's Government 'unwillingness to have her remain in the position of WHO/GPA Technical Officer'. Her appointment would expire on 30 April 1991, and the Organization would try to find another assignment for her. She was in Luanda from 6 February till 8 April 1991, and she asked the WHO Representative, for the text of the report about her that he sent to Geneva, a copy of which was also sent to the Resident Representative of the United Nations. He refused. The lady finally returned to Geneva in April 1991 where she started looking for work and tried to get copies of the documents sent by her supervisor. The Administration refused three times to show them to her, so she appealed to the HBA. In June 1992 the Legal Counsel informed her that the Director of Personnel was willing to file her supervisor's report of 17 January 1991 in a sealed confidential envelope along with signed statements from the Director of Personnel and the Legal Counsel himself denying the allegations by her supervisor.

In September 1992 this lady filed a second appeal to the HBA objecting to the failure to draw up a 'final' appraisal report and claiming disclosure of several items of evidence and reinstatement. In its report of February 1993, the Board rejected her appeal since it was not lodged on time. She then appealed to the ILOAT.

In this appeal she contended that her appointment was not renewed because she had spurned the sexual advances of her supervisor. She alleged that soon after his arrival in Luanda as the WHO country

Representative in 1990, he had invited her to his private quarters after working hours on the pretext of needing to put through an international telephone call. There he sought sexual favours from her. Having failed, he began humiliating her in front of others and in private, assuming 'a humorous and bantering manner' and trying to cajole her.

In October 1990 he ordered her 'not to get in touch with the government services' and denied her access to the AIDS programme office and to all normal facilities, including official vehicles. When she finally arranged to leave Angola in April 1991, he saw to it that she was stranded with her luggage at the WHO office without means of conveyance. Since it was too late to make other arrangements, she had to wait another five days to leave.

So damaging was the appraisal of her work that it prompted the Director of Personnel and the Legal Counsel to deny some of the allegations in writing. Later WHO established that it was indeed the supervisor who was to blame. However, instead of setting the record straight with the Angolan authorities, WHO personnel left a damaging report in the woman's file for over two years. This blocked her chances of lasting employment in WHO or any other international organization.

The lady claimed that under WHO's Manual paragraph ii 4.240, staff are entitled to know of, and have access to, any non-privileged material in their personnel files. This includes appraisal reports and any other document relating to performance and conduct. By failing to let her see her supervisor's comments, the Administration was in breach of the rules. She sought reinstatement in a suitable post with payment of salary and other benefits dating back to her termination, plus awards for material and moral damage. The Organization did not contest this woman's account, neither did it refute the allegations against the supervisor with, for example, a written denial by the accused official. So, the Tribunal concluded that this was indeed a case of victimization. The man she had named sent headquarters a highly adverse report about her in January 1991, which the Administration refused to show her.

The WHO admits that it should have formally stated that it regarded as 'without foundation 'the Angolan's Government allegation of unsatisfactory performance and that that view should have been communicated to all the parties concerned. Instead, it was decided to destroy the Representative's report on the grounds that it did not comply with the rules concerning appraisal reports. Only then was the woman given a copy. According to her, however, it was public knowledge among officials whose support she needed in order to obtain further employment. Thus, in the two years before the Tribunal heard her case, the woman only managed to find six months' work. Her career was in ruins, yet the official who had caused her troubles went unpunished. If the Organization was serious about wanting to deter sexual harassment it would surely have taken – and been seen to take – appropriate action. The assurance that their allegations will be taken seriously is what gives victims the confidence to come forward.

In conclusion the Tribunal passed judgment in her favour, as follows: 'She must be… reinstated as from the date of termination. Her salary, allowances and any other benefits to be reckoned at the rates applicable in Geneva. The assumption is that since her performance was without reproach, it would have continued to be so, she is therefore further entitled to any annual increments she would have been granted.

Any indemnities or occupational earnings she may have received since termination may be deducted from the amounts due, but she is entitled to payment of interest on all arrears at the rate of 10 percent a year. She must be granted a contract of employment for two years at the appropriate grade and step, and in a post matching her qualifications and experience. She was entitled to an award of damage for moral injury; to the amount of 25,000 Swiss Francs. She was also entitled to 6000 Swiss Francs in costs. Lastly, she claimed a performance appraisal report for the period May 1990 to April 1991. The Organization, not having strong views on the matter, offered to reinitiate the necessary procedures for the establishment of a report, should the Tribunal so order. The Tribunal 'so ordered.'

The net result was that WHO/AFRO had to pay out thousands of dollars from its meagre budget, already totally inadequate to meet the health needs of the disease-ridden region.

However, the saga wasn't over yet. When the accused WHO representative got wind of her allegations against him, he was deeply upset – all the more so, because he didn't hear the news from his superiors but read it in *Japan Times*. He promptly wrote refuting the accusation and requesting that WHO publish a denial. He also asked the Director General what arrangements the Organization had made to ensure his protection.

In November 1994 WHO appointed an *ad hoc* grievance panel to investigate the accusation. The panel's finding was that it had all been a big mistake – that no sexual harassment whatever had occurred. It recommended that the Representative and his family be sent a written apology; that the panel's findings be published in the press, particularly in Angola; and that he be granted financial compensation.

The Director General apologised for not telling him, offering him an apology and compensation for his costs. He also noted that 'there are significant contradictions between the Panel's conclusion and the allegation of sexual harassment; and that the Panel supported the view that the Representative was not guilty of sexual harassment.' Copies of the statement were sent to the Foreign Minister of Angola, the *Journal de Angola* and the *Japan Times*. The Organization then asked the Tribunal to review its judgment since the accusation of sexual harassment was found to be false. The Tribunal declined the request.

However, the Representative was still angry, and complained that when the case had been brought before the Tribunal, the Organization confined its reply to the issue of receivability, despite a warning from the Registrar. The WHO neither informed the accused man nor challenged the allegations, extraordinary though this seems. The Legal Counsel had written to the Personnel Administration expressing doubts about this man's honesty and integrity.

In mitigation, the Organization pointed out that it had already offered the man an unqualified apology, both in private and in public; it repeated this apology before the Tribunal. The Tribunal, however, decided that the Organization had slipped up and awarded the man US $ 10,000 in moral damages, plus 5000 Swiss Francs in legal costs. This was in addition to the compensation already paid to her. It seemed that whichever of the two was lying, they were both very convincing!

Sexual harassment on the increase

In recent years sexual harassment has been a major issue at the United Nations, especially among UNHCR relief workers and Peace Keepers in

Bosnia, the Democratic Republic of the Congo, Sierra Leone, Ethiopia and Eritrea. A survey conducted by ILOAT among 32 United Nations Organizations in 1997, found that an astounding 47 percent of the staff had experienced some sort of harassment or internal violence. Of these, 33 percent were sexually harassed, 29 percent suffered insults, 14 percent suffered moral and psychological harassment, 14 percent physical assault, and 10 percent were threatened.

Such harassment has a devastating effect not only on the victim, but also on the performance and efficiency of other employees, who often become anxious, stay away from work or even resign. Usually, it's simply a power game by a person in authority. Victims are left angry and frustrated, and often feel powerless to stand up for themselves. Commonly, sexual favours are sought in exchange for employment, promotion, salary increments or other benefits. Sexual favouritism occurs when a person in authority rewards only those who respond to his or her sexual advances, while denying others promotions, merit ratings or salary increases. Physical harassment ranges from touching to sexual assault and rape. It may include strip searching by, or in the presence of, someone of the opposite sex. Verbal harassment includes unwelcome innuendoes, sex-related jokes or insults, graphic comments about a person's body, inappropriate inquiries about some one's sex life and unwelcome whistling. Non-verbal forms include unwelcome gestures, indecent exposure and the display of explicit pictures.

As most allegations of sexual harassment are taken seriously by the ILOAT, their findings have sent a clear message that international organizations can and will be held liable for workplace harassment. It's been pointed out that failure to eliminate such behaviour could have a detrimental impact on the organization's reputation.

Another expensive bungle: ILOAT case 1432

In 1985 WHO appointed a woman doctor of dual nationality, France and Mauritius, as a consultant on a short-term contract. In 1986 she was granted a two-year fixed-term appointment to a medical officer post in the African Regional Office. She later became technical adviser to the Regional Director. However, in 1988 the Regional Director attested that it would be inadvisable for her to remain in Africa, as she had contracted an illness. He recommended a post ost for her in Geneva. Though not formally transferred from the African Regional Office, she was reassigned to Geneva from 1 January 1989 under a two-year contract.

Her reassignment was finally confirmed on 4 February 1991, but in September that year the Director of Personnel informed her that for budgetary reasons, her appointment would be terminated in December 1991. In November she had an end-of-service medical examination and in December she went on holiday to Mauritius. On 24 December she got a medical certificate from her own doctor recommending sick leave until 24 January 1992 and by another letter until 24 February. On 29 January 1992, she was informed that the Regional Director AFRO had reassigned her to Brazzaville as from 1 January. On 21 February the Director of Personnel, Geneva, informed AFRO that she could not be reassigned until a medical examination and other formalities had been completed. At the end of February, she left Mauritius for Geneva where she met the Regional Director of AFRO. By a memorandum of 13 March, the Personnel Officer AFRO informed her that for health reasons she was to be offered a post in Windhoek, Namibia. He sent her the post description signed by the Regional Director. The woman replied by fax indicating that she would prefer the Brazzaville post but would consider Namibia as a temporary assignment. In March the Personnel Officer, AFRO informed Geneva of the woman's reassignment to Namibia, and asked them to approve putting her on leave without pay from January 1 to 7 March 1992, so that her case could be sorted out.

In July the Personnel Officer AFRO asked the Director of Personnel Geneva to start the administrative process for reassigning her to Namibia. He refused. In August, the Regional Director AFRO intervened by writing to the Director General to clarify the woman's status. The Director General replied that he had ordered an inquiry, the findings of which had led him to endorse the decision of the Director of Personnel. In October 1992 the Personnel Officer, AFRO, informed the woman that she held no contract of employment with the Organization. The lady contested this and took two pleas to the ILOAT.

First, that her appointment did not expire on 31 December 1991 but was extended until 24 February 1992, the date on which her sick leave ended. The Organization acted arbitrarily by putting her on leave without pay for the whole period from 1 January to 7 March 1992, then refusing to treat her as an employee for that period.

Second, a contract had been properly concluded between her and the African Office for the Namibian post. Citing case law she submitted that a contract exists when all the essential terms have been agreed upon, and any point still pending is just a formality. She had reached full oral agreement with the Regional Director and the Organization had provided her airline tickets for Namibia. She had received written confirmation of the offer and had actually performed the duties of the post for one month.

After examining her appeal, the Tribunal concluded that the Organization had indeed reemployed her. She should accordingly have been granted leave without pay from 1 January to 7 March 1992 in accordance with Staff Rule 470.1 and the term of personnel decision in its cable of 27 March 1992. She was further entitled to pay from 8 March 1992 to 7 March 1994 plus interest at the rate of 10% a year from the date at which each sum fell due. Her pension should be reinstated in for the same period. In addition, WHO's attitude towards her constituted moral injury, the Tribunal found, although the decline in her health did not warrant an award of damages under this head. So the Organization was required to pay her moral damages in the amount of 10000 Swiss Francs, plus 7500 Swiss Francs for legal costs.

Thus, the fight between the Director General and the Regional Director over this woman's status ended in her favour, and once more the WHO had to shell out thousands in aid money to settle a bungle.

Revenge and the abuse of power: ILOAT case 1234

A Canadian Citizen who joined WHO in 1964 as Personnel Officer at Headquarters in Geneva was transferred to the WHO Regional Office for South East Asia in New Delhi in 1966 where he served as personnel officer for three years until his reassignment to the WHO Regional Officer Europe in Copenhagen, 1970. In 1977 he returned to Geneva, being promoted to Chief of Personnel after improving his qualification with a higher degree sponsored by the Organization. In 1986 he was granted a career service appointment, and in 1988 the then

Director General appointed him Director of the Division of Personnel and General Service at a salary grade D2. His career appointment was replaced with a fixed term of five years to expire on 30 June 1993.

Dr. Nakajima took over as Director General in January 1988 and split the Division of Personnel and General service into two, the Division of Personnel known as PER, and the Division of Conference and General Services known as CGS. A retired former WHO official was made acting head of the Division of Personnel and the Canadian man became Director of Conference and General Service. In July 1990 the Director General transferred him to the WHO's International Agency for Research on Cancer in Lyon, France, as Director of Administration and Finance, keeping his own grade and step D2 as before.

In October 1990 this man appealed to the Headquarters Board of Appeal against both his reassignment and the decision to remove him from his post as Director of Personnel and General Service. The Board found no evidence of personal prejudice but held that he had suffered moral injury. It recommended that he be reassured by letter that his career with WHO would continue at least until the mandatory age of retirement, 60. It also recommended that he be given priority for any Headquarters grade D2 or above appointment in personnel management.

The Director General did not agree with the Board's recommendations, but his appointment, due to expire in June 1993, was extended until March 1997, and he was supposed to serve in the new post until further notice. He appealed to the ILOAT, claiming that he was being victimised for two decisions he had made while Chief of Personnel which had offended Dr. Nakajima, then Regional Director, Western Pacific. The Canadian held that Dr. Nakajima was now seeking revenge by bringing someone over the age of 65 out of retirement to replace him. He protested that his appointment to the Agency in Lyon was farcical in several respects: it required financial and budgetary knowledge which he didn't have; it had necessitated turning someone else who presumably did have this knowledge, out of the post; and to crown it all, the Director of the Agency had not been even consulted about the matter.

The Tribunal found that the efficiency, competence and integrity of this staff were beyond reproach and that he had been transferred out of his area of expertise for no good reason replacing him by an over-age man whose supervisor he had himself once been. He had been also transferred to a work for which he was not equipped, with no explanation. Therefore, it was not convincing to say that the decision was 'in the interest of the Organization'. The Tribunal needed absolute clarity about the basis for that conclusion, to enable it to determine the grounds to set it aside.

In the end the Tribunal over-ruled the Director General. However, they were unable to order reassignment for him; all they could do was to quash the impugned transfer, and award him damages of 25,000 Swiss Francs for moral injury, plus legal costs of 10,000 Swiss Francs.

Resignation: the invisible cost. ILOAT case 1928

This case refers to an Italian lady who joined WHO/ AFRO in 1991 as a technical officer in the Human Resources and Fellowships Unit. Her fixed-term two-year contract was renewed twice. In August 1995, Dr. Ibrahim Samba, then new to his post as Regional Director, decided to abolish her post. Consequently, she was informed that her appointment would be terminated in December 1995, and that she could choose either separation by mutual agreement or application of the reduction-in-force procedure.

By the time her post was abolished in March 1996, no reassignment had materialized, hence she would be separated by mutual agreement with enhanced indemnity but without prejudice to her rights to a reduction-in-force procedure. The lady replied that she would not accept separation by mutual agreement, preferring reassignment world-wide under the reduction-in-force procedure. The committee studied her case and, being unable to offer her a post in her occupational group, allowed her to compete for a lower grade post. She opted for one in Kigali, Rwanda, one grade lower at P3.

She was duly appointed, and soon received two memoranda from the Regional Director criticizing her performance in her previous post. She took this as continuous harassment and informed him that she would not seek renewal of her contract when it expired in March 1997.

The Regional Director asked her to reconsider and offered her another post in the Regional Office in Brazzaville. She declined, and left the Organization of her own volition in March 1997. Before her resignation, however, the lady appealed to the Regional Board against the decision to abolish her former post. This Board recommended reintegrating her, and removing the Regional Director's memoranda from her personal file – which he agreed to do. She then went to the Headquarters Board of Appeal, which found that the failure to provide suitable reassignment and the decision to end her contract were tainted with prejudice. Moreover, she had not been treated like other staff in the same situation. The Board recommended allowing her to choose between reinstatement on a post truly commensurate with her experience, or the awarding of compensation.

She subsequently discovered that far from being abolished, her post had been reconstituted at a higher grade, and given to a newcomer. So she protested to the Tribunal that this smacked of personal prejudice, ill will and malice. Her plea was comprehensive: she covered the original appeal to the Regional Board impugning the decision to terminate her appointment pursuant to the 'flawed' reduction-in-force procedure; the failure to place her elsewhere; the Regional Director's prejudice towards her, and the WHO's failure to follow its own rules and procedures; the attempt to reconstitute her post with another title and a different post number; discrimination on the basis of gender and origin; and, to sum up, thoroughly unjust treatment.

In the opinion of the Tribunal the decision to terminate was never implemented, in view of the Brazzaville post she'd been offered. She had voluntarily accepted reassignment to another post; and she had declined the renewed contract offer in Brazzaville. So, the Tribunal could not blame the Organization, neither could it grant the subsidiary claim for damages. Nevertheless, the case – the tip of the iceberg – demonstrates the lengths to which some officials will go in harassing employees whom they do not like, by intentionally destroying their career.

How much acrimony could be avoided if training in conflict resolution were obligatory?

These few cases alone cost the WHO millions of dollars, all of which came from its regular budget. Many similar ones can be found on the ILOAT web site. The World Health Organization rarely settles appeals, preferring to fight to the end. But litigating an ILOAT staff appeal costs WHO a lot (CHF 200,000) even before judgement is made. If WHO loses, the costs soar. Most claims could be settled for less, but WHO simply refuses to settle before appealing to the ILOAT.

Numerous instances of staff harassment, conspiracy, mental torture, inhuman treatment and moral injury that resulted in mental cases, depression and even suicide, go unreported. Victims are afraid to speak out, fearing they will lose their jobs. Those who come from developing countries, especially women, are more victimized, as they cannot earn the same amount if they return to their own countries to work. 'Cut the throat' was the favourite phrase of one Regional Director of WHO/AFRO, held over his staff as a threat.

Most professional international civil servants enter the UN's service above the age of 30. If they are lucky, they stay for 10 years or more. If their appointment terminates before they reach retirement age it is difficult to secure employment elsewhere, because of their age and the specialized nature of their duties.

In 2002, 120 members of the UN Group on Equal Rights for Women were surveyed for their views on Morale and Work-Life Balance at the UN. The survey was forwarded by e-mail to colleagues far from headquarters, so that eventually 219 responses were received, 101 from New York and 118 from other duty stations. About 20 percent of the respondents were men, 80 percent women. About 48 percent were professional staff, 44 percent general service staff and 8 percent other categories. A key question was, how well was the UN was doing in its relations between employees and management? Seventeen percent thought it was doing a poor job; 50 percent thought there was considerable room for improvement; 17 percent thought the performance was average; 15 percent that it was pretty good, and one percent that it was outstanding.

For the 67 percent who felt that the United Nations had (at best) considerable room for improvement, three issues stood out. First, the need for a better balance between work and life in their programs.

Second, better career advancement opportunities – especially for General Service staff. Finally, they cited peoples' need to be recognized and feel appreciated for the work they do.

Had this finding been taken seriously, many of these expensive and unpleasant cases could, like my own, have been totally avoided. The ILOAT is probably never going to be redundant – but who knows how much of this petty-sounding acrimony could be avoided if training in conflict resolution were obligatory at a certain level? Just saving the costs of one such case would probably pay for this training the world over. Plus, it would provide constructive and useful work for thousands, instead of lining the pockets of bored lawyers in Geneva.

CHAPTER TWENTY-SIX

THE BIGGER PICTURE: WHO'S SUCCESSES AND FAILURES

*O*ne might imagine far more trauma would occur in view of the vast scale of WHO's operations, its answerability to 193 Member States, and the huge range of cultures, languages and creeds manifested in its staff and clientele. So why worry?

Some people would argue that individual staff who have been ill-treated – even grossly so – by the World Health Organization, are as insignificant as ants. The Organization, after all, employs some 10,000 people globally, which is not many in the light of its gargantuan tasks (the British Broadcasting Corporation alone employs 26,000). One might imagine far more trauma would occur in view of the vast scale of WHO's operations, its answerability to 193 Member States, and the huge range of cultures, languages and creeds manifested in its staff and clientele. So why worry?

That there is not more trouble is both good news and bad news. It is probably largely due to the ubiquitous rules and regulations, which occupy seven fat volumes and could no doubt be used, like statistics, to prove almost anything. That's the good news. The bad news is that these rules are a two-edged sword, often crushing the very idealism they seek to protect. They make staff averse to taking risks: 'never be too daring and certainly not innovative', is the message. This is an Organization that values caution, and drums out people who don't conform. Which might be okay if what the world needed was a bit of first aid. Unfortunately, with pathogens becoming ever more inventive in their efforts to wipe us out, we need more innovators at the helm.

A more significant case of Physician, heal thyself!' would be hard to imagine.

So, in case you're tempted to dismiss this dismal tale of human mismanagement, you should perhaps ask whether you simply prefer to assume that such a noble Organization can be entrusted to manage itself, because it's more comfortable to do so? Even if its troubles seem far removed from your life, just imagine someone telling you that bird flu is on the doorstep; or that Ebola fever has been diagnosed nearby. We straight away fervently start hoping that experts will speedily bring things under control. We know that in our present global village, every single one of us is vulnerable.

Much as we'd like to believe that compassion has been institutionalised, and WHO is IT, the truth is that as with liberty, there's eternal vigilance to pay. For too long WHO and other international bodies have traded on their successes. It is time to shine a spotlight on their weaknesses. Ghastly TV images of fly-blown bundles of bones parodying children, with vultures circling above should be and could be ended; we should demand more, and hold WHO accountable for its part in the global jigsaw puzzle.

Dr. Peter Piot, Executive Director of the joint UN programme on HIV and AIDS, has warned that new microbes are developing all the time, and that despite our progress and knowledge, we are at serious risk of global pandemics. The multi-drug resistant strains of many diseases could produce a plague more contagious and vastly more destructive than AIDS, because we will have no tools with which to fight it. We are only a hair's breadth away in some cases, such as multi-drug resistant tuberculosis. That's why these small voices, which flesh out the dry reports of many heavyweight critics, matter. For in some ways, the World Health Organization is sick indeed. And a more significant case of 'Physician, heal thyself!' would be hard to imagine.

There are many myths surrounding WHO, which blinker us to the truth about it. Myths are the essential beliefs, aspirations, ideals and dreams which hold a body together. They're vital when goals are as vague as the WHO's. 'Health for All' and 'a state of complete physical, mental and social wellbeing' sounds great, but as goals, they are about as concrete as water, and even less measurable.

International healthcare researcher Dr. John Peabody* has identified two key WHO myths:

- The Organization is a politically-neutral, technical agency that sets an international standard of social justice by improving health.
- The Organization is uniquely qualified to improve health in the vast and complicated international arena of divergent populations besieged by overwhelming diseases.

Their repetition is important, he says, and so are the success stories since they reinforce scientific professionalism and individual stamina of staff. The question is, are they true? While both have elements of the truth, the second, particularly, is being challenged as a wide range of new international health initiatives have been launched, due partly no doubt to the Organization's failure to learn from its mistakes. Since its inception, critics have observed the danger of decentralizing WHO without a clear definition of the relationship between the six regional offices and the headquarters. Argument in favour of decentralization centred on remaining close to the countries and people that are served, greater ease of coordination of services, and facilitating cooperative relations with subordinate government units. On the other hand, this has reduced the effectiveness of the headquarters in influencing the administrative apparatus aratus and preventing politicization. As a result, some member countries are unhappy because either their demands are not fulfilled by their regional office or they disagree with the priorities that are set by the programme committees. Funds trickling to the countries of greater need are too little and spread thinly over several projects and programmes resulting in low efficiency and effectiveness.

We will come to these, but first, let's unpack the history a little.

The pathogens

There's no question that, despite its failures, WHO has achieved much significant good for global health. By the time of its birth in 1948 it had over a hundred years' failed attempts at global cooperation from which to learn. Nineteenth-century plagues such as cholera and yellow fever caused months long quarantine restrictions on shipping. Between 1830 and 1847, two pandemics of cholera took their toll in Europe. Maritime trading nations such as France and Britain feared economic collapse even more than they did deadly disease, so with one eye on the common peril and the other on the worsening outlook of their maritime trade, they led the movement to mobilize international collaboration for control of epidemics. Thus, right from the start, politicians were key players. Their impetus gave birth to the earliest example of an international health organization (The International Sanitary Conference) in July 1851 in Paris, which was active for 50 years without accomplishing much.

In fact, the medical experts got booted out of the first International Sanitary Conference. Initially each country was represented by one diplomat and one doctor, but the doctors were boring: they insisted that health comes before commercial interests. Unsurprisingly diplomats saw money as being the better medicine, so they politely suggested that doctors 'did not fully grasp the political significance of international health regulations', and asked them to leave. Not a lot has changed in human nature since then.

Science was on the doctors' side, however, as the causes and prevention of some communicable diseases became known through scientific research. This proved the importance of medical and public health experts in the fight against communicable diseases. Thus, international cooperation gradually increased leading to the formation of a new international health organization in 1920 under the League of Nations. Alas, like so much else, it perished along with the League.

Post-World-War-Two leaders were determined to do better: the new United Nations charter declared splendidly that 'medicine is one of the pillars of peace'. And so, in 1948, that independent specialised agency, the World Health Organization, came into being. And, to do it justice it has – despite its failings – probably done more than any other UN agency to better our human predicament.

The fact that we are now, in the twenty-first century, facing more disease than ever, is unfortunately partly due to that very success. It led to an over-reliance on science and on single interventions such as the 'commando' approach – going in and striking with disease-specific magic bullets. We now know that this it is at best a temporary expedient; it fails to deal with the deep problems that affect health such as poverty, education, development and the environment. Worse, when drugs fail they produce a non-immune population exposed to fatal outbreaks with no tools to fight the disease.

However, this hindsight wisdom should not detract from WHO's early triumphs, which were magnificent. For instance, the yaws campaign.

How to fight a world scourge

In its first decade the WHO went straight into battle against yaws – a crippling and disfiguring disease afflicting 50 million people. Armed with the dramatically effective treatment of penicillin, the WHO drew up three prime battle strategies which were so victorious it seemed that in future, no disease would even dare start a war. They were:

1. The coordination of activities by means of international symposia, etc.

2. The training of staff in individual countries, through offering fellowships and other study plans.

3. The dissemination of appropriate medicine.

By these means 60 million people had been treated for yaws by 1960, largely ending the gross deformities which are its ultimate manifestation. As a result, these three critical tasks were held up as the gold standard for future campaigns, some of which, it has to be said, were outstandingly successful – the early vaccination plan for children, for instance. That's why, to this day, the 'yaws approach' still has its place. It is evident in the many technical meetings, consultative visits, fellowship trainings and medical supplies that are staple WHO activities.

Since its foundation one of WHO's greatest strengths has been leading the world in setting international technical norms and defining healthcare standards. This has been invaluable, creating uniformity and lack of ambiguity. However, when, in the 1970s, a broader concept of health emerged (encouraged by a great leader of the WHO, Dr.

Halfden Mahler, to whom we shall return), the usual strategies were less successful. People came to realise that real health depended on more complex socio-economic factors, such as access to water, hygiene and good nutrition, as we have seen in Namibia. This approach requires inter-disciplinary intervention, with many types of Organizations combining their skills. It was hard for an Organization such as WHO, with its top-heavy medical emphasis, to adapt. Critics say that its recent programmes include scores of ambitious activities for which it does not have the appropriate level of technical ability. Also, when it does try to cooperate rather than take the lead, it is uncomfortable in the role, according to a detailed critique by Gavin Yamey in the *British Medical Journal**.

Smallpox: WHO's greatest triumph

When WHO was founded, however, one can hardly blame its leaders for picturing a succession of future 'magic bullets' such as penicillin, which it was imagined would rid the world of scourges. Such was the pre-AIDS sanguinity that one professor wrote 'We have closed the book on infectious diseases. Eradication seemed not only a practicable but an inspiring ideal.'

Smallpox was an obvious first candidate because in 1966, this infectious fever was ravaging 15 million lives in 33 countries each year. It killed two million people annually and left survivors loathsomely disfigured, with pitted pox-marked faces. A single travelling carrier – or even his clothes – could set off a huge new outbreak. Tracking down isolated cases the world over was of course an immense challenge – even more so because an astonishing 95 per cent of smallpox cases were never reported to public health authorities. This was because in colonial days people's homes were often burned if a family member caught the disease: it seemed wiser to keep quiet. Moreover, in many cultures, vaccination was taboo. So it was a bold decision in 1966 to mount an all-out blitz in the form of a ten-year vaccination campaign, headed by an American, Dr. Donald Henderson.

Certain key features of the disease made the plan feasible: smallpox was not especially contagious; it had no animal reservoir; it was easily recognised and diagnosed, and there was an effective vaccine. The two superpowers were generous with funds, and gradually a multinational WHO team of approximately 50 full-time and 600 temporary medical workers spread out around the globe. Far from being Florence Nightingale types, their efforts frequently took on ruthless, military overtones, with the police being called in to invade houses and enforce vaccination. Few governments demurred, with such high stakes at play.

There is a passionate romance about some accounts of this battle, with WHO teams often risking their lives to track down smallpox carriers. These brave and dedicated people could recognise no borders, like the disease itself, and they had to be resourceful, breaking rules by crossing national boundaries, and offering monetary rewards to people for turning in cases. Often they were exhausted, and had to be spurred on like soldiers. One American scientist, caught in the Ethiopian rainy season, spent three days in a Land-Rover, stuck in a very thick wall of mud. They braved civil wars, floods, religious battles and a variety of geographic and logistical problems, armed only with their scientific knowledge and faith that success would make the world unite to fight other such battles.

Individual heroes emerged, and their stories, so unlike the normal obscurity of international civil servants, boosted morale. One such was Daniel Tarantola, an idealistic young French physician 'who dreamt of a world in which villagers in Burkina Faso had as much a right to expect an eighty-year life span as did *les parisiennes bourgeois*, according to Pulitzer Prize-winning author Laurie Garett. She wrote in her best-selling account, *Betrayal of Trust: the Collapse of Global Public Health*,. 'Tarantola had a vision for a new type of social order, and believed that with enough energy and Western money, anything was possible.'

Tarantola tackled Bangladesh, the toughest of terrains because of its massive population density and ancient smallpox endemicity. One story relates how he tracked down a smallpox carrier who also happened to be an infamous murderer. 'Without police protection,' says Garett, 'Tarantola approached the murderer and his outlaw gang in their hideout and faced down guns to immunize them. Word from the villagers was that the robbers had classic pockmarks on their faces and were spreading the epidemic throughout the countryside. They were right – the gang leader died of smallpox two days after Tarantola's courageous confrontation.'

Another young American physician, David Heymann, later to become Executive Director of WHO's Communicable Diseases Division, spent two years smallpox hunting in Bihar and Calcutta. Finally, in Merka, Somalia, the last case of smallpox was cured. On May 8, 1980, the World Health Assembly declared that 'The World and all its people have won freedom from... [this] devastating disease sweeping in endemic form through many countries since earliest times, leaving death, blindness, and disfigurement in its wake.' It was the first time in history that a disease had been entirely eliminated by human intervention.

What is interesting in the present context, however, is the shoddy way the WHO treated these heroes subsequently. Far from being congratulated individually for their magnificent efforts and given good posts, it was said that they were considered arrogant and thoughtless. This is because they violated too many of WHO's precious guidelines, having operated from a perspective quite beyond the average civil servant. 'Science really suffers from bureaucracy,' sighed Dr. Isao Arita, the Japanese who had succeeded Henderson as leader of the programme. 'If we hadn't broken every single WHO rule many times over, we would never have defeated smallpox.'

By 1968 fifty-six species of anopheles mosquito were not only resistant to DDT but, some people swore, they actually thrived on it.

Malaria: a different story

The malaria eradication programme (MEP), on the other hand, developed into a nightmare. The name is derived from the Italian *mala ari*, or bad air, and the feverish attacks the disease erupts into arise from parasites in the blood, inserted via the saliva of the anopheles mosquito. In 1955, when the eradication plan was mooted, malaria was striking down 300 million people globally each year, killing three million of them and leaving the rest forever susceptible to an attack. By 1957 there were two magic bullets: DDT, (dichloro-diphenyl-trichloroethrane) the powerful insecticide that, it was thought would kill the mosquitoes long enough to prevent re-infestation if sprayed over the insides of houses. And immunization with the drug chloroquine. Desk-bound bureaucrats dreamed of malaria graphs plummeting.

The story of what went wrong should have taught many lessons. And to some extent it did; yet as we later saw with AIDS, science and the vertical approach were too tempting, the alternatives too messy, for the 'experts' to abandon them. 'Eradicationists' says Gavin Yamey, 'remains highly prevalent within WHO.'

From the start of the MEP, nature refused to cooperate. On paper the idea of spraying houses seemed feasible, but on remote mountains where people inhabited tumble-down hovels with little in the way of walls, it fell apart. And mosquitoes had an annoying habit of biting people out of doors – and then, even worse, of developing resistance to DDT. By 1968 fifty-six species of anopheles mosquito were not only resistant to DDT but, some people swore, they actually thrived on it. Reaching every home was impossible in many countries, owing to the rough terrain and low population densities spread over vast areas. Not to mention wars raging here and there, which meant that some governments actually preferred to have mosquitoes around, to bite the enemy. Then people's bothersome customs, taboos and superstitions got in the way. Nature further emphasized that a little knowledge is a dangerous thing by rejecting DDT, which was by now part of the food chain. People who'd eaten it began to develop weird genetic mutations, amid other decidedly unhealthy symptoms. With American environmentalists now screaming that DDT should be banned, third-world countries became deeply suspicious of their 'benefactors', who insisted they use it. And to top it all, the parasites discovered a taste for drugs such as quinine and chloroquine. Substitutes such as malathion were developed, but of course, costs soared. From the 11 cents per person originally calculated, a colossal $2 per person, and counting, became the more realistic figure. And, too late, many countries who had been sold on eradication because they thought it would save millions on annual health-spend, now realised that maintaining their low infection rate would mean re-spraying for four years. They had no funds, for the worst-hit areas were, as always, the poorest.

The final straw came when the United States pulled out of the campaign. Having poured in a massive 40 percent of the total $1,339 million spent over ten years, America realised that eradication efforts were creating new problems as soon as they solved the old ones. For instance, population figures were mushrooming in areas where malaria had kept them down, so family planning became, and has remained, the new American priority.

Once again, WHO staff suffered in a way that could have been avoided. By 1965, there were some 381 WHO Malaria advisory staff running country, regional and international projects. Jobs weren't secure on the eradication programme, so it did not attract the best human resources, and there was a high staff turn-over. There were incidents of personnel not being paid for months, or of being suddenly dismissed. These were predominantly malaria experts, but since they offered no training in administration, they weren't as effective as they might have been in controlling the disease anyway. It was a prime example of that key WHO weakness, pinpointed in many reports: staff were top-heavy in medical expertise but lacking in other skills essential for running health services.

News seemed to travel fast among the mosquitoes: the disease surged back like a roller coaster. Sri Lanka had a million cases in 1955, hardly any in 1964 but half a million again by 1969. By 1977 cases in India had soared above six million. In sub-Saharan Africa, which has less benefited from the shortlived eradication programme, malaria continued to kill nearly a million children a year. Globally, as wonder drugs produced super bugs, there were three times as many cases of malaria in the 1990s as there had been in 1961.

Since 1999, a new approach has emerged. Known as 'Roll Back Malaria', it's the result of collaboration between many international bodies which play a strong role in health, including the Global Fund to fight AIDS, Tuberculosis and Malaria, the Organization of African Unity, the World Bank, academic institutions, the private sector and non-government organizations. Together with WHO/AFRO they have planned a major African Malaria Initiative.

However, in 2004 the respected British medical journal, *The Lancet*, reported that the current practices of WHO and the Global

Fund are inadequate to safeguard malaria patients in Africa. The disease is currently killing up to three million people every year, most of them children under five. Dr. Amir Attaran, an international health scholar, and others, reported that WHO is violating its own malaria policy by acquiescing to pressures to cut costs. Instead of promoting a new highly-effective treatment called artemisinin-class combination therapy (ACT), the so-called gold standard treatment when there is drug resistance, WHO approves the Global Fund's Plan to provide cheap but in-effective chloroquine or sulfadoxine-pyrimethamine. Attaran declared this policy indefensible and tantamount to medical malpractice. He held that prescribing such drugs at best wastes precious international aid money, and at worst, allows malaria patients to die. Considering the increase in deaths due to drug resistance, the authors say ten of thousands of children die every year as a direct result. ACT is 10 times more expensive than the traditional malaria medicines, so aid-giving agencies discourage poor debt-ridden African nations from buying it.'

WHO refuted these allegations, yet they could be a symptom of the oft-repeated judgement that the Organization is settling uneasily into its new partnership role, preferring to take the lead. And there are new fears arising from the independent route taken by massive funders such as the Bill Gates Foundation, which does its own thing, often preferring quick fix solutions to long-term sustainable good health. There is, now, no overarching world body with enough clout to enforce the deeper solutions which are part and parcel of good health. Perhaps it is unrealistic to expect one, given that the major determinants of health – poverty, education, development and the environment – are beyond the scope of WHO. Yet many critics agree that in failing to take a dynamic leadership role, WHO has lost ground. This was most clearly seen in its response to HIV/AIDS.

THE HIV/AIDS debacle

These people put 'URGENT' on a request for pencils!'

To do the Organization justice, no-one could have foreseen, when the first cases of a rare disease among the gay community in America and among heterosexuals in central Africa emerged in the early eighties, that, 25 years later, it would have swept the world, killing over 20 million people and infecting an estimated 34-46 million people more. However, it was arguably for just such a disaster that the WHO was founded, so it's instructive to look at why the Organization failed so dramatically to curb the pandemic. Eventually an entirely new body, UNAIDS, had to be set up, at enormous expense, largely due to lack of confidence in WHO.

Admittedly, AIDS is a disease like no other. It is exceedingly dangerous because it can be transmitted unwittingly, with no symptoms appearing for years. To prevent its spreading (and, since there's no cure, that's our best option) far more than drugs are needed. It means tackling sexual behaviour, psychology, sociology, nutrition, poverty and deep-seated cultural beliefs about gender. It requires a strong computer-linked health-service infrastructure, with proper record-keeping to avoid the risk of multi-drug-resistance. It requires organised community support. But perhaps most of all it requires strong, integrated leadership from the top down, to galvanise the world into fighting the disease. That, the World Health Organization could have provided – and did for awhile – but in the end, failed dismally at. Instead, there have been wasted years; years of petty fighting, lack of urgency and drift.

To backtrack a little, the virus (HIV) generally held responsible for the condition was discovered in 1983. There followed a period of world-wide moralizing and victim-blaming, wild recriminations, political squirming and intensive medical research. The World Health Organization, acutely aware of the unsettling aspects of AIDS, initially chose to ignore the emerging disease. From 1981 to late 1986 barely nothing concrete emerged from Geneva. Dr. Halfden Mahler then Director General, later confessed that WHO's response to the threat posed by the AIDS epidemic had been slow.

The WHO's Global Programme on AIDS (GPA) was set up in 1986, after various world conferences had been organised by other bodies. Its new office in Geneva was intended to serve as international clearing house for AIDS information and technical expertise. From 1986 to 1990 it was headed by Dr. Jonathan Mann, the much lauded, charismatic, American epidemiologist who had been researching AIDS in Zaire under the American-backed AIDS programme. At the start the

GPA had a total working budget of $4.5 million, a part-time secretary, and three epidemiologists, borrowed from other programmes. Mann's salary was initially paid by the US Centres for Disease Control. Such was his dynamism, however, that in less than two years he commanded a far-flung AIDS programme, a considerable staff, and a budget of over $50 million, with $92 million promised for 1989. The GPA grew to become WHO's largest single programme, and one of the largest in the entire United Nations.

You might think that in view of the millions affected by AIDS, Mann's fellow medics at Geneva would have welcomed this great start. No doubt some did, but jealousy was rife among programmes which had struggled for years on zero-growth budgets. Mann's celebrity status – he made headlines all over the world – aroused envy among the cautious career-plodders fighting such unglamorous things as diarrhoeal disease, from the glassy heights of the huge WHO block in Geneva.

Mann and his team sailed on regardless. While insisting that no AIDS donations should be at the expense of any other programme, Mann had no patience for people who quibbled and had no sense of urgency. He was quoted as saying, 'These people put 'URGENT' on a request for pencils!' But the team were frustrated by their rock-and-hard-place-situation, caught between the desperate AIDS crisis and the slow-moving WHO, where the concept of a genuinely dire emergency had almost no meaning. These complacent officials had no feeling for the heartbreaking struggles of people in a country like Namibia.

In 1987 the GPA outlined the need for a national AIDS programme in every country, to coordinate mass education campaigns. The Fortieth World Health Assembly passed the GPA's Global Strategy for the Prevention and Control of AIDS. And Jonathan Mann did something no WHO functionary at his level had ever done: he addressed the United Nations. For the first time the UN passed a resolution on a specific disease, formally endorsing WHO's leadership in the war against it. Never had the WHO seemed more relevant, in the public's eyes.

The high point came in 1988 when Mann brought together health officials from 148 nations to discuss AIDS at the vast Queen Elizabeth II Conference Centre in London. It was a coup for Mann's programme, for WHO, and for the millions of powerless AIDS victims. Even though the conference failed to curb the paranoia that led to over 80 countries trying to ban HIV-infected people from crossing their borders, it did provide a world wake-up call. Yet by the time the alarms sounded by Mann and his crew had woken everyone up, HIV was rampant; it had reached full-fledged epidemic status in all the major cities of North America and Western Europe, as well as sub-Saharan Africa. 'The GPA group felt justified in, figuratively speaking, yelling about AIDS at the top of their lungs. But yelling, figuratively or literally, simply wasn't done inside the World Health Organization,' wrote Laurie Garett. Back in Geneva, the medics muttered.

Their simmering resentment came to a head with a change of leadership at WHO. Dr. Halfden Mahler, the powerful leader with the `priest-like aura' who had garnered world-wide respect for, and belief in the Organization for 25 years – and with whom Mann had a great rapport – retired. In his place came the Japanese Dr. Hiroshi Nakajima, whom we have come across before in this narrative.

Dr. Nakajima had no time for Jonathan Mann. Dr. Nakajima did not share Mann's conviction that AIDS was a human right issue, and that the international community had to guarantee that any future therapies or vaccines would also be available, free, to the Third World countries where they were most needed. Contentious even before he took office, by the time he left it ten years later the WHO had 'sunk into a policy vacuum and was in danger of losing the initiative on international health issues' according to the London *Times*.

'Even Dr. Nakajima's most dedicated staff acknowledge that his severe difficulties in communicating are a major handicap for a United Nations leader', wrote Fiona Godlee in the *British Medical Journal*. But being reserved and a poor communicator were the least of his faults. Dr. Nakajima was a 'compromise operator', lacking the courage, skill and vision to fight the many necessary battles that were needed. He upset and demoralised the staff with his autocratic style and mass cronyism, leading him to double the number of discretionary directorial appointments, while bypassing the senior staff selection committee. As we have seen, complaints to the International Labour Tribunal flourished, but nothing much else did. Years later, Gavin Yamey summed up this period in the

BMJ: 'Demoralised, rife with rumours of corruption, and lacking in leadership, WHO floundered.'

Dr. Mann was one of the first victims. Dr. Nakajima was clearly uncomfortable with Mann's very public persona and high-profile AIDS programme, and in this, at least, he had the backing of envious WHO officialdom. Disease programmes, said Dr. Nakajima, should be managed in accordance with established WHO protocol. Utterly reasonable – except that established protocol couldn't cope with a mushrooming epidemic worse than any plague the world had ever known. In the middle of 1990 Mann resigned and was soon replaced by Dr. Michael Merson, who had been plodding along at WHO/HQ for most of his professional life. Dr. Merson understood WHO's protocol, and was safe. To our grief Jonathan Mann and his wife were among the victims of the tragic Swiss Air crash off Nova Scotia in July 1998. He died in the service of humanity.

The international AIDS community looked on in dismay.

Laurie Garett writes: 'Nearly all the disease cowboys who faced down epidemics during the 1960s, 1970s, and early 1980s soon left, disillusioned and dispirited by the Nakajima regime. Donors were also giving up on the World Health Organization, no longer convinced that the once-vital agency had the vision, will or resources to fulfil its mission. ....'

As the fallout of this political battle made itself felt in the world's AIDS control effort, the GPA began to lose credibility. In 1994, following discussions with other international bodies, the Economic and Social Council of the United Nations adopted resolution 1994/24 approving the establishment of UNAIDS, 'to which WHO will provide the administrative framework'.

UNAIDS is a multi-agency programme run jointly by WHO, the UNDP and the UN Population Fund. Its Executive Director is Dr. Peter Piot, a veteran AIDS researcher, who tried twice without success to get elected as successor to Dr. Nakajima in 1998 and to Dr. Brundtland in 2003.

However, a clear indication that the world no longer trusted the leaden-footed UN to handle this massive pandemic, even with the new AIDS body, was the setting up of new international health partnerships.

These have changed the landscape of global health, fragmenting it into a huge array of new initiatives and alliances. Some have called this a 'Balkanisation of efforts', pointing out that no-one is quite sure now who should be doing what. 'WHO still has to look for its place in the world,' comments Peter Piot.

One problem with the new global initiatives is that they are outside the World Health Assembly's governance and largely accountable to their donors – private foundations and rich governments. These initiatives are arguably weakening the UN's influence on how global health funds are spent, by choosing which interventions to fund (mainly communicable disease control); which strategies to pursue (predominantly vertical programmes) and which countries should receive support.

The biggest initiative is The Global Fund, a new public-private health funding mechanism with its own governing body, set up with a great fanfare, and impressive promises from donor governments. In April 2002 the Global Fund committed up to $616 million over five years to country-based projects tackling AIDS, TB and malaria. But by 2005, with a more realistic take on anti-retrovirals, the Fund was calling for a colossal $3.6 billion from donors.

'The fund was developed' said Daniel Tarantola, the disillusioned veteran of the smallpox campaign, 'in a spirit of wanting to create something very independent from the UN.' The Global Fund's major contribution has been to put health on the international political agenda. It has produced outstanding advocacy, making the compelling case that investing in health is vital for global economic development. Its major weakness is the lack of coherence between its mandate to control the three diseases and all the other efforts to do the same thing by alliances involving WHO such as Roll Back Malaria, Stop TB and UNAIDS.

Under Dr. Brundtland AIDS was less of a priority than stopping smoking, although to do her justice, she did succeed in regaining some credibility for WHO. However, a new era was ushered in the successor, Dr. Jong-wook Lee, for whom HIV/AIDs was a priority from day one prior to his sudden death. The late Dr. Lee pointed out that HIV/AIDS has cut life expectancy by as much as 20 years for millions in sub-Saharan Africa. Every day in the poorest African countries, 5,000 men and women and 1,000 children die of it. In the world as a whole only five percent of all those who require antiretroviral treatment for HIV/AIDS actually receive it. He declared this to be a global health emergency in September 2003, and set about raising funds for his 'three by five' campaign – three million on ARVs by 2005. Part of his strategy was for strengthened health systems across the board to address the widening gap between rich and poor countries; AIDS treatment would not be sustainable unless it was linked to stronger primary health systems.

Stephen Lewis, a Canadian diplomat and a one time UN's special representative for AIDS in Africa called the WHO decision to launch Three by Five the single most important and dramatic development in years. To meet its goal pilot projects throughout Africa will have to be scaled up rapidly from servicing a few thousand patients to tens and hundreds of thousands. This will require an extra US$ 200 million from Western countries to get underway. Out of the estimated 40 million people infected by HIV worldwide about six million need antiviral drugs. No country, according to Lewis, not even the USA, is paying an adequate share yet. He estimated that the Global Fund to fight AIDS, TB and Malaria needed $3.6 billion in 2005 alone. The fair share for USA would be $1.6 billion, but the Bush Administration's budget calls only for $200 million in support of this programme. With over 20 million people already dead, and still counting, Lewis emphasized the need for compassion to fight AIDS instead of resenting those holding out a begging bowl. In sub-Sahara Africa where 2.3 million people die each year of AIDS and 4.4 million need treatment, antiviral drugs were available last year to only about 100,000 people. 'Quite frankly that is an abomination,' Stephen Lewis concluded. Instead, we see large amounts of money still being spent for HIV/ AIDS sensitization workshops and seminars. There are also thousands of HIV/AIDS orphanages who lack adequate care and support. Part of the money could be utilized for poverty alleviation and education of the public at grass root level.

In 2005, a UN report on the subject issued the grimmest figures yet: more than 80 million Africans will die of AIDS by 2025, and another 90 million – more than one in 10 people on the continent – will become infected. Never has a strong World Health Organization been so sorely needed. Thankfully, befor his death Dr. Lee has set AIDS as his main target. He, laudably, wanted to treat three million Africans in a few years, trumping the two million target of President Bush. Yet due to the lack of public-health capacity, the high incidence of poverty, and the absence of political will in many African countries, this target was doomed to failure. There are all indications that the target of three million by the end of 2005 was not reached. Dr. Jim Yong Kim, Director of HIV/AIDS at WHO, was quoted by the British *Guardian* on 30 June 2005 as declaring, 'We are at one million, who would have guessed we would have got to this point by now? We are not going to make Three by Five but the point is that we are not going to stop.' With insiders claiming that Dr. Lee would have been a qualifying candidate to win the Nobel Peace Prize for promoting AIDS treatment in Africa, his untimely death has shattered the African dream of universal access to treatment by 2010.

*Peabody, John W. An Organizational Analysis of the WHO: Narrowing the Gap between Promise and performance...

Soc SCi Med, Vol 40, No 6, pp731-742 1995

**Yamey, Gavin Have the Latest Reforms Reversed WHO's Decline? First of 5 articles, *British Medical Journal*, Vol 325, 9 Nov 2002

Editor's Note

In mid-December 2004, the World Health Organization (WHO) released its annual *World Health Report*, the first under the leadership of the late Director-General Jong-wook Lee. Building on its earlier announcement of a plan to bring AIDS treatment to three million people by the end of 2005, the WHO called for a return to the goal of 'Health for All' adopted 25 years ago. The report calls for strengthening health systems across the board to address the widening gap between rich and poor countries, and it stresses that AIDS treatment will not be sustainable unless it is linked to the strengthening of primary health systems. The report thus presents a sharp contrast to the U.S. model of commercialized health care and the bilateral approach stressed by President Bush's new AIDS initiative. U.S. officials have used the weaknesses of national health care systems in African and other developing countries as an argument for a slower pace in funding for

AIDS programs. The WHO reverses that argument, stressing the need for immediate steps to build additional health care capacity.

This will be a critical test year for both multilateral institutions and the Bush administration, as well as national governments, to deliver on their promises to rapidly scale up treatment for almost six million people in need of immediate antiretroviral treatment.

'The principles defined at that time remain indispensable for a coherent vision of global health. Turning that vision into reality calls for clarity both on the possibilities and on the obstacles that have slowed and in some cases reversed progress towards meeting the health needs of all people. This means working with countries especially those most in need not only to confront health crises, but to construct sustainable and equitable health systems....

The report confirms that HIV/AIDS has cut life expectancy by as much as 20 years for many millions of people in sub-Saharan Africa. Every day in the poorest African countries, 5,000 men and women and 1,000 children die from HIV/AIDS.

Today only five percent of all those people living in the developing world who require antiretroviral treatment for HIV/AIDS actually receive it: a treatment gap which WHO declared a global health emergency in September 2003.

"The WHO goal of universal access to HIV/AIDS treatment, with the concrete target of providing treatment to three million people in the poorest countries by the year 2005 is a clear demonstration of how the principle of equitable access can be put into practice,' said the late Dr. Lee. 'Working with our partners, we will show that investments we make in treating people with AIDS can help to build up health systems for the benefit of all.'

The report suggests ways in which international support can counter some of the main healthcare systems' weaknesses, including critical shortages of health workers, inadequate health information, a lack of financial resources and the need for more government leadership aimed at improving the health of the poorest members of society. The report calls for rapid increases in training and employment of health care workforces, and stronger government-community relationships.

CHAPTER TWENTY-SEVEN
LONG LIVE WHO!

WHO is mighty in experience, but its labours will count for nothing if its staff cannot look at our world through the eyes of the least privileged. We have to understand their hopes and fears. As International Civil Servants, we exist to serve them; to help them realize their strength, their potential, and their aspirations. Between us we are in a unique position to put into action the world's idealistic plans for fighting global poverty and global sickness. This should be the common purpose that unites us, with all our multi-coloured cultures, languages, and creeds, under one umbrella-not pettiness, greed, corruption or despair.

I have told my story to encourage every international civil servant who has been the victim of injustice to speak out. They are manifold, but they keep silent about their grievances since they are tied to the United Nations by golden threads and dare not risk losing their jobs. Even after leaving the service, they often prefer not to write about what happened, for fear of losing possible consultancy work. I have spoken out, despite this risk to myself, in the hope that this will improve both the service and the lot of colleagues to come – on whom that service depends.

'Justice is connected with law, obligation, rights, and duties, and measures out its awards according to equality of merit', says Austin Fagothey in his classic *Right and Reason: Ethics in Theory and Practice*. According to that definition, justice was most certainly not served in my case, and still I ask, why?

I suspect the answer lies in the desperate desire of the Administration to exonerate itself from blame in order to avoid being sued. Sanya Damon, Andrew Damon's young widow, was an obvious candidate –

left to raise their three children alone, she was paid not one cent in compensation by the Organization which, in one way or another, had caused her husband's death. Neither the Namibian Ministry of Health nor the Ministry of Foreign Affairs raised this issue. Was it because Andrew Damon was a South African native?

At least WHO should have paid this widow part of the insurance claims of the vehicle that overturned in a clear road killing her husband who was on official mission. Even if the vehicle did not have insurance WHO would have done something for her in a form of compensation.

But there is still the nagging suspicion that instead, the Administration's desperate desire was to cover up foul play emanating from WHO's Country or Regional Office. We will never know. We do know that the Organization, of which the budget had been frozen for 13 years, chose to spend hundreds thousands of dollars, from under God knows what budget heading, by going to the Tribunal and the Namibian High Court to protect an employee who, at best, was incompetent at his job. At worst, he was a menace and a liability, who might yet cause the deaths of more eminent, skilled people the world can ill-afford to lose.

Who cares? Few people, because the money did not come out of the pockets of individuals but from the bottomless purse of faceless bureaucracies, sheltering so-called leaders and directors who have long since lost any consideration they may have had for staff; or concern for their Organization's reputation and effectiveness; or – above all – compassion for the millions of Africans dying of disease.

Thus, on 16 February 2004 the Prosecutor General of Namibia closed the file 'The State vs Niklaas Mootu' by informing the widow of Dr. Gregor Watters, that the High Court had ruled in favour of Mr. Mootu, finding that he indeed enjoyed diplomatic immunity from prosecution and could not be charged criminally with regard to the accident which killed her husband. However, this ruling need not automatically bring an end to the case. It merely settles the issue of immunity. It is still possible for the Prosecutor General, through the Namibian Ministry of Foreign Affairs, to formally request the new Director-General of WHO to lift the driver's immunity for justice to be served. I ask why if the Namibian government seriously wanted him brought to book, it didn't do that anyway? An obvious possibility to my mind, was that the whole High Court case against WHO was a farce, a charade to deter Mrs. Watters from pursuing her civil case. Perhaps WHO were party to this charade all the time. If not, I submit that it is the Prosecutor General's duty to apply now, to prevent similar obstructions of justice from making a mockery of local judiciaries, thereby threatening the security of international civil servants everywhere. The United Nations' Staff Association should also apply pressure for this to happen, since it is in the interest of thousands of UN employees who are deployed in hardship areas worldwide.

What happened to me can happen to others. Indeed, staff harassment and abuse of authority in United Nations organizations has reached an alarming level, and several cases are under investigation by independent bodies. The risk will increase unless drastic measures are taken to punish the wrongdoers. A few months after the Namibian car crash, when the WHO representative in Burundi was murdered at his residence and his body thrown in Lake Tanganyika, as mentioned in chapter 19, the police wanted to interrogate WHO staff, and sought permission from the Organization. It was granted immediately. Why, then, fight to the last in our case? It was, as the Tribunal finding put it, 'inconceivable'.

Power-mongering and the missing WHO millions

Perhaps the money to protect the driver was found from some extra-budgetary programme, donated by Member States to deal with TB, malaria, HIV/AIDS or one of Africa's many other dread diseases. The AFRO Regional Director, Dr. Ibrahim Samba was particularly successful in attracting such funds, and boasted of it at many meetings. He was not so forthcoming about the origin of the millions squandered on compensation and mismanagement as a result of his inept administration. But there is more to be said on the subject of unbudgeted WHO spending in Africa before we leave it.

We have already noted the uproar at the 1994 World Health Assembly when the WHO's external auditor, Sir John Bourne, announced that he had been prevented from examining the finances of the African Regional Office for two years. This was due to the disruption caused when Brazzaville became the centre of a war zone. The multi-million dollar Brazzaville WHO complex, complete with staff housing and technical equipment, was forced to close, and hundreds of staff had to be shuttled from country to country. Bourne said it was impossible to give any account of AFRO's spending of $122m, or their assets of $20m and liabilities of $21m. So, you see, to 'lose' a million here and there on silencing truculent staff, is not difficult.

To the outsider it might seem that the Administration could hardly be blamed for this disruption. The fighting was largely the result of an internal power struggle between the democratically-elected government and the opposition, fuelled by imperial power. During my time, the Regional Office had to close or decamp to another country three times as a result of civil and political unrest. This aggravated already poor communication between the region's 46 Member States. According to one diplomat it was easier for the Regional Office to get messages through to Geneva than to neighbouring countries. 'The Regional Director works in extreme difficulty,' he was quoted as saying. 'Coordinating regional activities is almost impossible.'

But the decision to site the WHO office in an unstable country such as the Congo/Brazzaville was a political one, pandering to demands that it be situated in Francophone Africa. The WHO's widely-criticized regional structure makes it vulnerable to such pressure. Many analysts have singled out the six regions as a reform priority; the body has 'one head and many brains', they say; both money and action should be directed straight at individual countries. Yet no leader has been able to reform the six regions of WHO because the political blocs have voting rights at the World Health Assembly, and they are not about to put themselves out of business. So, power-mongering in Africa continues to impinge on the Organization's effectiveness. In 1996 plans for what many consider an essential adjunct to health – a Regional Centre for Health and Environment to provide technical support in environmental health for the continent's 654 million people – had to be scuttled because of it. The South African Government generously offered to house the Centre, but most Francophone countries, doubtful of its location there, refused to vote funds from the regular budget. They directed the Regional Director to seek extra budgetary donations to build it, but Francophone interests still usurped regional ones, and funds weren't forthcoming. So it is that political blocs in every region which sabotages priority health programmes.

A premium on mediocrity: WHO/AFRO

When Dr. Ibrhaim Samba retired in 2005 after ten years in the post, an article in the *Lancet* commented on the 'astonishing' lack of interest shown in the selection of a new UN health leader. 'Familiarity with WHO and its African Office makes the lack of debate more understandable. This region has by far the highest disease burden coupled with the lowest level of economic development in the world, and is besieged by corruption, poor governance, political instability, and civil strife. Despite these constraints,' it continued, '*it is clear that the regional office could do better*. [our italics]. Indeed, many commentators are privately and scathingly critical of its composition and working practices. WHO/AFRO's weaknesses are typical of a large Organization: ineffective and self-serving central management with demoralised and unsupported rank-and-file staff.'

'At the heart of the regional office's ineffectiveness,' the article continued, 'is its acting as a political rather than a technical agency. Recruitment of senior staff is rarely based on competence or qualification.'

My experience as related here confirms this observation one hundred percent. For example, in 2001 WHO /AFRO put a chemical engineer in charge of health risk assessment and a biochemist in charge of occupational health in the newly established Directorate of Healthy Environments in Sustainable Development, under the cover of restructuring, while I was a Regional Adviser in Environmental Health. This made a mockery of the environmental health profession, and I protested vigorously. This was one of the reasons for my transfer to South Africa. There are many other instances of staff qualifications which bear no relation to the responsibilities of their posts. The Regional Director then appointed a medical geographer, a woman academician, to be Director of a Healthy Environments in Sustainable Development programme. This appointment was politically motivated, a favour to the government of the woman's country. As a geographer and academician, she knew little about the environmental health aspects of disease prevention. The senior staff, including myself, had difficulty working with her as she focused on poverty and ill health, undermining our efforts to speed up the provision of safe drinking water and basic sanitation, which would have controlled cholera and other communicable diseases. The community water supply and sanitation programme in AFRO which had evolved over the past 30 years, was suddenly scrubbed from the priority list. All the efforts made during the United Nations International Drinking Water Supply and Sanitation Decade (1981-1990) and through later initiatives such as AFRICA 2000 Water and Sanitation for All, PHAST etc, were undermined by AFRO in spite of the continued interest of the Member States in promoting this programme. WHO's partnership with UNICEF, UNDP, the World Bank, UNEP, Habitat and other international organizations, in the joint planning and implementation of community-based water supply, sanitation and hygiene education projects in the African Region came to a standstill. Until 2001 community water supply and sanitation was the only well-documented, effective and successful environmental health programme in AFRO and should have been promoted energetically.

Under the reorganised structure of the Directorate of Healthy Environment in Sustainable Development, the basic problems of water and sanitation, waste disposal and adequate housing were not prioritised. Although many countries have made substantial progress in these areas in the past three decades, we are still concerned about the rise of communicable diseases, particularly tuberculosis, cholera and other diarrhoeal diseases. It is vital to build on what has been achieved, instead of downgrading and marginalizing.

Meeting these crucial challenges to health and development in Africa is now a priority. WHO/AFRO receives 22 percent of the Organization's regular budget, more than any other region. In addition, extra-budgetary funds have increased substantially in the past decade, with due credit to Dr. Samba. The staff component in the Regional Office has increased from 240 to almost 800. However, according to a Russian health expert, Volemar Ermakov, writing in the *Lancet*, only four percent of their time is spent on disease prevention, whereas administration consumes 65 per cent. This bears out the questionable efficiency, competence and integrity which we have already discussed.

As we have seen, it is common WHO practice to inflict what in legal jargon is quaintly called 'moral injury'; or to terminate appointments or reassign staff to another duty station through personal prejudice. A regional director has, as Dr. Jonathan Mann was quoted as saying, 'potentially unlimited power of granting and taking away jobs and money. If someone at the regional office or a country representative opposes him, he can send that person to the remotest corner of his domain.' As a current (anonymous) WHO employee put it: 'To remain in one's post one has simply to do what the director asks, and the financial inducement, one might even say pressure to do this, is enormous.'

From top to bottom of the African Region this was a common scenario. In 1998, when the first term of the incumbent Regional Director was nearing an end, two highly-qualified and experienced public health experts emerged as rivals. They were the Director of Programme Management from Togo, and the Director of Communicable Diseases Control from Burundi. Before the election campaign got properly under way, they were reassigned to country offices and replaced with less experienced people. The incumbent Regional Director was duly elected for a second term.

'Unless WHO's African office is transformed from a political club to an effective health agency, its right to existence is questionable,' commented the *Lancet* in 2004.

Still the best referee?

In conclusion, the United Nations and its specialized agencies are under reform. No-one contests the need for their existence, or the significant role they play in creating a more peaceful and humane world. The World Health Organization is one of the most highly-respected of these agencies. Despite the controversies surrounding its leadership and performance, the Organization is still the best referee in global public health policy and provides its 193 Member States with effective tools and instruments to combat the numerous diseases that kill millions.

Several landmark achievements bear testimony to this magnificent work, of which we should all be proud. In addition to the smallpox triumph they include:

- A parasitic disease called onchocerciasis, or 'river blindness, no longer blights rural west Africa, thanks to a long multi-partner campaign. It's prevented 600,000 cases of river blindness and assured that some 18 million children in a 20-country area will never get the disease.
- Trachoma, a form of blindness resulting from chronic pink eye, is down 90 percent among Moroccan children younger than 10.
- With the launch of such policies as Health for All, primary health care and the code on breast milk marketing, the WHO has become a strong and effective advocate of change in health policy.
- The Framework Convention for Tobacco Control (FCTC), 2003, is an important example. For the first time in its history WHO exercised its powers to adopt a treaty, giving countries more tools to control tobacco use and save lives. Tobacco is the second leading cause of death globally, causing nearly five million deaths a year. It is the only legal product that causes the death of half its regular users. This means that out of 1.3 billion smokers, 650 million people will die prematurely.
- Most recently, the global strategies on diet and physical activity, reproductive health, and key resolutions on HIV/AIDS and road safety were all unanimously adopted. All these will infiltrate the minds, policies and practices of health officials the world over, as WHO's cutting edge policies have been doing for nearly 60 years.

WHO field staff continue to make personal sacrifices to further this work, knowing that at any time that sacrifice could be the ultimate one, as in the recent case of SARS. Dr. Carlo Urbani, the WHO infectious diseases expert in Vietnam, was such a hero. He first drew the world's attention to SARS, and was one of the first to die of it. When such a new disease, against which we have no defenses develops, WHO staff invariably become martyrs. They deserve the utmost respect and support.

At the start of the millennium, WHO was criticized for not having a strategy or sense of mission for global public health. For decades it had focused on the medicalised model, leaving such basics as clean water, sanitation, decent primary health care and good nutrition in the hands of local governments. But those governments displayed a remarkable range in sensibility towards those duties: at the top end of the scale was the Scandinavian cradle-to-grave, all-inclusive healthcare model; at the bottom, gross negligence such as existed in Mobutu's Zaire. Under the late Dr. Lee there was a new thrust towards balancing these two extremes so that, in his words: 'as well as poor people living in African villages feeling some benefit, wealthy countries would also feel they were getting value for their money'.

WHO is mighty in experience, but its labours will count for nothing if its staff cannot look at our world through the eyes of the least privileged. We have to understand their hopes and their fears. As international civil servants, we exist to serve them; to help them realize their strength, their potential and their aspirations. Between us we are in a unique position to put into action the world's idealistic plans for fighting global poverty and global sickness. This should be the common purpose that unites us, with all our multi-coloured cultures, languages and creeds, under one umbrella – not pettiness, greed, corruption or despair.

Let us therefore re-dedicate ourselves to the pursuit of that great good under the new leadership, of both Director General and Regional Directors. Hopefully they will usher in a new era, one ruled by justice and mutual respect, when staff rights will be honoured and all forms of harassment will finally come to end. We, the veterans, will then rejoice.

Long live WHO!

LIST OF SOURCES

Africa: Health for All? Focus Bulletin Jan 6, 2004.

Arumagam, Stanley. EQ: the new business leader's edge? Management Today, April 2003.

Bach, Paul. International Health. OUP1978.

Bate, Roger. WHO's on Last? A politicized and irrelevant global agency. BMJ 30 August 2003; 327:468.

Editorial. The Brundtland Era begins. The Lancet, Vol 351, Feb7, 1998.

Ermakov, Voldemar. Reform of the World Health Organization. The Lancet, Vol 347, June1, 1996.

Fleck, Fiona. South Korean WHO veteran has tough act to follow. BMJ, Vol 327, Aug 30, 2003.

Forss, Kim, Stenson, Bo, and Sterky, Goran. The future of global health cooperation; designing a new World Health Organization. Current Issues in Public Health 1996, 2: 138-142.

Friedman, F. Donor. Policies and third world health. Int. health Dev. 1989 Summer.

Garrett, Laurie. The Coming Plague. Penguin, 1995.

Garrett, Laurie. Betrayal of Trust: The Collapse of Global Public Health. Hyperiopn, 2000.

Godlee, Fiona. WHO in crisis. BMJ, Vol 309, Nov 1994.

Godlee, Fiona. The World Health Organization: the regions too much power, too little effect. BMJ, Vol 309, Dec 10, 1994.

Godlee, Fiona. The World Health Organization: WHO in retreat: is it losing its influence? BMJ, Vol 309, Dec 3, 1994.

Godlee, Fiona. The World Health Organization: WHO fellowships- what do they achieve? BMJ, Vol 310, Jan 14, 1995.

Godlee, Fiona. The World Health Organization: WHO at country level – a little impact, no strategy. BMJ, Vol 309, Dec 17, 1994.

Godlee, Fiona. The World Health Organization: WHO's special programmes: underminding from above. BMJ, Vol 310, Jan 21, 1995.

Godlee, Fiona. The World Health Organization: WHO in Europe: does it have a role? BMJ, Vol 310, March 4, 1995.

Godlee, Fiona. The World Health Organization: interview with the Director General. BMJ, Vol 310, March 4, 1995.

Hancock, Graham. Lords of Poverty. Macmillan, 1989.

Health for WHO? Interview with Timothy Stamps, new Scientist. International Labour Organization Administrative Tribunal (ILOAT) Judgement no 200-2010.

Kanter, Rosabeth. Leadership: it's the support system that counts. Management Today, April 2002.

Kanter, Rosabeth. Putting People at the heart of strategy. Management Today, May 2003.

Marchant, Joanna. WHO's way to health. New Scientist, Aprill, 2000.

Peabody, John W. An organizational analysis of the WHO: Narrowing the gap between promise and performance. SocSci Med Vol 40 No 6 pp 731-42, 1995.

Pellissier, Rene. Newton is dead. Management Today, July 2002.

Porter, Roy. The Greatest Benefits to mankind. A Medical history of Humanity from Antiquity to the Present. Fontana Press, 1997.

Robertson Geoffrery, QC. The ILO Administrative Tribunal (ILOAT). Special report prepared for the Staff Union of the International labour Organization.

Singer, Peter. Dream of a world where people come before power. The Times Higher Education Supplement February23, 2001.

Sparks, Donald and Green. Namibia: The Nation after Independence. Westview press, Boulder Colorado, December 1992.

Stenson, Bo and Serky, Goran. What Future WHO? Health Policy 28 (1994) 235-256.

Teferra Haile-Selassie. The Ethiopian Revolution 1974-1991. Kegan Paul International, 1997.

Under Surveillance. New Scientist, April 8, 2000.

Unhealthy ambitions. The Times (London) 19.9.2003.

Evolve or Die. The Lancet 7 August 2004.

The World Health Organization: a triumph of experience over hope. The Economist, May 26, 2001.

Walt, Gill. Globalization of International Health. The Lancet, Vol 351, Feb 7, 1998.

Wang, Yan, Collins, Charles, Tang, Shenlan, and Martineau Tim. Health systems decentralization and human resources management in low and middle-income countries. Public Administration and Development, Vol 22, pp, 429-453, 2002.

Wellington J.H. Southwest Africa and its Human Issues. OUP 1967.

Wend, Charles. African countries to cooperate on epidemic control. The Lancet, Vol 362, Jul 19, 2003.

WHO 2003-08: A Programme of Quiet Thunder Takes Place. The Lancet, Vol 362, Jul 19, 2003.

Yamey, Gavin. WHO's Management – struggling to transform a 'fossilised bureaucracy'. BMJ, Vol 325, Nov 16, 2002.

Yamey, Gavin. Have the latest reforms reversed WHO's decline? BMJ, Vol 325, Nov 9, 2002.

Yamey, Gavin. WHO in 2002. Why does the World still need WHO? BMJ, Vol 325, Nov 30, 2002.

Yamey, Gavin. WHO in 2002: Interview with Gro Harlem Brundtland. BMJ, Vol 325, Dec 7, 2002.

Zimbabwe: health system ranked worst in the World. Financial Gazette Zimbabwe 16.8.2001.

ABOUT THE WRITERS

Firdu Zawide was, until his retirement, an international civil servant for over 23 years. With great pride he served the World Health Organization in Sierra Leone, Zimbabwe, Congo/Brazzaville, Geneva and South Africa in the capacity, latterly, of Environmental Health Adviser, African Region. He travelled throughout the continent, supporting the 46 African Member States of the WHO in their struggle to improve the health of their people by providing effective environmental health services.

Zawide was born and grew up in Ethiopia. He studied Building Engineering at the Addis Ababa University and Public Health Engineering at the University of Newcastle upon Tyne in England. Later he was awarded WHO fellowship to study environmental aspect of river basin development in the United States of America, Puerto Rico and Egypt. He also holds MSc. degree in Environmental Management from the Imperial College of Science, Technology and Medicine, University of London. He is a long time Member of the Chartered Institute of Water and Environmental Management and most recently Member of the Chartered Scientist in England. He is also a member of the International Society for Environmental Epidemiology (ISEE} in the United States. Following retirement from WHO service he is actively engaged in promoting research in Environmental Health and has published several articles in peer reviewed international journals in the area of water, sanitation, hygiene (WASH) and food safety. He lives in the United States.

Hilary Bassett is an award-winning writer who lives and works in South Africa. She writes for many leading journals both nationally and internationally, and has won awards for her work on drug resistance tuberculosis, stroke and South Africa's health services. She is the author of 'The Help Directory' (Oxford University Press, 1996)